T0311634

ASIAN MODELS OF ENTREPRENEURSHIP
From the Indian Union and the Kingdom of Nepal to the Japanese Archipelago

Context, Policy and Practice

ASIA-PACIFIC BUSINESS SERIES   (ISSN: 1793-3137)

Series Editor
Leo-Paul Dana
Professor of International Entrepreneurship
Groupe Sup de Co Montpellier Business School, France

Published

Vol. 1   Guanxi and Business
        by Yadong Luo

Vol. 2   From Adam Smith to Michael Porter: Evolution of Competitiveness Theory
        by Dong-Sung Cho & Hewy-Chang Moon

Vol. 3   Islamic Banking and Finance in South-East Asia: Its Development and Future
        (2nd Edition)
        by Angelo M. Venardos

Vol. 4   Asian Models of Entrepreneurship — From the Indian Union and the
        Kingdom of Nepal to the Japanese Archipelago: Context, Policy and Practice
        by Leo-Paul Dana

Vol. 5   Guanxi and Business (2nd Edition)
        by Yadong Luo

Vol. 6   Islamic Banking and Finance in South-East Asia: Its Development and Future
        (3rd Edition)
        by Angelo M. Venardos

Vol. 7   From Adam Smith to Michael Porter: Evolution of Competitiveness Theory
        (Extended Edition)
        by Dong-Sung Cho & Hwy-Chang Moon

Vol. 8   Catalyst for Change: Chinese Business in Asia
        edited by Thomas Menkhoff, Hans-Dieter Evers, Chay Yue Wah &
        Hoon Chang Yau

Vol. 9   Asian Models of Entrepreneurship: From the Indian Union and Nepal to the
        Japanese Archipelago: Context, Policy and Practice (2nd Edition)
        by Leo-Paul Dana

Asia-Pacific Business Series – Vol. 4

ASIAN MODELS OF ENTREPRENEURSHIP
From the Indian Union and the Kingdom of Nepal to the Japanese Archipelago

Context, Policy and Practice

LÉO-PAUL DANA

University of Canterbury, New Zealand

 **World Scientific**

NEW JERSEY · LONDON · SINGAPORE · BEIJING · SHANGHAI · HONG KONG · TAIPEI · CHENNAI

Published by

World Scientific Publishing Co. Pte. Ltd.

5 Toh Tuck Link, Singapore 596224

USA office: 27 Warren Street, Suite 401-402, Hackensack, NJ 07601

UK office: 57 Shelton Street, Covent Garden, London WC2H 9HE

Library of Congress Cataloging-in-Publication Data
Dana, Leo Paul.
   Asian models of entrepreneurship : from the Indian Union and the
kingdom of Nepal to the Japanese archipelago : context, policy and
practice / by Leo-Paul Dana.
     p. cm. -- (Asia-Pacific business series ; v. 4)
   Includes bibliographical references and index.
   ISBN-13 978-981-256-878-6 -- ISBN-10 981-256-878-6
   1. Entrepreneurship--Asia. I. Title.

   HB615.D29 2007
   338'.04092--dc22

                     2006049225

British Library Cataloguing-in-Publication Data
A catalogue record for this book is available from the British Library.

First published 2007 (Hardcover)
Reprinted 2016 (in paperback edition)
ISBN 978-981-3203-33-4

Typeset by Stallion Press
Email: enquiries@stallionpress.com

Printed in Singapore

Dedicated to Naomï Josephine

Foreword

Welcome to the global entrepreneurial revolution. Around the world, free markets have replaced planned and command economies, even where political structures have not become democratised. As this has occurred, political leaders have come to understand that markets involve more than competition among sources of supply and demand, private property, a profit motive, and a freely fluctuating price mechanism. Markets are driven by entrepreneurs. The risk-taking, innovative entrepreneur represents the dynamic that makes the marketplace work.

Nowhere is the entrepreneurial revolution more in evidence than in Eastern Asia. Recent years have witnessed an amazing unleashing of the entrepreneurial spirit in this most populous region of the world. New business starts, new product and service introduction, new patent issuance, and new market creation are growing at historically high rates, and this is only a precursor of what is to come in the decades ahead. As Western economies such as those in Germany, France and the Benelux countries struggle to remain competitive under the weight of huge welfare states, the East is in the early stages of an entrepreneurial renaissance. And while this region lacks the kind of infrastructure that supports entrepreneurs in the United States and other highly entrepreneurial nations, it is only a matter of time before the gap is closed.

In this landmark book, Professor Dana makes it clear that entrepreneurship is a global phenomenon, but that much can be learned about the nature of entrepreneurial activity when we delve into the unique characteristics of different regions of the world, and more importantly, into the nations that make up those regions. Eastern Asia is a case in point. While researchers, policymakers and others tend to refer to this region as a common unit, nothing could be further from the truth. Asia is heterogeneous, with profound differences both among and within countries.

These country differences hold significant implications for entrepreneurship. One of the great myths in the field of entrepreneurship is the discredited notion that "entrepreneurs are born." The reality is that environmental circumstances play a much bigger role than genetics in explaining levels of entrepreneurship. Hence, we see wide variations in entrepreneurial activity across nations, and among geographic areas within a given nation. These differences become vividly apparent in the pages of this book — Dana juxtaposes the explosion in entrepreneurial growth within China against the struggles to build an entrepreneurial community in Japan, or the enlightened public policy leadership in Singapore against the crisis-driven developments in Korea.

Let us consider two questions. First, why do these differences exist? If the basic unit of analysis in the new world order is the entrepreneurial venture, what factors lead to a higher rate of new venture activity? The question is not simply one of starting businesses, but also the types of businesses that are created, and the sustainability of these businesses. Hence, certain factors might lead to relatively more technology-based businesses in Singapore, informal sector ventures in the Philippines, communal ventures in rural China, and "mom and pop" firms in Vietnam.

Dana's central thesis is that we can understand the developing entrepreneurial growth path in Asia only by considering a rich fabric of cultural, historical, social, political, economic and religious factors. He demonstrates that free markets alone are not enough. Critical roles are played by everything from Confucianism and the nature of the family unit, to government policies and social roles as they have historically been defined by society. In some instances, contemporary patterns in entrepreneurship can trace their roots back a number of centuries. In other cases, dramatic changes in the latter part of the 20th century are fuelling the entrepreneurial revolution.

Now consider a second question: why do these differences matter? There is growing evidence to suggest that those countries able to sustain greater levels of entrepreneurial activity benefit in number of critical ways — relatively higher increases in gross domestic product, more job creation, more creation of wealth, more empowerment of women and minority groups, and a general improvement in societal quality of life. As such, understanding how various factors facilitate or inhibit venture creation and growth is critical for explaining the long-term well-being of a country.

The importance of these differences is also apparent as we try to advance our understanding of entrepreneurship. To some degree, entrepreneurship represents a generic process no matter where it occurs. An opportunity must be identified, a business concept is formulated, perhaps a business plan is written, resources are acquired, the concept is implemented, and the venture is managed. Risks are taken, returns may or may not be generated, and growth may or may not occur.

And yet, some key aspects of entrepreneurship may not be so universal. Examples include: the relative importance of the individual versus the collective, the relationship between risk and return, the nature and role of failure, how performance is measured, the implications and uses of profits, levels of control within the venture, acceptability of debt and equity financing, and the roles of the entrepreneur, managers, employees, investors and others within the venture. In addition, certain values that are generically associated with entrepreneurship, such as achievement, competitiveness, individualism, and independence, may not be as significant depending on the geographic context within which ventures are created.

It is in this vein that Dana makes his most significant contribution. For us to understand the global nature of entrepreneurship, he concludes that we must move beyond a universal model or a Western model. Rather, we must recognise that unique models of entrepreneurship can be identified in different parts of the world, and the Asia Pacific region is an especially valuable source of such models. The range of factors identified within each of the 15 countries examined by Dana are not random influences on the entrepreneurial process; they can be construed in more systematic and logical ways. Thus, the book uncovers the Chinese model of gradual transition, the Royal Cambodian model, the *Doi-Moi* model, and others.

The reader is challenged to grasp these different models, and identify their commonalities and differences. Each approach has its own point of departure, and while relevant for its own country context, there may be lessons to learn regarding other contexts. The reader should look for transferable aspects of a given model or approach. In addition, insightful analysis by the reader will uncover potential advantages as well as defects and limitations of the approaches to entrepreneurship in each of these countries.

This is an important book, and one that comes at a critical time. Asia is in the midst of a dramatic transformation. Asian nations have joined the entrepreneurial revolution and will lead the revolution in the years to come. Our ability to decipher this complex part of the world is greatly aided by Dana's seminal work. It represents a comprehensive and well-documented treatment of the topic. While covering a considerable amount of geographic territory, the book does so in a concise and highly readable manner. In the final analysis, it is a book that challenges many of our basic assumptions and points us in important new directions. In this age of entrepreneurship we are reminded by Dana to look to the East, and reach much more deeply into the fabric of society, if we are to understand the future.

Michael H. Morris Ph.D.
Witting Chair in Entrepreneurship
Syracuse University
Syracuse, New York, USA

Preface

The earliest applied education in entrepreneurship that I have been able to find a trace of dates back to 1938, when Professor Shigeru Fijii taught at Kobe University in Japan. Seven decades later, academic interest in entrepreneurship is widespread. This book will familiarise the reader with a variety of entrepreneurship models and small business styles, found across East Asia. As noted by Harvie and Lee, "The term 'East Asia' can be said to be a terminological convenience referring to a geographically proximate group of countries on the western rim of the Pacific stretching from Japan, Korea and China in the north... (2002, p. 1)." The geographic scope of this book covers countries of East Asia, and also an emerging superpower, India. According to the Global Entrepreneurship Monitor findings, India has more persons active in start-ups and new firms than any other country in the world.

The best plan for one year is to cultivate grain; that for ten years is to cultivate trees; and that for a hundred years is to cultivate people. Once cultivated, grain may bring about a crop within the year; trees may bring about benefits lasting for a score of years; people may bring benefits lasting a hundred years.

— Chinese Proverb

Leo Paul Dana, BA, MBA, PhD
Editor Emeritus, *Journal of International Entrepreneurship*
University of Canterbury, New Zealand

Acknowledgements

The research leading to this book was conducted on location, in Asia. For travel to Asia, the author received funding from McGill University, from Nanyang Technological University, from the University of Oxford, and from the University of Pittsburgh.

In the process of preparing the manuscript, each chapter was sent to experts for review. The following kindly volunteered their time, providing inspiration, encouragement and constructive comments:

- Vishwanath V. BABA, Former Editor, *Canadian Journal of Administrative Sciences*, McMaster University
- Lady BORTON, Field Director, American Friends Service Committee, Hanoi, author of *After Sorrow*
- Kevin B. BUCKNALL, Griffith University, Brisbane, Australia
- Garth CANT, Trustee, New Zealand Geographical Society
- David P. CHANDLER, Professor Emeritus, Monash University, Melbourne, Australia
- Florence CHANG, Department of Business Administration, National Changhua University of Education, Changhua, Taiwan
- Jason C. H. CHEN, Graduate School of Business, Gonzaga University, Spokane, Washington
- CHEW Soon Beng, Professor of Economics & Director of the Asian Commerce and Economics Studies Centre, Nanyang Technological University, Singapore
- Yongho CHOI, Professor of Economics, Kyungpook National University, Korea
- Myrna R. CO, Open University of the Philippines

- Evelyne DOURILLE-FEER, Economist, CEPII, Paris
- Sophal EAR, University of California at Berkeley, California
- Ridwan GUNAWAN, Senior Vice President, PT Astra International, Jakarta
- William HIPWELL, Institute of Geography, Victoria University of Wellington
- Masaaki HIRANO, Waseda University Business School, Tokyo
- Earl HONEYCUTT Jr., Professor of Marketing & Chair, Department of Business Administration, Old Dominion University, Norfolk, Virginia
- Glenn HOOK, Professor of Japanese Studies, University of Sheffield
- Ming-Wen HU, Tamkang University, Taiwan
- Masahiro ISHIGURO, The Small & Medium Enterprise Agency, Japan
- Takayuki ITO, Good Samaritan Club, Japan
- Jan JOHANSON, Professor of International Business, Centre of International Business Studies, University of Uppsala, Sweden
- Katsuyuki KAMEI, Professor, Kansai University, Osaka, Japan
- Raymond KAO, Founder, *Journal of Small Business and Entrepreneurship*
- W. F. Fred KIESNER, Conrad Hilton Chair of Entrepreneurship, Loyola Marymount University, Los Angeles
- Winn KYI, General Manager, Myanmar Export Import Corporation, Merchant Street, Yangon, Myanmar
- Philippe LASSERRE, Professor of Strategy and Asian Business, INSEAD
- Byoung-Hoon LEE, Professor of Sociology, Chung-Ang University, Seoul
- LEONG Choon Chiang, Nanyang Technological University, Singapore
- Kenji MATSUOKA, Osaka University of Economics, Japan
- Nancy K. NAPIER, Professor of Business and Economics, Boise State University, Idaho
- Venkataraman NILAKANT, University of Canterbury, New Zealand

- ONG Chin Siew, Nanyang Technological University, Singapore
- Michael J. G. PARNWELL, Professor of South-East Asian Studies, University of Hull
- David. P. PAUL III, Monmouth University, West Long Branch, New Jersey
- Michael PENG, Ohio State University, Columbus, Ohio
- James PICKFORD, Executive Editor, *Financial Times*, London
- Edwina PIO, Auckland University of Technology, New Zealand
- Ms. Sheridan PRASSO, *BusinessWeek*
- Yoshio SAKUMA, Professor, Institute for International Economic Studies, Tokyo
- Michael SCHAPER, Small Business Commissioner, Canberra
- Salvador I. SIBAYAN, Open University of the Philippines
- Ming SINGER, University of Canterbury, New Zealand
- Luisa SOLART-LEE, Open University of the Philippines
- David I. STEINBERG, Director of Asian Studies, Georgetown University, Washington DC
- Tulus TAMBUNAN, Institute for Economic Studies, Research and Development, Indonesia
- Mitsuru TANAKA, Professor Emeritus, Kansai University, Osaka, Japan
- Naranhkiri TITH, Professor of International Economics and Asian Studies, John Hopkins University, Washington DC
- Sarah TURNER, Department of Geography, McGill University
- David WILLIS, Professor of Cultural Studies and Anthropology, Soai University, Osaka, Japan
- Myoe WIN, Director of the Ministry of Commerce Directorate of Trade, Yangon, Myanmar
- Richard W. WRIGHT, The E. Claiborne Robins Distinguished University Chair, University of Richmond, Richmond, Virginia
- Takashi YAMAMOTO, Centre for Entrepreneurship and Leadership Studies for Regional Economies, Akita International University, Akita, Japan

- Joon-Mo YANG, Department of Economics, Pusan National University, Korea
- Henry Wai-Chung YEUNG, Department of Geography, National University of Singapore
- Joseph Jermiah ZASLOFF, Professor of Political Science, University of Pittsburgh, Pittsburgh, Pennsylvania
- Tela ZASLOFF, University of Pittsburgh, Pittsburgh, Pennsylvania

In addition, I deem it appropriate to acknowledge the influence which Confucius has had on me.

If one learns from others, but does not think,
one will be bewildered.
If one thinks, but does not learn, one will peril.

— Confucius (551–479 BC)

Contents

Chapter 1

Introduction[1]

Cantillon (1755) described entrepreneurs as absorbing uncertainty caused by changing conditions, and thus contributing to the welfare of society. The aristocrat industrialist, Jean Baptiste Say defined the entrepreneur as the agent who "unites all means of production and who finds in the value of the products... the re-establishment of the entire capital he employs, and the value of the wages, the interest, and the rent which he pays, as well as the profits belonging to himself (Say, 1816, pp. 28–29)."

In this book, entrepreneurship refers to economic undertaking; this is based on the classical definition of the word, which can be traced to the German *unternehmung* literally translated as undertaking. The agents of entrepreneurship are entrepreneurs, from the French *entre preneurs*, literally meaning "between takers." The flagships of entrepreneurship are small and medium enterprises (SMEs).

While large corporations can greatly increase their efficiency and profitability, by outsourcing to specialised enterprises of lesser scale, entrepreneurs can benefit by focusing on niche markets. When having an economy of scale is not an issue, small firms may even have comparative advantages (vis-à-vis larger ones) in assembly, mixing or finishing. Thus, entrepreneurs need not compete with large firms. Instead, large and small firms can form symbiotic relationships, offering complementary services, thus improving a society's bearing capacity. Given that the flexibility of entrepreneurs, in the absence of excessive bureaucracy, helps them respond quickly to changing needs, entrepreneurship can

---

[1]The chapter draws on previous publications by the same author.

1

Exhibit 1.1   Agent of Enterprise; photo ©2006 Leo Paul DANA

Exhibit 1.2   Small-scale Retail Operation; photo ©2006 Leo Paul DANA

Exhibit 1.3   Flexible; photo ©2006 Leo Paul DANA

Exhibit 1.4   Decreasing Poverty; photo ©2006 Leo Paul DANA

Exhibit 1.5   India Encourages Cottage Industries; photo ©2006 Leo Paul DANA

Exhibit 1.6   British Colonial Experience in Bombay; photo ©2006 Leo Paul DANA

Exhibit 1.7   French Colonial Experience in Saigon; photo ©2006 Leo Paul DANA

also contribute to social development by providing local employment with relatively low levels of investment.

Today, it is widely accepted that entrepreneurship contributes to development, with a positive effect on society, creating employment, economic expansion, a larger tax base, and more consumer well being. This is increasingly supported by research, and governments around the world have acknowledged this.

Although interest in entrepreneurship as an academic discipline has spanned the globe, the phenomenon itself is expressed differently around the world. Furthermore, each government's policies affect entrepreneurship in different ways.

As will be shown, entrepreneurship differs greatly across Asia. Cultural values, government policy and a variety of other factors, including a nation's colonial experience, affect entrepreneurship.

Even the definition of "small business" varies. In Indonesia, for example, the government defines small industries as units of production with five to 20 workers. In Malaysia, "a small or medium industry" is defined

Exhibit 1.8   Manufacturer in Malaysia; photo ©2006 Leo Paul DANA

as "a manufacturer with up to 2.5 million ringgits in owner's equity." Environments with unlike histories and public policies shape entrepreneurship differently.

The East

The East is a career.

— Benjamin Disraeli, Prime Minister of England

The concept of "Asia" originates from the ancient civilisation of Mesopotamia and the eastern shores of the Mediterranean Sea. In Assyrian, *asu* means "east." It is likely that ancient Greek entrepreneurs adopted the term from Phoenician merchants, thus designating the land to the east. That was probably between 600 and 500 BC.

The Greeks cultivated relations with Asians, and trade expanded considerably. Both land and sea routes were further developed under the Romans,

Exhibit 1.9   French Car in Former French Colony; photo ©2006 Leo Paul DANA

Exhibit 1.10   Lama Temple in Beijing; photo ©2006 Leo Paul DANA

mostly to the Indian sub-continent. The Venetian explorer, Marco Polo, wrote accounts of his 13th century travels to India, China, and beyond. Before the arrival of the Europeans, there were many independent empires in Asia — at least a dozen in south-east Asia alone.

Exhibit 1.11   Hindu Temple in Singapore; photo ©2006 Leo Paul DANA

Exhibit 1.12   Synagogue in Singapore; photo ©2006 Leo Paul DANA

Exhibit 1.13 Cows Are Respected in India; photo ©2006 Leo Paul DANA

Beginning in the 16th century, European colonialism began to impose a new economic structure, and new patterns of trade emerged. Coffee, rubber and tea plantations were introduced. These being labour-intensive, workers were imported, thereby causing significant demographic shifts and changing ethnic distribution. Whereas Asia had formerly exported finished products, the colonies became exporters of raw materials and importers of manufactured goods. The emphasis on cash crops caused a move away from traditional self-sufficiency.

The mid-20th century saw a return to independence. In 1944, the Japanese declared Indonesia independent, effective at the termination of the war. The independence of the Philippines was declared on July 4, 1946. Ho Chi Minh declared Vietnam independent, on September 2, 1946. Laos, which was declared an associate state of the French Union in 1949, was granted full independence in 1953. Also in 1953, Cambodia declared its independence, which was recognised in 1954. Malaya became independent in 1957. Singapore obtained self-government from London in 1959, and independence from Malaysia, in 1965. However, nations continued to be influenced by their historical experiences.

Exhibit 1.14   China; photo ©2006 Leo Paul DANA

Exhibit 1.15   India; photo ©2006 Leo Paul DANA

Exhibit 1.16   Malaysia; photo ©2006 Leo Paul DANA

Exhibit 1.17   Singapore; photo ©2006 Leo Paul DANA

Exhibit 1.18   Thailand; photo ©2006 Leo Paul DANA

Cultural and religious differences are also important. Mahayana Buddhists (of the northern school) adopted the name "Greater Vehicle." They called the Theravada (southern) school the "Lesser Vehicle." The state religion in Cambodia is Hinayana Buddhism. In contrast, the principal religion of Vietnam is Mahayana Buddhism. In Tibet, the *Srunmas* are guardians of their faith.[2] In Malaysia, the religion is Islam. Singapore is officially multi-denominational, recognising Baha'i, Buddhist, Christian, Hindu, Jewish, Muslim, Sikh, Taoist and Zoroastrian religions.

Asia covers more area than North America, Europe and Australia combined. Nations of western Asia — Israel, Jordan, Lebanon, Palestine, Syria, and Turkey — are treated in Dana (2000b). Countries of Central Asia — Kazakhstan, the Kyrgyz Republic, Tajikistan, Turkmenistan, and Uzbekistan — are the focus of Dana (2002). The geographic focus of this book is the group of East Asian countries from India to Japan, including Cambodia, China,

---

[2] See Rock (1935).

Exhibit 1.19   Vietnam; photo ©2006 Leo Paul DANA

Indonesia, Korea, Laos, Malaysia, Myanmar, Nepal, the Philippines, Singapore, Taiwan, Thailand, and Vietnam.

Heterogeneity

Westerners sometimes speak of an Asian model of business or management, without considering the wide divergence within this vast geographic region. Yet, entrepreneurship, today, is shaped by cultural and historical factors. Not surprisingly, peoples with unlike experiences exhibit different approaches to management and entrepreneurship.

The Chinese and Indian minorities in Pacific Asia demonstrated a strong propensity for entrepreneurship. The same is true for Jews from Iraq and also for Armenians. Some chose entrepreneurship because they were unable to integrate into their host society; others did so because cultural values made it socially desirable for them. In other cultures, entrepreneurship is considered to be a less desirable option. Haley and Haley (1998) wrote that while merchants are exalted in Japanese culture, they are reviled in Chinese tradition.

Exhibit 1.20   Peddlers with Shoulder-Poles in Vietnam; photo ©2006 Leo Paul DANA

Attitudes toward entrepreneurship and entrepreneurs vary not only among countries but also within them. There are important differences among people of one nation. Goodnow suggested that the physical environment was among the causal variables, and he described China as "two countries in one (1927, p. 651)." The Chinese speak a variety of dialects and different dialect groups have their own clan associations, resulting in unique networks of entrepreneurs with distinct patterns of entrepreneurship. While most Chinese in Vietnam are Cantonese, 77% of the Chinese in Cambodia are Teochew, and 85% of the Chinese in the Philippines are Hokkien (Haley, Tan and Haley, 1998).

Within Indonesia, the Balinese are more tolerant of Chinese entrepreneurs than are the orthodox Muslims of Sumatra. Among the Indigenous hill-tribes of Sumatra, women are in charge of possessions, and traditionally a man's assets were passed on to a sister rather than to a spouse (Moore, 1930).

Exhibit 1.21   Magen Abraham Synagogue of Iraqi Jews in Ahmedabad; photo ©2006 Leo Paul DANA

In Kelantan and in Terengganu — on the east coast of the Malay Peninsula — pork-eating is not tolerated in public, as this act is considered offensive to the Muslims of this Malaysian province. In contrast, compatibility in religion, social customs and culinary habits allowed Chinese entrepreneurs to integrate easily into Thai society.

Also important is the fact that attitudes and behaviours are not always static. About Japan, Griffis wrote, "When feudalism had been abolished, in 1871, and the once-despised merchant was given honor and opportunity, he unfolded the pinions of a towering ambition and looked abroad to capture the markets of Asia (1923, p. 419)."

A characteristic which reappears across Asia is the existence of entrepreneurship networks that bind together entrepreneurs, based on trust. Numerous enterprises work together as a team, with little concern about core competencies. Group conformity prevails over individualism, and relationships

Exhibit 1.22   Well-networked in Beijing; photo ©2006 Leo Paul DANA

Exhibit 1.23   Sub-contracting; photo ©2006 Leo Paul DANA

prevail over constraints. Entrepreneurship networks transcend the limits of a small-scale enterprise.

Redding (1990) focused on Chinese enterprise — prominent in East Asia. The economic dominance of Chinese entrepreneurs often led to tensions. In response to ethnic discrimination, Chinese entrepreneurs often chose to have a low profile. Rather than develop their own brands, they usually preferred to act as subcontractors, wholesalers and retailers.

As will be shown throughout this book, there is no one best approach to entrepreneurship; rather, different nations adopt policy models, which are relevant to their respective history and culture.

Economic Sectors

Where governments have clung on to socialist ideology, there tends to be a large sector of the economy that is state-controlled, and it operates along side the traditional bazaar and the more modern firm-type sector. It is useful, therefore, to distinguish among these very distinct sectors of economic activity, which co-exist across Asia. The bazaar, the state-controlled planned sector, and the firm-type sector are components of the formal economy, some of the features of which are summarised in Table 1.1.

Table 1.1   Sectors of the Formal Economy

The Bazaar	State-Controlled Planned Sector	Firm-Type Sector
Focus on personal relations	Focus on bureaucracy	Focus on impersonal transactions
Segmentation refers to producers	Segmentation not considered	Segmentation refers to the market
Competition refers to tension between buyer and seller	Competition is deemed unnecessary, as the state declares a monopoly	Competition is an activity which takes place among sellers
Prices are negotiated	Prices are dictated by the state	Prices are indicated by the vendor

Exhibit 1.24   The Bazaar; photo ©2006 Leo Paul DANA

Exhibit 1.25   Among Traders; photo ©2006 Leo Paul DANA

In addition, the parallel economy includes informal economic activity; internal economic activity with no transaction; covert economic activity; and fictitious economic activity. Discussions of these shall follow.

The Bazaar

The bazaar is a social and cultural system, a way of life and a general mode of commercial activity, which has been in existence for millennia. In the bazaar, economic transactions are *not* the focus of activities; instead, the focus is on personal relationships. In this scenario, consumers do not necessarily seek the lowest price or the best quality. An individual gives business to another with whom a relationship has been established, to ensure that this person will reciprocate. *Reciprocal preferential treatment reduces transaction costs.*[3] The multiplicity of small-scale transactions, in the bazaar, results in a fractionalisation of risks and therefore of profit margins; the complex balance of credit relationships is carefully managed, as described by Geertz (1963).

Prices in the bazaar are negotiated, as opposed to being specified by the seller. In contrast to the firm-type sector, in which the primary competitive stress is among sellers, the sliding price system of the bazaar results in the primary competitive stress being between buyer and seller (Parsons and Smelzer, 1956). The lack of information results in an imperfect market and with few exceptions, such as basic food staples, retail prices are not indicated; rather, these are determined by negotiations. The customer tests price levels informally, before bargaining begins. It is often the buyer who proposes a price, which is eventually raised. As discussed by Geertz, the "relatively high percentage of wholesale transactions (i.e., transactions in which goods are bought with the express intention to resell them) means that in most cases both buyer and seller are professional traders and the contest is one between experts (1963, p. 33)."

Once a mutually satisfactory transaction has taken place, the establishment of a long-term relationship makes future purchases more pleasurable, and profitable. As noted by Webster (1992), building long-term relationships can be viewed as a social and economic process. Unlike Western relationship

---

[3]For a discussion of transaction costs, see Williamson (1985; 1996).

marketing, which is customer-centred, whereby a seller seeks long-term business relationships with clients (Evans and Laskin, 1994; Zineldin, 1998), the focus in the bazaar is on the relationship itself. In the bazaar, *both* the buyer and the seller seek a personal relationship.

Firms in the bazaar are not perceived as rivals of one another. There is minimal — if any — brand differentiation among merchants. Vendors do not necessarily seek to optimise monetary gain. Economic rationality is not always obvious.

In contrast to the Occident, where segmentation refers to the market, in the bazaar economy, segmentation refers to the clustering of producers and retailers; street-names reflect this. In Yangon — formerly Rangoon — the Chamber of Commerce and Industry is located on Merchant Street. The street-map of Hanoi includes Broiled Fish Street, Coffin Street, Fish Sauce Street, Gold Street, Jewellers Street, Paper Street, Silk Street, Sweet Potato Street, and Tin Street. Long gave an account of his observations in Hanoi, "Street names in the teeming native-Chinese section are a guide to the shopper. Each bears the name of the product traditionally sold there — silk, tin, scales, spice, brass, paper, jewelry (1952, pp. 315–316)."

Likewise, Passantino described the bazaar in Kunming, China, "There is also a street of beggars... There are streets for pig auctions and for prostitutes; there is one for banks... (1946, p. 142)." Even today, in the bazaar economy, shops still are clustered according to the goods offered therein.

When examining the bazaar, it is important to understand the relationships among the players within it, their organisation and their economic principles. The bazaar is a hub of information exchange. Buyers and sellers express intentions, and an intricate network of relationships facilitates transactions. As explained by Christian, "News spreads rapidly in a Shan States bazaar. Within the hour I was offered a half a dozen old pistols (1943, p. 504)."

While the entrepreneur described by Schumpeter (1912; 1928; 1934; 1939; 1942; 1947; 1949) is an innovator who causes disequilibrium to profit therefrom, the entrepreneur of the bazaar may simply identify an opportunity for profit — rather than create one. In this way, the entrepreneur of the bazaar corresponds to that of the Austrian school (Kirzner, 1973; 1979; 1982;

1985). Geertz (1963) and Dana (2000b) discuss, in detail, phenomena of the bazaar.

The State-Controlled Planned Sector

In transitional economies, state firms are remnants of the communist model — a doctrine first published in German (Marx and Engels, 1848), in Russian in 1882, and in English in 1888. This model assumed that a central office was in the best position to balance supply and demand. The focus of the state-controlled planned sector is thus neither on transactions nor on relationships, but rather on the state bureaucracy.

When the state produced everything, centralisation ruled out competitors. Barriers to trade, coupled with an import-substitution policy, ensured that competition is not a factor. Since demand exceeded supply, marketing was not necessary and segmentation was not considered. Prices became a function of the government's bureaucracy. Dalgic (1998) reported on an empirical study, which found that state-owned firms had much less of a market orientation, than did private companies.

The Firm-Type Sector

The firm-type sector is an economic institution, which involves a mode of commercial activity such that industry and trade take place primarily within a set of impersonally defined institutions, grouping people according to organisation and specialisation. It is assumed that profit-maximising transactions will occur based on rational decision-making, rather than the nature of personal relationships. The focus is transactions and these tend to be impersonal. Weber's (1924) thesis applies here.

In this sector of the economy, the decision space is occupied by product attributes; the buyer and seller are secondary, if not trivial, to the transaction decision. The interaction between the buyer and the product is deemed more important than that between the buyer and the seller. Transactions are based on economic rationality and are therefore impersonal in nature. Competition is an activity that takes place between sellers, who engage in segmentation, in

Exhibit 1.26   Small-scale Industry in Chennai (Formerly Madras); photo ©2006 Leo Paul DANA

order to partition the market into like-groups of predictable consumers. Prices are tagged, reflecting market forces.

While Western marketing principles (Gronroos, 1989) apply to this sector, market-orientation is linked to the maturity of the industrialisation process (Seglin, 1990). Where industrial development is limited, the framework for economic transition may have to rely more on new ventures and on joint initiatives.

The Parallel Economy

Under central planning, the lack of a legal market economy led to permanent shortages. Survival strategies often involved the emergence of entrepreneurs in the parallel economy, where inefficient regulations could be circumvented. According to Grossman (1977), this underground activity increased the overall efficiency of resource allocation under central planning. The problem is that a mindset evolved, equating efficiency with the evasion of regulation.

Recent years have been characterised by economic reform, regulatory reform, and change in the mindset of people. However, change in mindset has not kept up with changes in regulatory framework (North, 1990). Since these have not been evolving at the same pace, new problems have become associated with transition. As a consequence of their experience under central planning, people came to equate entrepreneurship with the avoidance of communist law. When new regulations were introduced to usher in market economics, people continued to circumvent business law. As noted by Feige and Ott (1999), during transition, evasion and non-compliance with new rules renders them ineffective. Thus, where economic reform has been faster than the ability of people to adapt, inertia has delayed actual transition. Štulhofer (1999) used the term "*cultura inertia*" to describe a collectivist legacy that has survived from the past. Especially among the elderly, there is still a distrust of the state, of banks and of legal institutions. Conditions in transitional economies thus make the parallel sector very popular, avoiding all forms of taxation. In transitional economies that lack developed market institutions, it is common to have a high proportion of underground activities. O'Driscoll, Holmes and Kirkpatrick (2001) reported a black market in Laos, larger than the formal economy.

The popularity of the parallel economy is no surprise, considering the low initial role of legitimate private enterprise, coupled with a high degree of liberalisation, and hindered by the lack of macro-stability in the absence of a sufficiently developed legal framework. As illustrated in Table 1.2, the parallel economy may be informal; internal; covert; or fictitious.

Informal Economic Activity

Barter, selling from an impromptu stall and itinerant vending are considered forms of informal economic activity. Unrecorded cash sales circumvent taxation as well as regulation.

Table 1.2   Activities of the Parallel Economy

Category	Examples
Informal Economic Activity (with business transaction)	Barter, street vending, unrecorded cash sales
Internal Economic Activity (with no business transaction)	Subsistence agriculture, hunting, fishing
Covert Economic Activity (with illegal business transaction)	Prostitution, smuggling, trade in illegal drugs
Fictitious Economic Activity	Foreign devil company

Exhibit 1.27   Unrecorded; photo ©2006 Leo Paul DANA

In some economies, private enterprise is concentrated in the informal sector. This is illustrated by the large numbers of self-employed vendors in the profitable distribution of goods and services. The law is often bent, but authorities generally tolerate the sector. A relevant discussion from Dana (1992) is presented concisely by Chamard and Christie (1996).

For some entrepreneurs in transitional economies, legal transactions may be limited to informal barter. The transition from such a traditional system to a modern cash economy will require cognitive innovation. A prerequisite will be for people to internalise new notions of measurability, to encourage the use of cash. New elements of formality, and impersonal structure, will have to be introduced and internalised, before new institutions can function effectively. At the World Economic Forum in Davos, Somavia (2006) argued that cultural barriers often hinder transition from the informal economy to the formal sector.

Internal Economic Activity

This category of economic activity is best described as internal, because *no business transaction* takes place. Wealth is created, but nothing is sold for profit. That which is created is consumed or saved for personal use. In transitional economies, internal subsistence activity is often necessary, as a means to adapt to rapid reform.

Examples of internal economic activity include subsistence agriculture, and subsistence fishing. Both are legal, but involve no market transaction external to the producer. These are, therefore, forms of internal economic activity.

While internal economic activity exists, as an activity of choice — even amid the most advanced and industrialised backdrop (Dana, 1995a) — for some people in transitional economies, this is the only strategy for survival.

Covert Economic Activity

This category of economic activity involves business transactions, which are illegal, and therefore conducted in a covert way, in order to avoid punitive measures from law-enforcing authorities (Haskell and Yablonsky, 1974; Henry, 1978). Prostitution, which Cantillon (1755) considered a form of entrepreneurship, often falls in this category.

Covert activity promises fast cash. Glinkina (1999) predicted the growth of covert economic activity, in some environments. In Cambodia, illegal logging has been an economically significant covert activity. In Myanmar, smuggling has been on the rise (O'Driscoll, Holmes and Kirkpatrick, 2001).

Fictitious Economic Activity

Fictitious economy has been created to facilitate circumvention of the law; this "implies speculative transactions and different kinds of swindles with a view to receiving and transferring money, including contrived rent-seeking (Glinkina, 1999, p. 102)." In Vietnam, for instance, "foreign devil" companies have been used to set up fictitious economic activity.

Melting Pot Pluralism and Structural Pluralism

Where groups with unlike spheres of values co-exist, the result is a pluralistic society. Norwegian anthropologist Frederik Barth[4] placed great emphasis on the existence of different spheres of values. Central to his discussion is the concept of the entrepreneur being an essential broker, mediating boundary transfers in this situation of contacts between cultures. By being active in the transformation of a community, entrepreneurs are the social agents of change.

Enterprise is very much influenced by the nature of pluralism. It is, therefore, important to distinguish between **melting pot pluralism**, and **structural pluralism**. When people, from different cultures, share activities in a secular mainstream arena, the expression of cultural differences tends to be limited to private life. Often, employment is shared in a common sphere of life, while cuisine, customs, languages and religion are a domestic concern. This form of socio-economic pluralism is referred to as **melting pot pluralism**, and this is descriptive of the situation in Singapore.

In contrast, **structural pluralism** involves a society with different cultures that do *not* share a secular mainstream arena. In such a case, there is minimal interaction across cultures. Rather, each ethnic group has its distinct institutions, and members of a given community have a lifestyle that is incompatible

---

[4]See Barth (1963; 1966; 1967a; 1967b; 1981).

Exhibit 1.28   Multilingual Trader; photo ©2006 Leo Paul DANA

with that of people from other backgrounds. This type of pluralism is prevalent in Xinjiang (China).

Toward an Understanding of Transition

Cambodia, China, Laos, Myanmar and Vietnam are among many countries referred to as being in transition to a market economy. As China prospers, it is useful to keep in mind that transition requires more than funding and infrastructure. Transition also involves mindset. Business takes place between people, and the interaction between the parties does not take place in a vacuum, but rather it is part of a social system, as discussed by Hakansson (1982).

Central to transactions are the cultural assumptions of a social system. In the West, these are implicit because it is assumed that everyone knows about them; marketing takes place in the context of a firm-type economy. In transitional economies, environmental factors must not be ignored. As discussed by Huntington (1996), globalisation has not led to a single world culture.

The move to a market economy — transition — is process-driven, and this necessitates the understanding of people and their culture. The focus of the following chapter, therefore, is culture.

Exhibit 1.29   Far from Globalisation; photo ©2006 Leo Paul DANA

Throughout this book, unless otherwise specified, statistics were provided by government sources. The symbols $ and ¢ refer to the currency of the United States.

Chapter 2

Culture and Enterprise[5]

Introduction

Globalisation may have given rise to a global village, but has not produced a homogeneous world culture. Instead, there are different belief systems, each with its set of customs. This is important because culture shapes managerial assumptions. While that which goes on around the negotiation table is important, everything that surrounds a deal is equally influential — spoken or unspoken.

Many managers report frustrations when doing business in Asia, particularly when delaying tactics appear during negotiations. Du Ding-Ping, in his book about how to do business with Americans, explains that delays help the Chinese during negotiations with Westerners. Perhaps knowing this may be a good reminder of the Western notion that "patience is a virtue" and that it might be beneficial to adhere to this virtue when doing business with Asians. Developing the ability to be patient and tolerant can surprisingly speed up negotiations; inflexibility and haste may, more often than not, lead to a bad relationship, what the Chinese call *guanxi gao jiang*.

Business increasingly involves interaction with foreign suppliers, employees, distributors, clients and government officials. Each operates in a particular environment, where interactions involve implicit and explicit assumptions. This is a function of the complex belief systems, cultural values and attitudes that dictate accepted norms of conduct.

---

[5]This chapter draws heavily on material published in an article commissioned by the *Financial Times* (Dana, 2000c).

Exhibit 2.1   Respecting Ancestors during the Ghost Festival; photo ©2006 Leo Paul DANA

It is of crucial importance for people in business to understand cultural differences. Yet, many Westerners often fail to acknowledge the extent to which culture affects enterprise.

It is not a matter of noting the "different ways" that "those" people have; it is considerably more useful to understand the rationale behind these ways. Everything has a reason, and actions may have implications. In contrast to the short-term focus of many companies in the West, Asians often have a longer-range plan. Also, Asian entrepreneurs are generally reluctant to share their implicit assumptions with outsiders.

Many Asians have mastered the comprehension of Western culture and have developed the ability to adapt to it; they have built on the knowledge conveyed to them by a variety of sources. In contrast, Westerners seldom have the patience to master an Asian language, let alone one of its cultures. Complex cultural environments require fluency not only in words, but also more importantly in understanding of what is not said — and this takes time, patience and dedication to learn. Westerners may argue that time is money and they cannot afford to learn everything it takes before even discussing a deal. In the long term, however, more knowledge does pay off.

Exhibit 2.2 At a Wedding in Nepal; photo ©2006 Leo Paul DANA

The Chinese Experience

The dominant culture in Asian business is that of the Chinese. This is not surprising, considering that ethnic Chinese are well represented in the realm of business around the world and very concentrated in Asian countries. In Ho Chi Minh City — formerly Saigon — for instance, 12% of the population is ethnic Chinese, and this group controls half of the local economy.

Given the widespread influence of Chinese culture, one would think that it is appropriate for Western businesses to take the time to learn something about this culture and how it affects business; yet, even large and global players have made costly errors. In 1979, Northern Telecom was approached to provide new switching equipment for China. The communications giant underestimated the importance of "face" and embarrassed Chinese officials. When the company tried to get a deal with China in 1987, the Chinese officials remembered that Northern Telecom had "walked away from negotiations in 1979." This time, the tables were turned: although Northern Telecom was eager to do business, the Chinese negotiators were not.

Exhibit 2.3   Chinatown in Singapore; photo ©2006 Leo Paul DANA

Networking as Viewed from the Occident

Networking involves calling upon a web of contacts for information, support and assistance. Aldrich and Zimmer (1986) integrated social network theory into the study of entrepreneurship. They linked entrepreneurship to social networks. Carsrud, Gaglio and Olm (1986) also found networks important to the understanding of new venture development. Aldrich, Rosen and Woodward (1987) studied the impact of social networks on profit, as well as on business creation; they found network accessibility significant in predicting new venture creation. Likewise, Dubini and Aldrich (1991) found networks central to entrepreneurship. Gomes-Casseres (1997) focused on the alliance strategies of small firms. Anderson (1995) and Johanson and Associates (1994) studied the effect of business networks on internationalisation of firms. Indeed, networks can influence a firm's degree of internationalisation (Dana, Etemad and Wright, 2000).

Boissevain and Grotenbreg (1987), in their study of the Surinamese in Amsterdam, suggested that access to a network of contacts is an important resource for entrepreneurs. They noted, for instance, that networks could provide introductions to wholesalers and warnings of government inspections. In their study of Asians in Atlanta, Min and Jaret (1985), found family networks to be a source of manpower for entrepreneurs. Analysing Asian entrepreneurs in Britain, Aldrich, Jones and McEvoy found that their sample benefited from "certain advantages denied non-ethnic competitors (1984, p. 193)." They found a strong internal solidarity in the ethnic enclave. Given that the possibility of exploiting opportunities appears to be linked to the internal organising capacity of a group — such as creating an ethnic network — Auster and Aldrich (1984) concluded that the ethnic enclave reduces the vulnerability of small firms, by providing an ethnic market and also general social and economic support, including credit. Others who focused on ethnic minority enterprise include Aldrich and Waldinger (1990), Cummings (1980), Dana (1995a), Jenkins (1984), Light (1972; 1984), Light and Bonacich (1988), Min (1984; 1986–7; 1987), Portes and Bach (1985), Portes and Jensen (1987; 1989; 1992), Sanders and Nee (1987), Waldinger (1984; 1986a; 1986b), Waldinger and Aldrich (1990), Waldinger, Aldrich and Ward (1990), Waldinger, McEvoy and Aldrich (1990), Ward (1987), Ward and Jenkins (1984), Wong (1987), and Wu (1983).

Networking in Asia

Aspects of networking reflect historical, cultural and demographic factors. In contrast to the situation prevailing in many industrialised countries, where voluntary migration prompted members of some immigrant minorities to create networks to help other members of their community (Acs and Dana, 2001; Boissevain and Grotenbreg, 1987; Brenner and Toulouse, 1990; Dyer and Ross, 2000; Iyer and Shapiro, 1999; Light, 1984), much of the demographic shifting in Asia resulted from forced migration.

Migration to Central Asia was largely the result of civil engineering, rather than a voluntary migration of entrepreneurs with a high need for achievement (McClelland, 1961). In Central Asia and in Indochina, the situation has been such that there has been considerable emigration, as opposed to immigration. Despite the absence of immigrant networks in these environments, there are nevertheless ethnic networks and these take on a distinct flavour. Muslims in Central Asia, for instance, have developed networks of like-minded co-ethnics in neighbouring countries, and this has enhanced opportunities for trade. International transactions are facilitated by the fact that members of ethnic networks speak the same language, and share similar values, influenced by the same religion.

In spite of the political divide, which separated the Kazakhs in China from those in the Soviet Union, the Kazakhs in China feel that they have more in common with their co-ethnics in the republics of Central Asia, than with the Han-Chinese who rule them. The Han-Chinese read Mandarin and eat dishes that include pork. The Kazakhs — like the Uygurs and other Muslims in China — are often trained in Arabic script, and of course they would feel uncomfortable at a table where pork has been served. Indeed, entrepreneurs are comfortable doing business with like-minded people, whom they understand, and with whom they get along.

Inevitably, entrepreneurs form networks (Dana, 2001). Where civil servants are poorly paid, it is no secret that bribes are welcome. In these scenarios, business networks include government officials, as well as entrepreneurs.

Roles in Society

Confucianism teaches that people are *not* equal. To this day, people in China are defined by their role in society and contribution to it. Status is influenced by relationships and these are attached to implicit duties and obligations. People are viewed as relation-oriented beings, regulated by cardinal relationships that dictate an individual's obligations — *renqing* — toward other people. Observance of proper relationships is essential for the smooth functioning of society.

In Laos, for instance, the ethnic Chinese have become highly successful entrepreneurs, partly thanks to the lack of a local entrepreneurial culture. Business activities in this country have not been traditionally associated with high social status. Stemming from religious beliefs, cultural values in Laos emphasise the elimination of desire. Since commerce was traditionally perceived as a means to satisfy desire, social forces discouraged enterprise, and trade has

Exhibit 2.4   He Knows His Role in Society and Contribution to it; photo ©2006 Leo Paul DANA

usually been the role of those with inferior social standing. The communist takeover further discouraged entrepreneurial spirit.

In Laos, culture makes it important to extinguish unsatisfied yearnings. An important doctrine, here, focuses on suffering caused by unsatisfied wishes. Assuming that an unsatisfied craving causes suffering, then suffering can be eliminated if its cause — desire — is suppressed. According to this ideology, a respectable person strives to eliminate a perceived material need, rather than working toward the satisfaction of materialistic wants. Not surprisingly, ethnic minorities, especially the Chinese, dominate private enterprise, in Laos.

Guanxi

In the Chinese realm of business, a special relationship — *guanxi* — involves the exchange of favours, usually involving position or rank. It is similar to insurance, inasmuch as favours are registered — like premiums — so that benefits may be obtained if and when required. *Guanxi*, composed of two words, *guan* — meaning "to close up" — and *xi* — "to tie up" — expresses the notion of being an insider to a relationship network that involves obligations. *La guanxi* refers to the act of getting on one's good side.

While Western business-people usually have a general understanding of this concept, relatively few Westerners realise that the mutual obligation is a function of one's ability to help, explaining why the weaker party accepts to receive more, in exchange for less. Furthermore, *guanxi* is not easy for Westerners to develop. *Guanxi* is intuitive, rather than rational, and it is not limited to business hours.

In the West, relationship marketing — the pursuit of customer loyalty — involves the fostering of long-term alliances with customers; in a similar fashion, *guanxi* involves building a long-term relationship, based on trust and mutual exchange, in order to secure customer loyalty and good working relations. *Guanxi* forms a bond among buyers and sellers and between suppliers and producers.

Westerners seeking joint venture partners in China should seek the ideal partner using connections maintained through *guanxi*; simultaneously, the foreigner would benefit by linking up with a company that has enough *guanxi* to get things done efficiently in China. For companies regulated by legislation such as the American Foreign Corrupt Practice Act, this is not an easy task; difficulty increases if and when a joint venture is established and the venture must maintain the *guanxi* of counterparts in China. Furthermore, it is important to look at the whole — not simply the parts.

Guanxi has long been important in Chinese business circles. The West has known contract law since the 1700s; the purpose of such legislation is to give business an assurance that deals will be honoured. In the absence of an elaborate contract law, the Chinese have relied on *guanxi* for the same assurance. When a relationship is more valuable than a transaction, then it is likely that the transaction will be smooth. Who would tarnish a relationship for a single transaction? No contract is necessary. The sense of obligation would come from the relationship, rather than a piece of paper.

On the other hand, in the absence of a strong relationship, there exists the possibility that one of the parties might ignore a contract. Although it had 18 years remaining on its lease, McDonald's was evicted from a Beijing site in favour of a newcomer with stronger *guanxi*. In Chinese circles, it is therefore more crucial to monitor a relationship than a transaction. Where a strong relationship exists, problems can always be solved. The long-term benefit of *guanxi* becomes obvious. During the process of cultivating *guanxi* within business relationships, customer loyalty evolves naturally, while bonds are created with suppliers and with creditors. *Guanxi* rests on the moral premise of *renqing*, as a justification for social exchange. In a Chinese cultural setting, *guanxi* is the norm for carrying on business.

Adapting to the Environment

One might argue that Western companies also value relationships and that these hold mutual obligations. There is, however, an important difference between the Chinese and Western views of relationships. *In the West, successful transactions lead to good relationships. In Chinese circles, one builds relationships in order to initiate transactions; the common belief is that if a relationship is built properly, then profitable transactions will follow.* As explained by Peng and Heath (1996) reciprocal preferential treatment reduces transaction costs.

Exhibit 2.5   Well-informed about the West; photo ©2006 Leo Paul DANA

Every region has a predominant culture and there are many intricacies intertwined into each one. Just as Europe hosts many different cultures,[6] there is neither one single culture nor one single way of doing business in Asia. The key for those attempting business there is to have patience and to learn as much as possible about what is important to each company, manager and worker.

As stated so well by Lasserre and Schütte, *"The West cannot expect to compete successfully with Asia as long as the Asians know more about the West than the West knows about Asia (1995, p. xv)."*

---

[6]See Dana (2005, 2006).

Chapter 3

Cambodia[7]

Indochina

This chapter is about Cambodia, one of the countries (the other two being Laos and Vietnam[8]) the land of which was formerly referred to as *Indochine française* — French Indochina. There are some important differences, as well as similarities, among the constituents of this region. As explained by Moore and Williams, China and India were the cultural parents of Indochina, making it a "mosaic of Indian and Chinese cultures (1951, p. 462)." Hindus sparked the native genius of the early Khmers, while Chinese officials lent their culture to the Annamese. Under colonial rule, the whole region used the same currency, the Indochinese *piastre* — issued by the Bank of Indochina.

It would be naïve, however, to overlook significant differences within this region. Traditionally, in Cambodia, the ownership of land was strongly individual in nature. In contrast, a tradition of communally owned land existed among the Vietnamese. Long observed:

> Unlike Viet Nam, which took China as its teacher, Cambodia and Laos received much of their art, religion, and language from India. Both countries resemble Thailand more than they do their Indochinese neighbor... Nor has Cambodian writing been changed to Roman letters like Viet Nam's; it uses graceful, rounded lines of Sanscrit (1952, p. 312).

---

[7] This chapter is based on information obtained from a variety of sources, including: the Ministry of Commerce and the Ministry of Finance and Economy. The chapter includes material that first appeared in Dana (1999b; 2002).

[8] Literally, Vietnam means "people of the south."

Indeed, in contrast to the adjacent area — today corresponding to southern Vietnam — which had its status changed to that of a colony and its alphabet changed to the Roman one, Cambodia had relatively little Occidental influence. Cambodia retained its monarchy and its script.

Williams wrote, "Between the India of unrest and stormy China is an oasis of peace and beauty — French Indo-China, composed of one colony and four protectorates (1935, p. 487)." Zasloff (1988) examined post-war Indochina. Vietnam became independent on September 2, 1945, Laos on July 19, 1949, and Cambodia on November 9, 1953.

In the 21st century, there are still important differences to be found when comparing the Kingdom of Cambodia, the Lao People's Democratic Republic, and the Socialist Republic of Vietnam. Their paths to transition follow quite unlike models.

In Cambodia, a true veritable transition has taken place. This involves complete "restructuring" under the constitutional monarchy. Cambodia has already privatised most state-owned enterprises, and import licenses have been abolished for most items. O'Driscoll, Holmes and Kirkpatrick (2001), described Cambodia as being freer[9] than any other transition economy of Asia. They showed that the government in Cambodia is less of a fiscal burden than is the case in the other countries of Indochina. Nevertheless, as observed by Prasso, "compared to neighboring Laos and Vietnam, which have also struggled to recover from an era of war and bloodshed, Cambodia remains far behind in its ability to establish the most basic building blocks of economic recovery... Domestic savings rates are stunningly low compared to other Asian countries (2001, p. 2)."

O'Driscoll, Holmes and Kirkpatrick (2001) showed that Cambodia has less black market activity than any other transitional economy in Asia. They also revealed that the economies of Laos and Vietnam each have more government intervention than is the case in Cambodia. While Cambodia has fewer restrictions on foreign direct investment, than other countries described in this book, Laos has the most.

---

[9] Beach and O'Driscoll defined economic freedom, as "the absence of government coercion or constraint on the production, distribution, or consumption of goods and services beyond the extent necessary for citizens to protect and maintain liberty itself (2001, pp. 43–44)."

In contrast to situation in Cambodia, the leadership of Laos is still recognised as being communist and even transition is centrally planned. Weighted by bureaucracy, nothing changes fast here.

In Vietnam, the Communist Party has taken steps, to "renovate" the economy with some transitional measures; yet, there has been no attempt to "restructure." The state has been slow to implement structural reforms, and this has been a concern for investors. Foreign direct investment fell from a high of $8.3 billion in 1996, to a total of $1.6 billion in 1999.

Cambodian law includes royal decrees, as well as legislation influenced by the United Nations Transitional Assistance in Cambodia (UNTAC). In contrast, the legal system of Laos is largely based on traditional customs and Soviet practice. The law in Vietnam blends communist theory with the French Civil Code.

Cambodia's merchant marine is seemingly large, as the government offers a flag of convenience to owners of foreign vessels. In contrast, Laos has one ship registered over 1,000 GRT. Vietnam has about 150 Vietnamese-owned ships registered.

In Cambodia, literacy among males is 48%; among females, it is 22%. In Laos, the figure is 70% for males and 44% for females. Vietnam is relatively more educated, with a literacy rate of 97% among males and 91% among females. Not surprisingly, the level of poverty varies too. In Cambodia, 36% of the people live below the poverty line, while the statistics for Laos and Vietnam are 46% and 37% respectively.

In addition to differences among the countries of Indochina, there is also heterogeneity within each country. Most noticeable is the ethnic Chinese minority, very active in enterprise. Over half a century ago, Moore stated, "keen traders, Indochina's 500,000 Chinese dominate many businesses (1950, p. 508)." Centrally planning has since come and gone, and the Chinese are still involved in entrepreneurial activity.

Cambodia

Cambodia covers 181,035 square kilometres. It lies on the Gulf of Siam, bordering Laos, Thailand, and Vietnam. Cambodia is among the least developed countries in the world. Traditionally, the people of Cambodia — known as Khmers — were not inclined to become entrepreneurs, as enterprise was not seen as contributing to Buddhist society. A merchant class developed after independence, but during the 1970s, the Khmer Rouge — officially the Communist Party of Kampuchea — extinguished private enterprise in this country. More recently, the ownership of property was legalised, and the nation embarked on a comprehensive programme of transition to a market economy.

According to O'Driscoll, Holmes and Kirkpatrick (2001), Cambodia ranks higher in economic freedom than any of the following: China, Kazakhstan, the Kyrgyz Republic, Laos, Myanmar, Tajikistan, Turkmenistan, Uzbekistan and Vietnam. The same study also calculated average tariff rates and found Cambodia to have the lowest of all these countries. As well, that study noted less government intervention in Cambodia than in any other country on the above list; comparing the fiscal burden of governments, Cambodia scored lowest.

Exhibit 3.1   Buddhist Society in Cambodia; photo ©2006 Leo Paul DANA

Historical Overview[10]

About 2,000 years ago, much of that which is Cambodia today belonged to the Kingdom of Funan — a prosperous nation frequented by merchants travelling between India and China (for a detailed account, see Chandler, 1999). At the time, Mahayana Buddhism flourished alongside the religion and culture of the Hindus.

During the 6th century, the Kambu'jas — literally "those born from Kambu" — established a kingdom in the interior of present-day Cambodia. Chinese travellers knew this kingdom as Chenla. Its people associated themselves with Kambu, a figure of Indian mythology and the nation became known as Kampuchea, a derivative of Kambu'ja.[11]

In 802, a Khmer prince declared himself a universal monarch, and founded a dynasty that lasted until Angkor was abandoned in the 16th century (Chandler, 1999). During the Angkorian period — 9th to 15th century — the civilisation stretched into parts of today's Laos, Thailand and Vietnam. Indravarman, who ruled from 889 to 910, built an elaborate irrigation system. Jayavarman VII, who ruled from 1181 to 1201, built a new capital — Angkor Thom.[12] During the 13th century, the nation gave up Hinduism, in favour of Buddhism. The official language of the Hindu priests was also abandoned.

Over the next two centuries, several tributary states — in what is now Thailand — declared their independence and invaded Cambodian territory (Chandler, 1999). The capital city shifted away from Angkor to the region of Phnom Penh.

In 1860, King Norodom ascended to the throne. Fearful of nearby Siam, in 1863, he asked France to provide protection, and he subsequently signed a treaty with Napoleon III, making Cambodia a French protectorate. In 1904, King Norodom was succeeded by King Sisowath, who reigned until 1927.

---

[10]This section benefited greatly from the personal assistance of David P. Chandler, PhD, Professor Emeritus of History, at Monash University, and Adjunct Professor of Asian Studies at Georgetown University. Professor Chandler is recognised as the leading authority on Cambodian history.

[11]The Portuguese later modified *Kambu'ja* to *Camboxa*. The French adapted it to *Cambodge*. When anglicised, the name became "Cambodia."

[12]*Angkor* means "the city," in Khmer, while *Thom* means "large."

Exhibit 3.2   French Colonial Architecture in Phnom Penh; photo ©2006 Leo Paul DANA

King Sisowath was succeeded by King Monivong, who died during the early phases of Japanese occupation. Prince Norodom Sihanouk — born on October 31, 1922 — was crowned king, in 1941. After the Japanese surrender, in 1945, France made Cambodia an autonomous state within the French Union — but retained control over its diplomatic, financial and military affairs.

In 1953, the *Royaume du Cambodge* — Kingdom of Cambodia — declared its independence, which was recognised in May 1954 by the Geneva Conference. Self-sufficient in food, the new kingdom enjoyed economic growth and became a net exporter of rice (Ear, 1995; Prud'Homme, 1969; Steinberg, 1959). In 1955, Sihanouk abdicated, but remained for 15 years the leading political figure in Cambodia.

Although Cambodian-American relations deteriorated after Cambodia rejected the American economic and military aid programme, in November 1963, Cambodia remained officially "neutral." Radio Phnom Penh subsequently stepped up anti-American propaganda (Abercrombie, 1964). For a lucid account of Sihanouk's policy of neutrality, see Hamel (1993).

Exhibit 3.3　Cambodian Independence Monument; photo ©2006 Leo Paul DANA

In 1969, the United States began bombing suspected communist camps in Cambodia. The population of Phnom Penh was slightly more than half a million at the time, and Cambodia was agriculturally prosperous.

In March 1970, General Lon Nol staged a successful coup d'état. Sihanouk was deposed and moved to Beijing. The country was renamed the Khmer Republic. Chantrabot (1993) gave a detailed account of that era.

On April 30, 1970, American and South Vietnamese troops attacked Cambodia. During the following years, hundreds of thousands of people were killed, and many fled from rural areas to Phnom Penh. By 1975, the capital city was home to two million people.

On April 17, 1975 the Khmer Rouge, a group whose goal was to transform the nation into an agrarian peasant-dominated Maoist co-operative, overran the republic. Under the leadership of Saloth Sar — who used the pseudonym Pol Pot[13] — the Khmer Rouge transformed the nation (Jackson, 1989), as the new regime confiscated private property, banned currency and

---

[13]For a discussion, see Chandler, Kiernan and Boua (1988).

changed the name of the country to Democratic Kampuchea. Millions of city dwellers were ordered to evacuate their homes and to migrate to the countryside; they were told that these measures were being taken in order to avoid bombings by the United States.

Cambodians interviewed by the author explained that the Khmer Rouge communists slit the throat of their prisoners, in order to save ammunition. Women's nipples were removed with pliers, and victims were left to scorpions.

Border clashes between the Khmer Rouge and the Vietnamese led to an invasion by Vietnam on December 25, 1978. On January 7, 1979, Vietnam toppled the Khmer Rouge regime. Again, the name of the country was changed, this time to the People's Republic of Kampuchea. Currency was re-introduced and people were again permitted to reside in towns.

Since the Khmer Rouge had killed the urban landlords, Phnom Penh was desolate at the time. Nevertheless, it was quickly populated as anybody could claim whatever property they wished, on a first come, first serve basis. People returned to Phnom Penh, but infrastructure was lacking.

Rice fields were abandoned as masses flocked to urban areas. Famine followed. During the 1980s, the Soviet Union and Vietnam contributed food to Kampuchea.

In September 1989, Vietnam withdrew its troops, and the State of Cambodia was established. However, the Khmer Rouge kept a hold of gem-rich lands neighbouring Thailand. Rumours spread that currency might be banned again and people dumped riels to buy gold; the currency tumbled.

In 1991, the United Nations brokered a peace accord known as the Paris Agreement, which was signed in October that same year. On October 31, the United Nations Security Council agreed to establish the United Nations Transitional Assistance in Cambodia (UNTAC).

The Khmer Rouge continued fighting in the jungle, and in January 1992, riots broke out in Phnom Penh — with the return of nominal Khmer Rouge leader, Khieu Samphan. On February 28, 1992, the United Nations Security Council voted to send a force of 22,000 to Cambodia.

Although the signing of the peace accord strengthened the riel, the influx of United Nations peacekeeping troops contributed to higher prices and subsequent devaluation. Retailers and even government ministries began refusing local currency. Inflation, in 1992, was 177%, while per capita GNP was $150. Government employees were earning low wages and often pursued sideline opportunities.

The 1993 constitution re-established the monarchy. Norodom Sihanouk was crowned king, once again, on September 23. In 1994, the literacy rate edged up to 35%.

During the first weekend of July 1997, a coup d'état by Hun Sen — holding the position of Second Prime Minister — overthrew Prince Norodom Ranariddh, the so-called Prime Minister of Cambodia at the time. The nation was scheduled to join ASEAN — along with Laos and Myanmar — on July 23, 1997. However, on July 10, the members of ASEAN decided to postpone admitting Cambodia into the association. The last Khmer Rouge fighter surrendered in December 1998.

On April 30, 1999, Cambodia officially joined ASEAN. The other members were Brunei, Indonesia, Laos, Malaysia, Myanmar, the Philippines, Singapore, Thailand and Vietnam.

In 2006, New Zealander Jane Nye, the 28-year old editor of the *Cambodian Scene* magazine, had her throat slashed during a robbery at a bar in Phnom Penh. The entrepreneur who owned the bar was stabbed to death.

Changing Policies and the Royal Cambodian Model

Under colonial rule, Cambodia's public policy was dictated by France, which was actually more interested in neighbouring Cochin-China — the area around Saigon, as Ho Chi Minh City was then known. In Cambodia, the French left the economy to market forces, but taxes raised in Cambodia were used to develop Cochin-China. Large-scale rubber plantations in Cambodia — which belonged to Europeans — imported workers from the area known today as Vietnam, justifying this by a claim that the local people were less productive.

Since Cambodia, Laos and the other constituents[14] of French Indochina used the same *piastre*, this facilitated such "imports."

French control ended with the independence of Cambodia. The *Banque National du Cambodge* (National Bank of Cambodia) introduced the local currency — the riel, which was pegged to 23.3905 mg. of gold. From 1953 to 1970, Sihanouk implemented a policy of national socialism. In the 1955 elections, the *Sangkum Reastr Niyum* (People's Socialist Community) won every seat in parliament. Although socialist policies were introduced, about 80% of the farmers remained the proprietors of the land that they farmed. Most of the farmers cultivated rice, and many raised animals. In urban areas, the ethnic Chinese controlled the economic sphere; 77% of these were Teochew Chinese from Guang Dong Province, in China.

Sihanouk introduced his first economic plan in 1956. It was a two-year plan, the budget of which the United States paid 57%, China 23% and France 17%. Only 3% of the budget was raised by Cambodia. The two-year plan emphasised the role of capital, but ignored private investment and entrepreneurship. The plan was renewed for another two years, beginning in 1958. After that, the Planning Ministry began to set longer plans. The first of these covered 1960 to 1964.

In 1963, private banks were nationalised and austerity measures resulted in many tariffs being doubled. A new economic plan covered the period 1964 to 1968 and another the years 1968 to 1972.

In April 1975, the Khmer Rouge implemented an unprecedented policy reform. During the last two weeks of April, the Khmer Rouge evacuated Phnom Penh, forcing every urban resident out of the city and into slave-labour camps in the countryside.

The regime proclaimed 1975 as Year Zero (Ponchaud, 1977). Private property, in theory and in practice, ceased to exist. The Central Bank was blown up, other banks were closed, currency was abolished, postal service ceased to exist, and the regime caused the death of over 1.5 million[15] Khmers — out of a national population of about seven million — eliminating intellectuals,

---

[14]These were Annam, Cochin-China, and Tonkin, later consolidated as Vietnam.
[15]Vietnamese sources claim the figure to be 3 million.

landlords, entrepreneurs and the business sector. Market activities were banned and all commercial transactions were outlawed. In addition to a change in clothing, individuals were allowed only two items of private property, namely a bowl and a spoon. The urban areas, including the capital city, Phnom Penh, were depopulated and would remain empty for over three years. All flights to and from Democratic Kampuchea were halted — except a fortnightly flight linking Phnom Penh with Beijing. The regime designed a four-year plan for the period 1977 to 1980. In 1977, people were required to participate in communal cooking and eating, as Pol Pot banned the private ownership of pots and pans.

When the Khmer Rouge regime was driven from power in 1979, trade resumed, but in the absence of a national currency; commerce relied on barter or foreign money. Only in March 1980 was currency reintroduced, and then only within the context of a socialist economy. Cigarettes, condensed milk, kerosene, rice, soap and sugar were subsidised by the state, but goods were rationed.

During the 1980s, the government devalued the Kampuchean currency. In 1984, $1 bought 7 riels; by the end of the decade, $1 was worth 380 riels.

After the 1989 withdrawal of the Vietnamese from Cambodia, reforms enhanced the economic environment for entrepreneurs to operate in the private sector. The local authorities divided farmland and distributed it to those living on it. In the urban areas, the Law of Private Ownership allowed persons to claim title to property occupied, and even to sell it.

In August 1991, the National Assembly passed the Law on the Management of Exchange, Precious Metals and Stones. This legislation contained 20 articles governing foreign exchange, precious metals and gems. In November, the Foreign Exchange Decree supplemented this law.

By 1992, three quarters of the economy was in private hands. Some entrepreneurs operated from their homes, while others lived in their shops. Smaller-scale vendors set up impromptu stalls. Petrol was sold on roadsides, in used soda-pop bottles.

Entrepreneurs were required to pay a signage tax and, therefore, many merchants — including prominent retailers in Phnom Penh — opted to have no sign.

Exhibit 3.4   Roadside Vending in the Capital City; photo ©2006 Leo Paul DANA

A new constitution introduced the Royal Cambodian Model in 1993. Article 56 specified that the kingdom would have a market economy. In an attempt to improve the inadequate infrastructure, in November 1993, the kingdom participated in the formation of Royal Air Cambodge, to supplement the operations of state-owned Kampuchea Airlines. Royal Air Cambodge was established as a joint venture, 60% owned by the government and 40% by a Malaysian affiliate of Malaysia Airlines (MAS). Linking Phnom Penh with Bangkok, Guangzhou, Ho Chi Minh City, Hong Kong, Kuala Lumpur and Singapore, Royal Air Cambodge became the largest airline in Cambodia. Yet, between 1994 and 2001, the firm lost over $30 million. In September 2001, flights to Ho Chi Minh City were suspended. On October 16, 2001 the airline stopped flying.

In August 1994, liberal laws were implemented to encourage entrepreneurship in the kingdom. A problem, however, was that a very lenient implementation of public policy allowed latent corruption to persist. Also in 1994, special zoning laws were introduced, to limit development in the area of Siem Reap; only small-scale ventures were allowed near Angkor Wat, and large hotels were required to be four kilometres away. Nevertheless, entrepreneurs could bribe officials and obtain exemptions. In the French daily *Figaro*, Desjardins (1997) dubbed Cambodia the "Kingdom of Corruption."

In 1994, the dollar traded at 2,400 riels and the inflation rate fell to 26%, but fighting escalated. Brown and Zasloff (1999) provided a detailed account of peacekeeping efforts. In 1995, although the Khmer Rouge continued to control its stronghold — in the northwest of the country — economic growth approached 5%; per capita GNP was $215, while inflation stood at 3.5%. The average value of $1 was 2,451 riels in 1995, 2,624 riels in 1996, and 2,938 riels in 1997. Then came the Asian Crisis. By 2006, $1 bought 4,230 riels.

Pluralism

The Chinese always had a significant impact on the economy in Cambodia. Gold, silver and coins were introduced to Cambodia by the Chinese, and Chinese traders flourished at Angkor. Immigrants from China came to dominate the realm of business.

Traditionally, the ethnic Khmers tended to be attracted to occupations related to agriculture, government service, and monastic life; commerce and industry were occupations that were left to ethnic minorities. Muslims controlled the cattle trade, commercial fisheries and the weaving industry. The ethnic Chinese engaged in international trade and in retailing.

Abercrombie reported on the situation during 1964:

Nearly a third of Phnom Penh's population of 403,500 are Chinese. Together with Vietnamese importers, shopkeepers, and moneylenders, they dominate the city's — and the country's — commerce. In the shops strange goods caught my eye: dogmeat sausages, incense sticks, begging bowls, silver elephants, betel leaves, Chinese comic books, brass hongs, and bamboo flutes (1964, p. 518).

Notice that the above account does not mention Khmer entrepreneurs. Elaborating on the ethnic Chinese, in Cambodia, Abercrombie explained, "Rarely holding citizenship, they maintain their own language, customs, and schools (1964, p. 526)."

Today, Cambodia is among the most homogeneous countries in Asia. There are, nevertheless, relatively small minority groups. The ethnic Chinese community is concentrated in entrepreneurial activities. The Vietnamese in Cambodia are often associated with fishing-related occupations. Although both of these minorities have suffered persecution in Cambodia — especially the Vietnamese — the Chinese are emerging as an important economic force, and Chinese aid is crucial to the well being of the current regime. Cambodia is also home to some 200,000 Cham Muslims and members of the Khmer Loeu hill-tribe.

The Nature of Entrepreneurship

Entrepreneurship in Cambodia developed rapidly after independence from France. In 1955, there were 650 small and medium-scale factories in Cambodia. By 1968, there were almost 4,000. Most entrepreneurs, however, were not industrialists. Many were speculators who tried to make fast money in alcohol, beef, gold, land, tobacco, salt and other commodities. These people also contributed to economic instability.

The economy collapsed during the era of the Khmer Republic, which lasted from 1970 to 1975. Manufacturing declined due to shortages of inputs. The republic financed its deficit by printing money and imposing a 60% Value Added Tax (VAT) on cigarettes.

White (1982) reported on covert economic activity in Cambodia. The article described entrepreneurs dealing in contraband goods smuggled to Kampuchea from Thailand. These included cigarettes, medicines, soap and watches.

A decade later, the *Far Eastern Economic Review* ran a cover story (Chandra and Tasker, 1992) describing the widespread activities of Thai entrepreneurs who were extracting gems from Cambodia.

In 1995, the *Washington Post* described Cambodia as a "pre-emerging market." That same year, *Paris Match* reported that prostitution was Phnom

Exhibit 3.5   Rice or Sex or Both?; photo ©2006 Leo Paul DANA

Penh's leading industry, with 10,000 prostitutes in town and another 10,000 elsewhere in the country. The prominent French magazine explained that virgins were rented for 2,500FF[16] before being discounted to 200FF. While opium was worth 150FF per gram, a bag containing 200 grams of cannabis cost 10FF. Marijuana was traded openly and commonly added as flavouring, in soups.

Meanwhile, some entrepreneurs made 6-year old children work in factories. Other children became entrepreneurs themselves, taking advantage of arbitrage opportunities, selling food and drinks to long-distance travellers on boats, buses and trains.

Desjardins (1997) described how government employees in Cambodia were selling, for personal gain, rubber and wood that belonged to the state, in addition to medicines donated by foreign parties, and meant for free distribution.

---

[16]The French franc (FF) was the currency of France until the introduction of the euro (€) on January 1, 2002. The euro was valued at 6.55957 FF.

Exhibit 3.6   Successful Woman Entrepreneur; photo ©2006 Leo Paul DANA

On March 7, 1999, the *Japan Times* (1999) described poverty-driven Cambodian entrepreneurs dealing in rare animals and their products. In Phnom Penh, an entrepreneur offered an endangered sun bear for sale, for $600.

Licensed and regulated by the central National Bank of Cambodia, VisionFund Cambodia provides business training and small loans (averaging $70 in 2004) to micro-entrepreneurs in seven Cambodian provinces. Its loan portfolio is $3 million and it boasts a repayment rate of 99.8%. Most of the clients are women.

Toward the Future

Earlier, this chapter summarised findings of O'Driscoll, Holmes and Kirkpatrick (2001): Compared to China and to other transitional economies, Cambodia ranks relatively high in economic freedom. Average tariff rates are lower in Cambodia than in than China, and elsewhere. There is less official government intervention in Cambodia than in many other countries. Comparing the fiscal burden of governments, Cambodia scored very low on the list. Yet, further investigation suggests that this may be an optimistic picture.

Naranhkiri Tith, Professor of International Economics and Asian Studies, at John Hopkins University, explained to the author: "Tax burden is low because of the inability to tax and not because of the willingness not to burden the tax payers; tariff is low because room must be left for corruption… and the official government intervention is less but corruption — a form of unofficial government intervention — is pervasive."

Although most enterprises in Cambodia are privately held, entrepreneurship in this kingdom is concentrated in grey or black-market areas. Casinos and shady banks are said to launder money. Can causal variables be identified?

One explanation is that the historical experience of this nation makes immediate gains more attractive than waiting for an uncertain future. All middle-aged Cambodians can remember the day money was made useless; the result is a predisposition to reject currency as a medium for savings, and for large purchases, Cambodians often use the *damleung* (1.2 ounces of gold) to buy property, and *the chi* (0.13 ounces of gold) for items such as televisions (Prasso, 2001).

Exhibit 3.7   Grey Market; photo ©2006 Leo Paul DANA

Exhibit 3.8   For Sale Only Today; photo ©2006 Leo Paul DANA

Entrepreneurship in Cambodia is largely short-term in nature, due to high risks and uncertainty. People use a young tree for firewood, as they are impatient to wait seven years for it to produce rubber. A more long-term orientation would be desirable in the future. In Cambodia, however, institutions are weak and traditions are strong.

Chapter 4

China[17]

Introduction

The People's Republic of China (PRC) — commonly referred to as mainland China, or simply China — covers 9,596,960 square kilometres, neighbouring Afghanistan, Bhutan, India, Kazakhstan, the Kyrgyz Republic, Laos, Mongolia, Myanmar, Nepal, North Korea, Pakistan, Russia, Tajikistan, and Vietnam. China has shores along the East China Sea, the South China Sea, and the Yellow Sea. In 2005, the Chinese economy grew 9.9%, making it the world's fourth after the United States, Japan, and Germany (Alderman, 2006).

Since the 1970s, liberalisation of the Chinese economy led to dynamism among SMEs (Wang and Yao, 2002). Unlike the situation prevailing in much of Eastern Europe, in Cambodia and in other states that have abandoned communist ideology in favour of capitalism, entrepreneurship in the PRC was introduced by the government as a supplement to the socialist economy.

Despite its success, in June 2001, China's Prime Minister Zhu Rongji declared that he was slowing down transition in the PRC, due difficulties created by economic reform. Ahlstrom and Bruton (2002) suggested that

---

[17]This chapter is based on information obtained from a variety of sources, including: the China Council for the Promotion of International Trade (CCPIT); the China Individual Labourers Association; the China International Trust Investment Co. (Beijing); the Department of Science and Technology for Rural Development; the Economic Management School of Shanghai University of Technology; the Industrial and Commercial Bureau; Kunming Foreign Economic Relations and Trade Commission; the Ministry of Agriculture, particularly its Department of Township Enterprise; and the Ministry of Foreign Economic Relations and Trade, Market and Trade Development Division. Travel to China was funded by Nanyang Business School. The chapter includes material that first appeared in Dana (1998a; 1999a; 1999b; 1999d; 1999e; 2002).

Exhibit 4.1   Fast Growth in Shanghai; photo ©2006 Leo Paul DANA

Exhibit 4.2   Entrepreneurship as a Supplement; photo ©2006 Leo Paul DANA

Exhibit 4.3   Informal; photo ©2006 Leo Paul DANA

Exhibit 4.4   Self-employed Woman; photo ©2006 Leo Paul DANA

entrepreneurial firms employ specific tactics in order to navigate China's often hostile institutional environment. According to Minniti, Bygrave, and Autio (2006), the prevalence rate of informal investors is higher in China than in Thailand.

While the *guoying qiye* — literally, state-run enterprise — is the Chinese term to describe a collective enterprise, the *siying qiye* is defined as a private enterprise owned by entrepreneurs and providing employment for eight or more people. Smaller firms, with fewer than eight people are referred to as *getihu*. Twenty percent of entrepreneurs in China are women (Smith-Hunter, 2006).

Historical Overview

China's first dynasty, the Xia, was established over 4,000 years ago. In 221 BC, Emperor Qin Shi Huang of the Qin dynasty (221 BC to 206 BC) united China, centralised his authority over the nation, banned slavery, and initiated the transition to feudalism.

The Hans (206 BC to 220 AD) entrenched the feudal system in China[18] and allowed the export of silk. During a horse-buying mission in 138 BC, Han-Chinese traders realised that Central Asian merchants were willing to pay a high price for silk, and this soon became China's main export. Agriculture, handicrafts, shipbuilding and weaving were developed during the Han dynasty. Also during this era, the armillary sphere and the seismograph were invented in China. Table 4.1 summarises Chinese history according to dynasties.

Chinese entrepreneurship developed without institutional support. Rather than foster entrepreneurship, several emperors attempted to discourage the activities of entrepreneurs. Traditional Chinese law, influenced by Confucian principles, forbade merchants from wearing nice clothes in public. The law also forbade them from riding horses or from travelling on wagons.

For many years, international trade occurred not because of encouragement by rulers, but rather in spite of state intervention. Boulnois (1963) gave

---

[18] See Edwards (2004).

Table 4.1   Historical Periods in China

Dynasty/Era	Period	Economy
Xia (Hsia)	2205 BC to 1766 BC	Slavery
Shang	1766 BC to 1122 BC	Slavery
Western Zhou	1122 BC to 770 BC	Slavery
Spring & Autumn Period	770 BC to 476 BC	Transition
Warring States Period	476 BC to 221 BC	Transition
Qin (Ch'in)	221 BC to 206 BC	Feudalism
Han	206 BC to 220 AD	Feudalism
Wei	220 to 265	Feudalism
Jin	265 to 420	Feudalism
Southern & Northern	420 to 589	Feudalism
Sui	590 to 617	Feudalism
Tang	618 to 907	Feudalism
Five Dynasties	907 to 960	Feudalism
Song	960 to 1279	Feudalism
Yuan (Mongol)	1279 to 1368	Feudalism
Ming	1368 to 1644	Feudalism
Qing (Manchu)	1644 to 1911	Feudalism
Modern Era	1911 to 1949	Bourgeois
Post-war Era	1949 to 1952	Rehabilitating
Planned Economy	1953 to 1978	Centrally planned
Opening Policy	1979 to 1992	Planned-commodity
Transitional	1993 to date	Socialist-market

an account of Huang Ch'ao, who massacred 120,000 traders in China — Christians, Jews, Mazdeans and Muslims. The same author cited the Arab writer Abu Zaid Al-Hasan who wrote about China banishing Western merchants — Christians, Jews and Nestorians. In 1424, Emperor Hung-His of the Ming dynasty banned foreign expeditions, and in 1426[19] China closed its borders to keep out foreign influence. Emperor K'ang-hsi of the Qing dynasty banned foreign travel.

The first Westerner to sail into China's Pearl Delta was Captain Jorge Alvares, in 1513. There, he found Guangzhou (Canton), already a great trading city at the time. In 1553, officials in Guang Dong accepted bribes from the

[19] For a discussion of the Chinese military defeat of 1426, see Lamb (2004).

Exhibit 4.5   Famous for 2,000 Years; photo ©2006 Leo Paul DANA

Portuguese who wished to conduct trade in Macao. When the Portuguese discovered that the Japanese were willing to buy Chinese silk while the Celestial Empire prohibited business dealings between Chinese and Japanese merchants, Portuguese entrepreneurs prospered as middlemen between the two.

In 1557, China allowed Portuguese merchants to establish homes and warehouses in Macao. The Portuguese supplied ivory from Africa and cotton from Goa, as well as cannons, clocks and mirrors from Europe. In exchange, Chinese entrepreneurs brought porcelain, seed pearls, and silk. Exporting silk from Macao to Japan proved to be highly profitable for the Portuguese entrepreneurs who were happy to be paid in silver. They then used the silver to pay for Chinese goods, which they sold in Europe.

During the 1600s, English entrepreneurs decided to get silk and tea directly from China. A problem, however, was that Chinese consumers wanted nothing from England. This obstacle was resolved when Chinese entrepreneurs gave English traders silver in exchange for opium from India. The silver was then used to acquire silk and tea in China. Toward the end of the 18th century, the English also purchased from Chinese merchants a fine cotton fabric known as nankeen. In 1821, the English began using Hong Kong as a base for opium vessels.

Exhibit 4.6   Still Smoking; photo ©2006 Leo Paul DANA

The year 1839 marked the start of the Opium War between China and the English. In 1841, the latter occupied Hong Kong Island, and in 1842 the Treaty of Nanking ceded Hong Kong to the British. In 1860, Queen Victoria also acquired the Kowloon Peninsula and later leased the New Territories for a period of 99 years. In 1887, Portugal forced China to sign the Draft Agreement of the Sino-Portuguese Meeting. This was followed by the Sino-Portuguese Treaty of Peking,[20] allowing Portugal perpetual administration of Macao.

The Sino-Japanese War, which lasted from 1894 to 1895, resulted in a shift of dominance from China to Japan (Scidmore, 1910). By signing the the Treaty of Shimonoseki, China agreed to stay out of Korea, ceded a large portion of eastern Manchuria to Japan, and gave up its sovereignty over Taiwan.

By 1898, Shanghai was one of the world's great trading centres (Bishop, 1899). Large numbers of Jews from Iraq settled in Hong Kong, Ningbo, Shanghai and Tianjin. Among the prominent Jewish entrepreneurs in China were the Kadoories and the Sassoons. In 1903, Sir Jacob Sassoon, brother of

---

[20] Peking was romanised from Beijing.

Exhibit 4.7   Shanghai Waterfront; photo ©2006 Leo Paul DANA

Sir Edward Sassoon and son of Elias, donated the Ohel Leah Synagogue, part way up Victoria Peak. Sir Matthew Nathan, governor of Hong Kong became president of the synagogue, and the main street in Kowloon — Nathan Road — was named after him. Large numbers of Ashkenazi Jews began arriving in China during the Russo-Prussian War of 1905; many settled in Harbin, Manchuria. Simpich called Manchuria the "promised land of Asia (1929, p. 379)."

In 1911, overseas Chinese entrepreneurs financed Dr. Sun Yat-Sen's bourgeois-democratic revolution, which overthrew the Qing dynasty. On December 25, 1914, Yünnan[21] Province announced its separation from the Chinese Empire (Passantino, 1946). After WWI, many thousands of Chinese men chose to go to France to work at restoring the French republic (Williams, 1919).

A great famine came about in 1920.[22] The Communist Party of China was established in 1921. Chitty (1922) discussed economic life in China at the

---

[21] For details about the Nashi, Indigenous people of Yünnan, see Rock (1924; 1930).
[22] For a discussion, see Robinson (1923).

Exhibit 4.8   Shanghai Home of Sir Elly Kadoorie until 1949; photo ©2006 Leo Paul DANA

time. China was exporting up to 4,800 tons of silk annually. Things changed, however, when three quarters of its silkworms were found to be diseased in 1923 (Boulnois, 1963). Chinese sericulture was no longer a major force in international markets. In order to re-establish a significant market presence, the International Committee for the Improvement of Sericulture in China then purchased healthy silkworms in France and Italy. Yet, the 1920s were bleak. A revolution took place in 1926,[23] followed by the Agrarian Revolutionary War that lasted until 1937. In 1928, Nanjing became the nation's capital city, and the name of China's former capital, Peking, was changed to Peiping (Moore, 1933).

When the Japanese arrived in 1931, Manchuria was home to 13,000 Jews, many of these entrepreneurs with an impressive network, including two Jewish banks. Yet, these Jews did not mix with the Indigenous Jews of China.[24]

Williams (1935) correctly described China during the 1930s as stormy, in more ways than one. During 1932, Harbin was flooded for several weeks; Coville noted, "Many Russian and Chinese boatmen ferried across... to make a little pocket money rowing people around town (1933, p. 243)." The Shanghai Library was built in 1934.

The Sino-Japanese War — also known as the War of Resistance against Japan — started in 1937.[25] Between January and September 1938, nearly

---

[23] For a discussion, see Chapman (1928).

[24] For a discussion of the Indigenous Jews of China, see Bainbridge (1907).

[25] For a discussion, see Eigner (1938).

Exhibit 4.9   Shanghai Library Clock Tower; photo ©2006 Leo Paul DANA

200,000 Chinese worked on the Burma Road,[26] an all-weather highway linking Kunming, with Rangoon — as Yangon was called at the time. Outram and Fane described how the "opening of the Burma Road turned sleepy Kunming into a bustling metropolis. Capital and largest city of Yünnan Province, the ancient community slumbered half-forgotten until 1939. Even the opening of the narrow-gauge railway from Haiphong, French Indochina seaport, nearly thirty years before, failed to rouse it from lethargy. Suddenly trucks by the hundred poured into the city, which became a distributing center for the Chinese armies (Outram and Fane, 1940, p. 654)." The Japanese occupation of Burma was tragic for China, as Burma had been the principal base for Allied aid to China (Christian, 1943).

By the time the war was over, in 1945, millions of Chinese had been killed. Brown (1944), Stewart (1944) and Lowdermilk (1945) gave detailed

---

[26]For a discussion of 21st century opium trade along the Burma Road, see Webster (2003).

Exhibit 4.10   Ashkenazi Ghetto in Shanghai; photo ©2006 Leo Paul DANA

accounts of enterprise in wartime China. When Hong Kong fell to the Japanese, many entrepreneurs fled from occupied Hong Kong to China.

In 1945, capitalists in western China declared the independence of the Turkestan Republic. Following the National Liberation War — which lasted from 1945 to 1949 — on October 1, 1949, Mao Zedong proclaimed the establishment of the PRC. Turkestan was subsequently absorbed into the PRC.

From 1949 to 1952, the PRC focused on "the task of rehabilitating the national economy (Hong, 1990, p. 11)." The First Five-Year Plan, covering the years 1953 to 1957, gave rise to a centrally planned economy in China. Entrepreneurship in the PRC was eliminated, in favour of a system of state production and co-operatives. By mid-1950, about 20,000 refugees poured in every week from the PRC to Hong Kong (Long, 1954). With 80,000 seats, the Peking Workers' Stadium was completed in 1959 (Shor, 1960). Until 1978, business was production-oriented, based on a plan. Prices were fixed and advertising was banned by law.

The Chinese Model of Gradual Transition

In 1978, Deng Xiaoping declared that the PRC needed to "reform and open up," thus setting the nation on the road to economic liberalisation — with an open-door policy. The state moved away from Maoism, reduced its control of the economy, and business became increasingly oriented toward sales. Private enterprises — including foreign participation — were permitted. Some prices were allowed to float. Advertising was legalised.

In 1979, the State Council of China officially endorsed a policy allowing entrepreneurship to contribute to economic development, not as a replacement of central planning, but rather as a supplement to the socialist economy. Regulatory reform legalised entrepreneurship, and by 1980 there were over one million entrepreneurs in China.

The government also recognised *zhuanyehu* — "specialised households." These were families who were given permission to operate family businesses. Enterprises included animal husbandry, carpentry, construction, embroidery, and fish farming. Self-employed farmers were permitted to cultivate apples, beans, corn, grapes, pears, persimmons, rice, sorghum, soya beans, sugar

Exhibit 4.11   Live Chickens; photo ©2006 Leo Paul DANA

beets and tangerines. A new constitution was adopted on December 4, 1982. Taxation was subsequently introduced (Wei, 2001).

The Chinese proverb, "*A single spark can start a prairie fire*," led to the "Spark" Programme, an important scheme that was launched in 1986, to promote entrepreneurship in rural areas of China. Through this programme, the State Science and Technology Commission encouraged the establishment of several thousand new ventures. Special incentives were offered to entrepreneurs who harnessed a technology deemed to be appropriate for rural industry. This included enterprises involving agriculture, aquaculture, food processing, light industry, textile manufacturing, and the production of components.

In 1992, the Fourteenth National Congress of the Communist Party of China proposed the establishment of a socialist market economy. During the early 1990s, annual growth reached 13.4%, as the orientation of firms was shifting toward the market. In 1993, the China Council for the Promotion of International Trade hosted a world conference in Beijing to

Exhibit 4.12   Beijing; photo ©2006 Leo Paul DANA

Exhibit 4.13   Bank of China; photo ©2006 Leo Paul DANA

encourage entrepreneurship. Devaluation of the yuan, in 1994, helped Chinese entrepreneurs increase their competitiveness in export markets. The state also introduced a variety of incentives for entrepreneurs who export. This included tax exemptions and easy access to financing via specialised banks. An overview of entrepreneurs in China, during the early 1990s, appears in Chow and Tsang (1995).

In 1995, legislation declared 339 cities and counties open areas in which entrepreneurship could thrive, as a supplement to socialism. The Financial Security Law came into effect in October 1995. This legislation affects entrepreneurship inasmuch as it covers different forms of security: deposit, guarantee, lien, pledge and mortgage. Land-use rights and social facilities were placed on the list of assets, which could be mortgaged.

The All-China Federation of Industry and Commerce — with more than 80,000 members — established its Information Centre in 1995. Its

Exhibit 4.14   Inviting Investment; photo ©2006 Leo Paul DANA

major functions are: to provide assistance to foreign entrepreneurs, in finding Chinese partners for joint ventures; to perform market analysis; to provide consulting services to foreign entrepreneurs; to organise trade shows; to organise technology exchanges; and to assist foreign entrepreneurs. The federation also publishes periodicals of interest to entrepreneurs.

Until April 1996, foreign entrepreneurs benefited from Value Added Tax (VAT) exemptions and exemptions from customs duties on imported capital equipment. These were then withdrawn, thus putting foreign and local entrepreneurs on equal footing with regards to investment incentives.

In 1997, domestic growth in the PRC slowed down, and in 1998, the state responded by launching an elaborate programme of government spending on infrastructure. In 1998, the State Economic and Trade Commission of China was restructured such as to include a Department of Small and Medium Enterprises.

From a level of 43% in 1997, average tariffs have been significantly reduced; yet, imports are subject to VAT. However, Chinese entrepreneurs are

Exhibit 4.15   Slow; photo ©2006 Leo Paul DANA

often exempted from sales tax. Thus, it may be said that the effective tariff rate is close to 40%, thereby protecting local entrepreneurs.

In July 2001, President Jiang Zemin made news with his declaration that the Communist Party of China should recruit capitalists. He said this would boost the "influence and cohesiveness" of the party. That same month, the PRC passed new rules on intellectual property. Anderson, Li, Harrison, and Robson (2003) noted the increasing role of small business in China.

In 2005, the State Council released 36 articles on non-public economy. For the first time, the central government supported the entry of non-public firms into sectors previously reserved for monopolies. A three-tier system exists in China today:

(1) Consumer staples, raw materials and industrial materials are supplied by the state and prices dictated by the government. This is truly a state-controlled planned sector.

Exhibit 4.16   Protected; photo ©2006 Leo Paul DANA

(2) For other products — as determined by the state — prices can vary within a range dictated by *guojia wujia guanliju*, the State Price Bureau. This may be described as a hybrid sector.

(3) In contrast to the state-controlled planned sector, a free-market system allows the market to establish prices of some products.

One Country, Two Systems

In 1984, the Sino-British Agreement pronounced the reversion of British Hong Kong to China, effective July 1, 1997. This was conditional on the PRC creating a Special Administrative Region, conforming to the concept of "One country, two systems." Hong Kong reverted to Chinese rule, but the Special Administrative Region of Hong Kong was allowed to keep its own legal and judicial system, as well as capitalist economy, until 2047.

Along the same lines, in April 1987, Portugal signed the Joint Sino-Portuguese Declaration and Basic Law. This allowed the PRC to take back Macao, on December 20, 1999.

There are, nevertheless, important differences between Hong Kong and Macao. Although both were built on entrepreneurship, their industrial sectors evolved differently. Entrepreneurs in Hong Kong benefited from the government's laissez-faire policy, including favourable tax treatment. In contrast, beginning in 1981, Macao adopted an increasingly interventionist approach.

Hong Kong has at least 300,000 small and medium enterprises, which are flexible, and cost-effective. While their product mix is increasing, the typical size of an order is shrinking.

Many entrepreneurs in Hong Kong are concentrated in the service industries. Others have manufacturing plants, outside Hong Kong. Entrepreneurs from Hong Kong have financed over 170,000 joint ventures in China, and these employ some 10 million people — twice the labour force in Hong Kong. According to unpublished sources at the Hong Kong Trade Development Council, two fifths of the exporters in Hong Kong, have operations in two or more economies.

The Trade Development Council of Hong Kong operates the SME Service Centre. This is a one-stop shop for entrepreneurs in search of information about technology acquisition and internationalisation.

In contrast, entrepreneurs in Macao tend to be small-scale producers of low-technology goods, including artificial flowers, ceramics, clothing, electrical products, electronics, firewood, footwear, furniture, machinery, optical devices, plastic goods, textiles and toys. Dana (1999e) provided a detailed contrast of differences between entrepreneurship policy and practices in Hong Kong and those in Macao.

Pluralism

While the Han-Chinese comprise the majority of China's population, the country is also rich with minority groups.[27] There are 55 recognised national minorities in the PRC.

---

[27] See Wong (1984).

Exhibit 4.17   Han; photo ©2006 Leo Paul DANA

In Xinjiang,[28] the largest administrative region in China, the Han-Chinese are a minority, and most people are Muslims. The Indigenous people in Xinjiang are Uygurs — Muslims with Indo-European features. Members of different ethnic communities have distinctly different tastes. A particular favourite among the Hui is soup made of flour. In contrast to the Hans who use chopsticks, the Kazakhs in Xinjiang eat with their hands; these people enjoy smoked meat and horse intestines as well as mutton with noodles eaten without utensils. The Kirghiz prefer eating rice mixed with milk, and they exhibit a preference for horse's milk. A popular meal among Uygurs consists of hand-pulled noodles mixed with bits of lamb and vegetables, savoured with strong tea. They enjoy fried *sanzi* — made from dough — and a variety of steamed foods including buns and dumplings; they also like roasted cubes of mutton on skewers. They eat *zhuafan* with their fingers and their favourite cake is *nang*. For the Xibe people, a special meal includes sheep entrails. The

[28] For a detailed analysis of Xinjiang, see Dana (1998a).

Mongolians, the Uygurs and the Xibe drink milk-tea. As for the Kazakhs and the Kirghiz, their favourite drink is fermented mare's milk, known in Central Asia as *koumis*, and in China as *manaizi*. In major centres, Western food has also made inroads, with chains such as Kentucky Fried Chicken (Dana, 1999d).

A Muslim Uygur, in Xinjiang, sells *nan*, flat bread with *plov* — rice mixed with religiously prepared halal mutton — along with *shashlik*, i.e., halal mutton broiled on charcoal. On another street, Han entrepreneurs sell tofu, noodles, dumplings, dogmeat, fried vegetables, white rice and eggs cooked in tea. Pluralism is structural in nature, as members of the different ethnic groups do not share a secular mainstream arena. Whereas the Han-Chinese introduced a firm-type economy to Xinjiang, the non-Han sphere of activity is concentrated in the bazaar economy.

Among the non-Han peoples in Xinjiang are Kazakh and Kirghiz minorities; these are also Islamic, with a Turkic language. In contrast to the Uygurs who have been cultivating the land, the Kazakhs and Kirghiz have retained their traditional nomadic lifestyle, which includes breeding camels[29] and horses, both of these for meat and for milk as well as for transport.

Among the Kazakhs, horseback courtship is still practised, as a suitor must kiss his woman, on the gallop. Although Kazakhs, in Xinjiang, engage in agriculture on a limited scale, many are herdsmen, and their entrepreneurial spirit is strong. Clark (1954) described the thousands of families of Kazakhs in Xinjiang who opted to trek 3,000 miles, in order to escape communist control in China.

While the Hans speak Mandarin, the Uygurs speak a Turkic tongue, written with an Arabic script. The Uygurs have more in common with their Turkic neighbours of the formerly Soviet, Central Asian republics, than with the Han-Chinese. Perhaps because they are often looked down upon by Han-Chinese, the Uygurs do not generally identify with Chinese nationality, but rather consider themselves to be under Chinese occupation.

---

[29]Wulsin (1926) provided a comparison between camels owned by Chinese people and those owned by Mongols in China.

Rather than wearing Chinese slacks, Uygur women sport colourful dresses or skirts with matching, brightly coloured scarves. Among the Uygurs, both men and women wear a colourful head cover. Daggers are fashionable among Uygur, Kazakh, Kirghiz and Mongolian men.

The Uygurs continue to cultivate cotton, grapes and melons. Local green grapes are still dried in the traditional manner, producing export-quality raisins with no pits. At local markets, such as that in Turpan, donkey-carts wait for local loads. Closer to the Kyrgyz Republic, trucks at the Kashgar market represent major international business. While some Uygurs have opted to urbanise, many have decided to remain in rural areas, residing in rectangular farmhouses with scuttles on flat roofs.

Recently, a new class of international merchants has been emerging with a pan-Turkic scope. Rather than doing business with Han-Chinese, the Muslims of Xinjiang express a preference to trade with co-religionists from the Turkic republics of the former Soviet Union. While the majority of the world's international trade takes place in the firm-type economy, Uygur traders thrive in the bazaar.

Perhaps the most striking bazaar is at the Horgas Pass, to the south-west of Bortala. Like other towns of the Silk Road,[30] the settlement was impoverished when caravans stopped passing through it. In 1971, all international activity was banned here, as the border with the Soviet Union was closed. The local inhabitants had no electricity, no running water, and no trade.

In 1983, the border was re-opened. Entrepreneurs carried 20 million kilogrammes of goods across this border in 1984, according to information obtained by the author during an interview in Kazakhstan. Trade was predicted to surpass 500 million kilogrammes a year, in the early 21st century.

The demise of the Soviet Union meant little to the average Chinese individual. However, the independence of the five formerly Soviet Central Asian states — Kazakhstan and the Kyrgyz Republic in particular — had a great symbolic lift for Uygurs, for Kazakhs and for Kirghiz living in Xinjiang. These Turkic-speaking minorities had historical, religious and cultural links

---

[30]This term refers not to one road per se, but to a web of inter-weaving paths that linked towns and bazaars.

with their Turkic-speaking neighbours in the Commonwealth of Independent States.

Uygur entrepreneurs in Xinjiang began to rebuild commercial links between east and west. In Khorghus, formerly a Silk Road town, now on the Kazakh side of the Kazakhstan-Xinjiang border, a new bazaar is sprawling. A unique feature along the border of China and Kazakhstan is "The Bazaar for Entrepreneurs from Both Sides." This market has an entrance in Xinjiang and another in Kazakhstan. Uygur entrepreneurs from Xinjiang bring beer, vodka, sugar, candies, clothing, leather goods, sporting apparel, toys, housewares, tools, cigarettes and jewellery, all of which they sell to buyers from Kazakhstan, including Kazakhs and Russians, most of whom arrive by bus. Thus, pan-Turkic trade is on the rise, as Muslims in Xinjiang conduct business with Muslims in republics of the CIS.

Although the bazaar is not simply a means to monetary reward, it is producing wealth among the Uygurs. More importantly, it allows Uygurs to socialise among others sharing similar cultural values. The flow of commerce is still fragmented into numerous transactions between individuals, just as it was generations ago. This allows the sharing of cigarettes over tea, and it helps to spread risks.

Officially, all of China has only one time zone, which is the same as that of Beijing. Uygurs function according to their own unofficial time zone. Uygur entrepreneurs, in Xinjiang, are more concerned with conducting business with Kazakhstan and the Kyrgyz Republic, than with pleasing politicians in China's capital; although Han-Chinese in Xinjiang respect Beijing time, most Uygurs set their watches two hours behind the official time of China. This presumably facilitates pan-Turkic trade between Uygurs and entrepreneurs in Kazakhstan and in the Kyrgyz Republic; more importantly, it is a highly symbolic gesture.

Given that the Uygurs have a Turkic culture and that they speak a Turkic language, this has facilitated trade with bazaar entrepreneurs in the rapidly developing, newly independent republics of Central Asia.

Toward the Future

Yu and Stough noted that "the Chinese government that not only implemented a successful top to bottom economic reform, but also preserved much

Exhibit 4.18   Beijing Time in Shanghai; photo ©2006 Leo Paul DANA

of its socialist political system, is taken as the most influential determinant of entrepreneurship development (2006, p. 48)." Across the PRC, entrepreneurship has become a supplement to socialism and industrialisation is viewed as a complement to agriculture. Unlike other economies, which rapidly abandoned communism, the PRC is liberalising its economy slowly, thus avoiding spiral inflation. As well, its township enterprises are helping the nation industrialise, while avoiding uncontrolled urbanisation. In the longer term, sustained growth will likely require privatisation of state enterprises and a free flow of labour.

Meanwhile, local and foreign entrepreneurs are playing an important role in the economic and social development of China, despite tight control by Beijing. Heavy investment has been pouring in from overseas Chinese entrepreneurs, and the PRC today has the world's second largest GDP.

China's model of transition is likely to bring increasing prosperity to its people. MacDonald warned, however, "But development has been uneven and the losers number in the hundreds of millions. Their growing dissatisfaction with their plot poses a threat to China's stability and economic progress (2005,

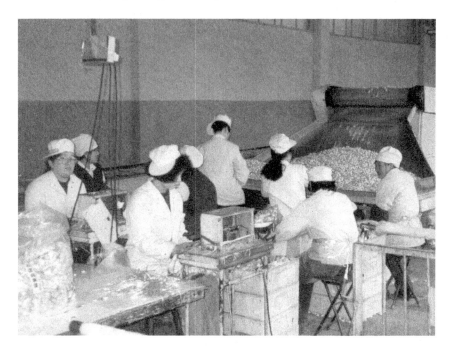

Exhibit 4.19   Working at Full Capacity; photo ©2006 Leo Paul DANA

Exhibit 4.20   Investment Transforming China; photo ©2006 Leo Paul DANA

Exhibit 4.21   Exhibit Demonstrating Western Ways in China; photo ©2006 Leo Paul DANA

Exhibit 4.22   Not among the Wealthy; photo ©2006 Leo Paul DANA

p. B.2)." As Becker stated, "China's race to riches comes at a high cost to both land and people (2004, p. 69)." At the World Economic Forum, in Davos, Bhagwati (2006) cautioned not to assume that China's rapid growth was sustainable.

Chapter 5

India[31]

Introduction

Situated in southern Asia, the Indian subcontinent has over 7,000 kilometres of coastline along the Arabian Sea and the Bay of Bengal. The Republic of India is the world's fastest growing free market economy; it a vibrant country, covering an area of 3,165,596 square kilometres. The federation shares borders with Bangladesh (formerly East Pakistan), Bhutan, China, Myanmar (formerly Burma), Nepal and Pakistan.

As noted by Johnson, "India's middle class is bigger than the entire 300 million population of the US (2006, p. 1)." India is very tolerant of minorities and its multicultural society includes Hindus and Muslims living peacefully with people from many different religions.

Dana (2000a) observed that a combination of historical factors, including the caste system,[32] British occupation, cultural values and government regulations, formerly limited innovative entrepreneurship in India. Kanitkar and Contractor wrote, "handicaps to entry into business ownership have been far too many given the traditional, conservative, orthodox Indian society (1992, p. 5)." In recent years, however, efforts have focused on changing the mindset and creating entrepreneurs by giving youngsters the self-confidence to become

---

[31]This chapter is based on information obtained from a variety of sources, including: the National Bank for Agricultural and Rural Development, and the World Association for SMEs, in Delhi. Travel to India was provided by the University of Pittsburgh. Travel within India was provided by the World Association for Small & Medium Enterprises. The chapter includes material that first appeared in Dana (2000a).

[32]For discussions of the caste system, see Gadgil (1959); Medhora (1965); and Weber (1958). Hazlehurst (1966) focused on merchant castes.

Exhibit 5.1   Vibrant with Entrepreneurial Spirit; photo ©2006 Leo Paul DANA

Exhibit 5.2   Cochini Jewess; photo ©2006 Leo Paul DANA

Exhibit 5.3   Cochin Synagogue, Built in 1568; photo ©2006 Leo Paul DANA

Exhibit 5.4   Association of Kerala Jews; photo ©2006 Leo Paul DANA

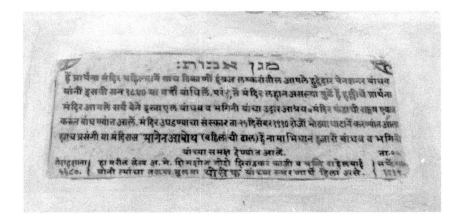

Exhibit 5.5   Multilingual Sign in Alibag; photo ©2006 Leo Paul DANA

Exhibit 5.6   Beth El, Built by Iraqi Immigrants to Calcutta; photo ©2006 Leo Paul DANA

high achievers. Raghavendra and Subrahmanya (2005) found that inter-firm co-operation has increased collective efficiency in India, with a significant influence on capability.

Historical Overview[33]

The early history of India stretches back to the Mohenjodaro and Harappan times with well laid out cities, a script, and possible evidence of trade. During the Vedic times, with the flourishing of philosophical treaties on life, intricate writings on medicine, astronomy and mathematics, there was the caste system into which individuals were classified based on their birth. The four castes were: (i) the Brahmins or priestly class; (ii) the *kshatriyas* or warrior class; (iii) the *vaishyas* or merchant class; and (iv) the *shudras* or those at the bottom rung of this social hierarchy, who did menial tasks. The untouchables, or *harijans*, fell out of this system. The *shudras* and untouchables were those who would do work such as the burying of animal carcasses and the cleaning of waste, or in today's terminology waste management. The caste system resulted in occupational specialisation, with the *vaishya* class becoming the merchants, the overland traders, the maritime investors for waterborne trade, and intermediaries between the European powers; today their scions form the top management and owners of many of the large industrial organisations and conglomerates in India.

During the Buddhist period of ancient India, along with the travelling monks were travelling merchants, whose wealth allowed the construction of caves for residence on the trade routes between various villages and cities. Such caves were often lavishly decorated, along with the carved images of deities and donors, and can still be viewed in states such as Maharashtra. The caves were the dwelling place for monks during the monsoon season, and also served as five-star hotels for the merchants. The Buddhist period also saw the flourishing of major universities such as Nalanda and Taxila, resulting in a wave of Chinese monks who came to India to study and take back their learnings and relics to

---

[33]This section benefited greatly from the personal assistance of Edwina Pio.

China. Merchants also used the Silk Road of the first century, which served as a significant boost to trade with many countries.

It was the traders and merchants who were the early entrepreneurs in India, and the *vaishya* class became and still is highly specialised in scanning the environment and setting up businesses. The early entrepreneurs developed intricate systems for credit and forward trading to further their entrepreneurial activities such as buying ships, goods, and investing in cargo and land. The *vaishya* class was largely the source for subcastes such as the Marwaris or Banias in northern, eastern and western India. In southern India the merchants were primarily the Nattukottai Chettiars.

In 1700, the East India Company established a formal system of government for Bengal. At the time, India's share of world income was about 23%, approximately the same as Europe's (Singh, 2006).

In 1784, the British government took control of the East India Company. Entrepreneurs from various lands saw commercial opportunities in India. In 1790, Shalom ben Ovadiah HaCohen — a famous Baghdadi Jew — moved from Aleppo (*Halab*), in Syria, to Bombay. He was followed by other Jewish

Exhibit 5.7   Paid for by David Sassoon, the Magen David Synagogue Was Completed in 1861; photo ©2006 Leo Paul DANA

Exhibit 5.8   The David Sassoon Library; photo ©2006 Leo Paul DANA

entrepreneurs from Baghdad and from Basra; Jewish entrepreneurs also came to India from Persia and from Yemen. In 1832, David Sassoon moved to Bombay where he became a magistrate of the cotton industry. His son Abdullah Sassoon revolutionised the weaving industry in Bombay, helping Bombay become an important manufacturing centre. In 1903, the Sassoon family built the Sir Jacob Sassoon School, next to the Magen David Synagogue, in a predominantly Jewish neighbourhood of Bombay.

Until the late 20th century, the Jewish Club, on V. P. Ghandi Road in Mumbai (formerly Forbes Street, Bombay), served as a meeting place for Jewish entrepreneurs. In 1985, Giani Zail Singh, president of India, graced the festivities celebrating the centennial anniversary of the Knesset Eliyahoo Synagogue, on V. P. Ghandi Road, and the Post Office issued a stamp for the occasion.

The Marwaris are a community who specialised in domestic trade. Their enterprises complemented those of English entrepreneurs, who allowed the Marwaris to become prominent in a diversified industrial economy. In contrast, other groups of Indian entrepreneurs had experiences of another

Exhibit 5.9   The Jewish Club; photo ©2006 Leo Paul DANA

kind. During the 1800s, the British discriminated against those communities (such as the Bengalis) who competed with English entrepreneurs in international commerce. Many Indian entrepreneurs were thus pushed out of the business realm. During the 1880s, local firms with established reputations were defrauded by British partners, an action which led to more withdrawals from the business sector. Consequently, Nafziger concluded that "the lack of indigenous entrepreneurship... stems in part from the discrimination and duplicity of the British in the 19th century (1971, p. 30)." Nevertheless, until the turn of the century, Indian entrepreneurs were central to the geographic expansion of manufacturing industries (Medhora, 1965). Dilke (1894) gave a detailed account of India during the late 19th century. Between 1912 and 1945, industrial production, in India, doubled (Balakrishna, 1961). During the 1920s and 1930s, the Jains (especially the Marwari Jains) shifted their activity from trading to manufacturing. This was a break away from scriptural teaching.

Williams (1942) provided a war-time account of the British colony. "Tryst with destiny," were the words of India's first prime minister, Jawaharlal Nehru, to describe independence on August 15, 1947. India became a republic in 1950 and the constitution, coming into effect on January 26, 1950, indicated specifically that the state, not entrepreneurs from the private sector, would play the decisive role in building up the national economy.

The Small Scale Industry Organisation was established in 1954, for the purpose of planning the growth of small businesses as supplements to the efforts of large industries.

Formerly French Pondicherry was transferred to India in 1954. Decimal system coinage was introduced in 1957. Goa, under Portuguese rule since 1510, was incorporated into India in December 1961.

Patel (1987) gave a historical account of entrepreneurship development in India. "The first programme to convert potential entrepreneurs into actual owner-managers of manufacturing businesses was held at Ahmedabad in April 1970 (Sebastian and Thakur, 1994, p. v)."

In 1975, unemployment in Rajasthan led to urbanisation. That year, Barefoot College began promoting rural handicrafts, providing artisans with access to credit and also marketing outlets. Barefoot College encourages people to take risks, to innovate, to improvise and to experiment.

Economic liberalisation took effect in 1991. The official exchange rate was abolished in 1993.

Exhibit 5.10   The Regal Motion Picture Cinema; photo ©2006 Leo Paul DANA

During the 1990s, government policy in India focused on technological development. Wani, Garg, and Sharma (2003) suggested that "to develop and transfer technology for SMEs in India, effective interaction of academic institutions with this sector will be the first step in this direction (2003, p. 71)." Wani, Garg, and Sharma (2005) also emphasised the importance of developing technology-based entrepreneurship.

At the 2004 World Economic Forum, Mirai Chatterjee spoke on behalf of India's Self-employed Women's Association. At the 2006 Meeting, in Davos, India was a star player.

The Impact of Culture and Social Structure[34]

Pio (2005b) examined everyday Indianness of the work culture and the future dreams of an Indian export hub; it appears that culture continues to be an important force in the nature of entrepreneurship. Indeed, culture is central in explaining the social acceptability and perceived utility of entrepreneurship. Ever since McClelland's (1961) investigation of need for achievement, entrepreneurs have been viewed in the West as those with a high need to achieve. In contrast, the economy of India traditionally reflected Indian culture and social structure. Pio (2005a) explained how religious and philosophical concepts still have practical applications in industrial management in India; she argued that Indian culture does not segment the spiritual from the secular, and that spirituality is intrinsic to being Indian. "*A person's specific* dharma *is interpreted through his role in life, and every role has certain expectations of* dharma *to be fulfilled* (Pio, 2005a, p. 4)."

An ascetic religious group, the Jains, became traders — not because of an entrepreneurial spirit based on materialism, but — due to ritualistic reasons; trading was an occupation free from conflict with religious requirements. Jains who follow Jainism are known as entrepreneurs and have been in textiles and diamonds in western India as well as other parts of the world, for example in Africa. One more group of Indians who have thrived on their business acumen are the Sindhis (from Sindh). Both the Jains and Sindhis are closely aligned to Hinduism in their beliefs. Other early entrepreneurs were merchants

---

[34]This section benefited greatly from the personal assistance of Edwina Pio.

from the Islamic religion such as the Bohras from Gujarat, the followers of Zoroastrianism the religion of the Parsees, and the Baghdadi Jews who settled in India.

Under colonial rule, Marwari enterprises complemented those of English entrepreneurs who permitted them an important role in a diversified industrial economy. Today, Marwaris have the reputation of having business acumen and are considered to be a very enterprising group. Likewise, Banias are considered to be thrifty and with an eye on business opportunities.

As noted by Mishra, "In India there are many castes that are categorised as business castes... Most of the business castes (the erstwhile *vaishya*) are now classified under 'Other Backward Castes' for purposes of government regulations (2005, p. 305)."

While the caste system reinforced the practice of following a family occupation, this impeded class mobility (Dana, 2000a). In fact, Nafziger (1971) noted that leading entrepreneurs often belonged to communities in which caste divisions were not rigidly observed.

In India, according to Kakar (1978), people are more sensitive to emotional affinity in the workplace than to work and productivity. According to Sinha (1978), work — as an end in itself — is not valued in India. Sinha (1984) explained that work is done with involvement only when done for a nurturing superior. This supported McClelland's (1975) suggestion that people in India generally performed their work as a favour to their employer.

"In India, the Planning Commission, central and state governments recognize that women should be in the mainstream of economic development. In particular, the development of microenterprise for women is seen as an appropriate way to attack poverty... (Ghosh, Gupta, and Dhar, 1998, p. 158)." Yet, Porter and Nagarajan suggested that there "may be a bias in Indian culture against women who engage in entrepreneurial activities outside the home (2005, p. 41)." The practice of *purdah* keeps women at home.

A Holistic Approach to Entrepreneurship

Across India, there are countless advocates of holistic management. This is a philosophy which attempts to synergise basic elements, in order to get optimal results. The holistic approach, for instance, encourages an all-encompassing

Exhibit 5.11   Family Firm; photo ©2006 Leo Paul DANA

Exhibit 5.12   For a Nurturing Superior; photo ©2006 Leo Paul DANA

Exhibit 5.13   Work as a Favour, Calcutta; photo ©2006 Leo Paul DANA

Exhibit 5.14   Emancipated Women; photo ©2006 Leo Paul DANA

integration of the intellectual with the physical and the spiritual. Mental, material and moral aspects are involved.

Although schools teach facts, educational institutions are often lacking when it comes to personality development. It is the belief of many that entrepreneurship personality can be taught, and that this should be done at a young age. This could lead to more effective members in society.

Various agencies participate in holistic entrepreneurship development. To coordinate and oversee their activities, the Ministry of Industry established the National Institute for Entrepreneurship and Small Business Development (NIESBUD). Among the many programmes of this institute is one entitled, "Training Trainers for Barefoot Managers."

In line with the observation that over-population greatly nullifies the effect of overall development, it has been deemed in the national interest to promote birth control. For this reason, a non-governmental organisation, the Progress Harmony Development (PHD) Chamber of Commerce and Industry has become involved in propagating the message of population control. Its Rural Development Foundation has been organised to act with a holistic approach.

Likewise, the Entrepreneurship Development Institute of India (EDII) takes a holistic perspective with very impressive results. Located near Ahmedabad, in Gujarat, the EDII promotes independent thinking, creativity, and a spirit of innovation. Its Rural Entrepreneurship Development division promotes micro-enterprise and provides micro-credit. The EDII sponsors research, provides education and training — including its own educational video series — and publishes an academic journal on entrepreneurship. Perhaps the most unique contribution of the EDII is its summer camp, an entrepreneurial adventure for youth to learn achievement, a concern for excellence, creativity, innovation, leadership, problem solving, and systemic planning.

Toward the Future

Today's merchant princes include the Ambanis, Birlas and Tatas, the Premjis and Narayanamurthys, as well as the Indians of Silicon Valley such

Exhibit 5.15   Densely Populated Bombay; photo ©2006 Leo Paul DANA

Exhibit 5.16   Traffic in Calcutta; photo ©2006 Leo Paul DANA

Exhibit 5.17   Micro-enterprises; photo ©2006 Leo Paul DANA

Exhibit 5.18   Rural Entrepreneur; photo ©2006 Leo Paul DANA

Exhibit 5.19   Sidewalk Stall; photo ©2006 Leo Paul DANA

as Kanwal Rekhi, many of whom are returning to India to invest and manage start-up as well as top performing IT companies. "Indian family-run businesses have been developing rapidly from firms with limited goals that valued loyalty more than ability into dynamic professionally-managed corporates capable of taking on global competition (Skaria, 2006, p. 48)."

While India continues to be a patriarchal society, today there are a number of Indian women entrepreneurs many of whom are highly educated and run their own businesses, as well as the larger segment of Indian women who are starting their own micro-enterprises through micro-financing schemes. This is quite a change from the past; women in the early history of entrepreneurship are hard to find, though it is possible that like today many of them were the hidden supporters, the invisible women who stood behind their men and brought up the children. It is important to note that the merchants would marry among their own caste, and even today one finds that arranged marriages, often to keep the wealth in the family, as well as to keep the "purity" of the caste, continue.

"With Manmohan Singh, the prime minister, calling for the 21st century to be the 'Indian Century,' the geopolitical ramifications of the country's rise are attracting attention (Johnson, 2006, p. 1)." Challenges facing India, however, include the liberalisation of government regulation; this was discussed by James

Exhibit 5.20　　Patriarchal Society; photo ©2006 Leo Paul DANA

Exhibit 5.21　　Toward a Bright Future; photo ©2006 Leo Paul DANA

F. Hoge at the World Economic Forum, in Davos, January 25, 2006 (Hoge, 2006). At the same Forum, Bhagwati (2006) cautioned not to assume that India's rapid growth was sustainable. Nevertheless, Internet entrepreneurs in Bangalore are preparing taxes for people in faraway places, reading X-rays for doctors around the world and tracing lost luggage.

The national economy is growing. Jain reported, "organised retail is expanding at a rate of 40 to 45 per cent each year (2006, p. 4)." In the long run, this will have an impact on small neighbourhood shops.

Chapter 6

Indonesia[35]

Introduction

Comprised of 13,667 lush islands, Indonesia is the world's largest archipelago. Its total land area is 1.92 million square kilometres. Entrepreneurs, here, are concentrated in labour-intensive industries where the use of traditional methods result in a competitive edge. Popular sectors include clothing, foodstuffs, footwear, furniture, leather, metal products, pottery and wooden products. Most manufacturing takes place in small-scale establishments.[36]

The Central Bureau of Statistics, in Jakarta, defines small industries as units of production using five or more workers, but less than 20. More traditional are the cottage household industries — units with up to four people, usually family members. Officially, entrepreneurs are required to obtain a basic business permit, *Surat Izin Untuk Perusahaan*. However, there are hidden costs involved, as civil servants often require an abusive bribe before issuing a permit. Therefore, it is common for entrepreneurs not to have one. When officials come around and hassle them, cigarettes and cash are used to avoid fines. Thus, it is easy to function without a permit, but as noted by Parnwell and Turner (1998), without one, it is impossible to obtain institutional credit.

---

[35]The chapter is based on information obtained from a variety of sources, including: the Capital Investment Co-ordinating Board; the Central Bureau of Statistics; the Department of Co-operative and Small Entrepreneur Guidance; the Department of Commerce; the Department of Industry and Trade; the Directorate General of Small Industries; the Institute for Economic Studies, Research and Development; the Ministry of Co-operatives; the Ministry of Finance; the Ministry of Tourism, Post and Telecommunications; and the National Agency for Export Development. The chapter includes material that first appeared in Dana (1999b).

[36]See also Tambunan (1992).

Exhibit 6.1   A Native of Indonesia is the Gibbon; photo ©2006 Leo Paul DANA

Exhibit 6.2   Indigenous Musician; photo ©2006 Leo Paul DANA

Exhibit 6.3   No Permit; photo ©2006 Leo Paul DANA

Exhibit 6.4   Bank Indonesia; photo ©2006 Leo Paul DANA

Indonesia has introduced a unique model, a special guidance scheme to assist entrepreneurs in clusters. The state identifies clusters of entrepreneurs in the same economic sector and in the same geographic region. The clusters — *sentras* — are provided with training, facilities and subsidies.

Small-scale farmers of vanilla beans co-operate in local farming associations facilitating exports. Their vanilla is used in Ben & Jerry's ice-cream, and sold around the world.

Historical Overview

The original people of Indonesia were short and dark-skinned. About 5,000 years ago, Indians and Malays arrived. Buddhism was brought from India, almost 2,000 years ago. When merchants spread Islam to the region, Hindus who resisted Islam moved to Bali.

During the 15th century, the Portuguese came in search of spices. The Dutch arrived, and subsequently established the Dutch East India Company in 1602. The Dutch created the Netherlands East Indies, which they governed between 1799 and 1942. The Portuguese kept eastern Timor until 1975.

In contrast to the British who tried to dissolve the caste system of India, the Dutch opted to develop relations with the Indonesian elite. Descendants of Javanese royalty were invited into the civil service.

Under Dutch rule, Indonesia had three classes. Dutchmen were in control of the higher levels of public administration, as well as the banks and large-scale enterprises such as the Royal Dutch Shell Company. The Indonesians were farmers, and some had small-scale businesses. The Chinese were traders and money-lenders.

Prior to the Depression, a small number of large-scale merchants prospered. During the 1930s, peasants turned to cash crops. Eventually, the market was saturated with micro-traders, each one making a marginal living.

In 1942, Japan took over Indonesia. In 1944, Japan proclaimed that Indonesia would become independent once the war ended, and independence was formally declared after the Japanese surrendered in 1945. The Dutch attempted to reinstate their government, but the United States threatened to cut off Marshall Plan assistance to the Netherlands, unless the Dutch let go of their former colony (excluding the western portion of Papua New Guinea). In 1949, Sukarno led Indonesia to independence, and became the first president of the republic.

In 1963, Indonesia annexed the western portion of Papua New Guinea, calling it Irian Jaya. Unlike other Indonesians, the people here are primarily Papuan.

A failed coup by communists, in September 1965, was followed by a blood bath. Thousands of Chinese Indonesians were slaughtered in 1966.

Exhibit 6.5   Nutmeg, an Important Spice; photo ©2006 Leo Paul DANA

In 1967, General Soeharto took the place of Sukarno. That year, Indonesia became a founding member of the Association of South East Asian Nations (ASEAN). The other founding members were Malaysia, the Philippines, Singapore and Thailand. In 1976, Indonesia annexed formerly Portuguese Timor.

During the 1980s, non-tariff barriers were converted to tariffs, and tariff rates were lowered. Financial services were deregulated. Income tax rates and property taxes were reduced. In 1989, foreign direct investment was freed from most controls. In 1990, $1 bought 1,828 rupiahs (Rp).

A political patronage system, under Soeharto, allowed nepotism and corruption to thrive. Soeharto gave the flour monopoly to his friend Liem Sioe Liong. In partnership with Soeharto, Chinese entrepreneurs controlled 70% of the private sector. The gap between rich and poor widened. Street peddlers were fined Rp 1,000, or imprisoned, for operating at road junctions. In 1992, the collapse of Bank Summa shook confidence in the banking sector.

The rupiah tumbled during the financial crisis of 1997. From its level of Rp 2,450 per dollar in July 1997, it fell to Rp 16,500 in January 1998. Devaluation led to inflation.

Exhibit 6.6   Soeharto Featured on the 50,000 Rupiah Note; photo ©2006 Leo Paul DANA

Angered over increases in the prices of milk and rice, in January 1998, Indonesians looted stores reported to be charging excessive prices. Shops owned by Chinese entrepreneurs become the focus of aggression. This happened in several Javanese towns, including Jember, Kragan and Losari. On February 13, in Pamanukan (Java), about 600 people attacked every store owned by Chinese entrepreneurs. The rioters hurled stones at some shops and burnt others down, using cooking oil.

By March, prices for food staples had risen by as much as 300% in local currency. In April, seven banks were closed down. These were: PT Bank Centris International; PT Bank Deka; PT Bank Hokindo; PT Bank Kredit Asia; PT Bank Pelita; PT Bank Subentra; and PT Bank Surya. In May, the prime lending rate rose from 36% to 45%, and more price increases led to new riots in Bandung (Java) and Medan (Sumatra). On May 12, looters ransacked Jakarta. *Newsweek* reported that 4,940 buildings were damaged. According to Reuters, damage affected 4,168 stores, 383 offices, 24 restaurants, 13 public markets, 12 hotels and nine service stations. Riots, in Solo (Java), prompted 600 ethnic-Chinese families to move away. Many wealthy Indonesians left the country. Tourism in Indonesia dried up.

Following the 80% plunge in the value of the rupiah, many foreign parties were reluctant to honour letters of credit that had been issued in Indonesia. Being flexible and less reliant on formal markets and formal credit, SMEs (with

Exhibit 6.7   Among the Well-to-do; photo ©2006 Leo Paul DANA

Exhibit 6.8   Among Few Inbound Travellers; photo ©2006 Leo Paul DANA

Exhibit 6.9   Postal Delivery Was Interrupted During Riots; photo ©2006 Leo Paul DANA

up to 50 workers) were found to have weathered the financial crisis better than was the case among larger firms (Tambunan, 2005).

Soeharto was forced to step down in May 1998, and his vice-president, Dr. Bacharuddin Jusuf Habibie began to lead Indonesia out of the Asian Crisis. Nevertheless, the economy contracted by about 4% in 1998, while inflation approached 80%. In 1999, much attention was shifted to ethnic fighting on eastern Timor, where separatists clashed with federalists. Finally, it was resolved that the 1999 national elections be followed by a referendum on the future of self-rule in Timor. After the crisis, formerly legal tender banknotes were made obsolete.

As part of an autonomy package to quell separatism in Aceh, in 2003, Aceh courts were granted the freedom to apply Shariah law. Public canings were hence legalised.

A devastating tragedy in 2004 was a tsunami that caused consider-able damage to Indonesia among other places. Mydans (2005) reported that Indonesia received billions of dollars in aid, but that relief efforts were delayed by bureaucratic requirements. An earthquake in 2006 caused yet another setback.

Exhibit 6.10   No Longer Accepted; photo ©2006 Leo Paul DANA

Ethnic Diversity

The population of Indonesia is quite diverse. On the island of Lombok (east of Bali and west of Sumbawa Island), people practise a unique form of Islam, called *Wektu Telu;* followers retain many animist or spiritualist beliefs. Entrepreneurs from Nusa Tenggara dominate towing services. Further west, entrepreneurs from Tegal, on the island of Java, have a reputation for being in the food business; many own street-side food stalls — known as *warung tegal* or *warteg* — catering to low income people. Even further west, Bataks from North Sumatra are clustered in the sale of oil products and the servicing of vehicles. Madurese entrepreneurs are famous for owning satay stalls.

On the island of Java, a small number of Jews reside in Surabaya. Of Iraqi origin, their community has given rise to many entrepreneurs with international networks spanning the world, with hubs in India, Singapore, North America and Europe.

Across Indonesia, the Chinese minority has been successful in entrepreneurship. Chinese entrepreneurs have dominated distribution networks for food and other essentials. Ethnic Chinese entrepreneurs from Pontianak (West Kalimantan) are traders in building materials.

Exhibit 6.11   The Only Synagogue in Indonesia; photo ©2006 Leo Paul DANA

Exhibit 6.12   Inside; photo ©2006 Leo Paul DANA

The Chinese in Indonesia

During the 1800s, the Dutch welcomed Chinese traders in Indonesia, and entered into business partnerships with them. Thus, the success of ethnic-Chinese entrepreneurs in Indonesia dates back to the *Vereenigte Oost-Indische Compagnie* (United East Indies Company), which granted them monopoly leases. Later, the Dutch colonial government did the same, further contributing to the economic success of Chinese entrepreneurs on these islands. Even when the monopoly leases were phased out, at the end of the 19th century, former lease-holders continued trading.

By 1900, there were 227,000 ethnic-Chinese in Java and another 310,000 on other Indonesian islands. They included self-employed artisans, builders, contractors, furniture-makers, manufacturers, money-lenders, repairmen, shippers, shopkeepers, smiths, speculators, suppliers, and tanners; they owned abattoirs, gambling dens, grocery stores, pawnshops, real estate and warehouses.

As explained by Kahin (1952), sharp trading practices used by aggressively competitive Chinese entrepreneurs contributed to the rapid growth of *Sarekat Dagang Islam* after 1909. This propagated anti-Chinese sentiment, and by 1912 anti-Chinese riots were a reality in Surabaya and Surakarta.

The 20th century saw demographic and social changes among the Chinese in Indonesia. Fluent in Dutch, the children of established families strayed away from their family businesses, and drifted toward salaried professions. The more recent immigrants did not integrate into the established community. Many newcomers became peddlers or low-wage labourers. This caused an increasing gap between the existing Indonesian Chinese and new arrivals from China. During the 1920s, however, many Chinese wage-workers became small-scale merchants. By 1930, according to the census of that year, there were 1,230,000 Chinese residing in Indonesia.

Among the Chinese immigrants who arrived in Indonesia, in 1938, was Liem Sioe Liong. During the 1950s, he befriended an army supply officer, who later became President Soeharto. Through his Salim Group, Liem Sioe Liong became Indonesia's most successful entrepreneur, with 300 companies producing cars, cement, chemicals, cooking oil, flour, milk, noodles and steel.

During the rule of Sukarno (1945–1966) anti-Chinese pressure prompted 119,000 ethnic-Chinese people to leave Indonesia. Those who stayed were prohibited from being entrepreneurs in rural areas. The rational was that Indigenous Indonesians should have a chance to be merchants. Under Soeharto, the Chinese were barred from government office and most professions. The lack of alternatives encouraged them to concentrate their efforts in the commercial realm.

During the 1950s, new legislation prevented the Chinese from living in certain towns. This included the locally-born Chinese (Peranakans), as well as ethnic-Chinese immigrants (Totok). The objective was to give a competitive advantage to the Muslim *pribumi* people. Customs regulations also prohibited the import of Chinese medicines and/or printed matter in Chinese characters.

The Soeharto regime followed with a policy favouring the *pribumis*. These people were entitled to favourable credit terms, and they had easy access to permits. Indonesians could acquire permits, and they did. Then, they sold them to Chinese entrepreneurs, with immense mark-ups.

The Chinese community in Indonesia has been very heterogeneous, with differences based on origin and on socio-economic class, as well as on the degree of assimilation. The diversity within this population has prompted some commentators to suggest that these people can hardly be considered one entity (Rigg, 1997). Nevertheless, *pribumi* anti-Chinese sentiment seldom makes distinctions (Turner, 2003b).

Throughout Soeharto's rule, the identities of the Chinese in Indonesia (about 3% of the population) were politically contested. The government erased the diverse cultural identities of the Chinese, placing priority on assimilation (Turner, 2003b).

In June 1998, there were about seven million ethnic-Chinese in Indonesia. This represented 3.5% of the country's population. Yet, ethnic-Chinese entrepreneurs owned 70% of the private sector in Indonesia. In September 1998, ethnic-Chinese entrepreneurs controlled 170 conglomerates in Indonesia as well as 5,000 medium-sized firms and 250,000 small enterprises. According to Yeung (1999), the overseas Chinese controlled 80% of corporate assets in Indonesia in 1999. Although the Chinese in Indonesia adopted Indonesian names, they never fully integrated with the Indigenous population. Half of Indonesia's Chinese are Hokkien.

Culture and Entrepreneurship

Penujak, on the island of Lombok, is home to potters who use the *turun temurun* method of making pottery. Since the 1500s, this skill has been passed on from mother to daughter, using no tools other than a round stone and a wooden paddle.

In Sukhara, a village of 3,000 people, also on Lombok, about 600 families are self-employed weavers. The men grow cotton and the women weave it into cloth, which is sold in larger towns, such as Sweta. Families also grow cloves, coffee, garlic, rice, soya beans and tobacco for personal use.

Indeed, many Indigenous Indonesians are self-employed, inasmuch as they are subsistence farmers. However, market-oriented entrepreneurship is not central to the culture here. In Javanese, the word for trader also signifies "tramp," or "foreigner."

In contrast, the ethnic-Chinese, in Indonesia, have thrived in entrepreneurship. One causal variable may be their culture, but it should also be emphasised that they were given few alternatives, as they were barred from many other occupations open to Indigenous Indonesians. By the same token, Indigenous Indonesians complained that ethnic-Chinese entrepreneurs also created barriers to entry.

As ethnic-Chinese entrepreneurs became increasingly successful in Indonesia, Javanese would-be-entrepreneurs complained that Chinese entrepreneurship was a de-facto barrier to entry, inhibiting the Javanese from becoming self-employed. The Chinese had more experience in business, more capital, better networks, and international contacts.

Public Policy on Entrepreneurship

At the National Level

President Sukarno, who ruled from 1945 to 1966, introduced anti-business policies to Indonesia. The Land Reform Bill of 1960 redistributed property;

individuals were limited to 7½ hectares, the equivalent of approximately 19 acres.

Beginning in 1969, Indonesia implemented a series of five-year national development plans. These typically emphasised development in rural areas. The first two plans focused on agriculture.

In 1973, Indonesia introduced its Small Enterprises Development Programme (SEDP). This was a subsidised credit scheme to help cottage industries and small-scale Indigenous enterprises controlled by *pribumis*. The SEDP was discontinued in January 1990.

The Third Five-Year Plan (1979–1984) began giving assistance to clusters of similar types of small firms — known as *sentras*. These will be discussed in a separate section.

The Fourth Five-Year Plan (1985–1989) established a framework for the development of national industry. Among the plan's objectives was finding solutions for major problems facing small-scale entrepreneurs, in financing, marketing and technical problems.

As the price of oil dropped, Indonesia deregulated large sectors of its economy. In October 1988, Indonesia launched important bank reforms, which reduced capital restrictions.

In October 1989, policy changes allowed foreign entrepreneurs to have 100% ownership of an enterprise in the Batam Economic Zone, for a period of five years. Also, private firms were permitted to set-up industrial estates.

The Fifth Five-Year Plan (1989–1994) emphasised entrepreneurship and the development of small industries. The plan called for tripling private sector investment in targeted industries, including agriculture and tourism. The plan focused on small-scale and household industries, especially those outside urban areas. In January 1990, the SEDP was replaced by the *Kredit Usaha Kecil* (KUK), an unsubsidised credit scheme. The Directorate General of Small Industry was created (within the Ministry of Industry) with the purpose of financing the new ventures of competent entrepreneurs. The *Kredit Investasikecil* — the government's small-scale investment credit scheme — made it possible for small-scale industries to obtain capital for the purpose of purchasing fixed assets. As well, *Kredit Modal Kerja Permanen* — the permanent working capital credit scheme — allowed firms to receive working capital loans, through banks, at subsidised rates. Also, the (central) Bank of Indonesia started a Small Enterprise Development Project, the purpose of which was to train loan officers and to simplify lending procedures.

During the 1990s, the banking sector was liberalised, but Soeharto asked banks to increase lending to small firms. Until 1992, the seven state banks of Indonesia specialised in different sectors: Bank BNI met the needs of manufacturers and traders; Bank Bumi Daya served plantations; Bank Dagang Negara focused on mining; Bank Exim financed international trade; Bank Pembangunan Indonesia specialised in finance for transport; Bank Rakyat Indonesia financed farmers; and Bank Tabungan Negara mobilised public savings.

In 1992, reforms blurred the distinction between different banks. Indonesia's new Banking Law was passed in February 1992, and in August, Indonesia's seven major state banks became joint stock enterprises. This was a move away from bureaucratic regulations and toward profitability. A problem with this restructuring, however, was that it became expensive for entrepreneurs to borrow capital. Also in 1992, the Directorate General of Small Industry adopted an official policy of promoting entrepreneurs who employed between five and 19 workers. Since then, the Directorate General has focused on helping entrepreneurs with marketing, production and financing problems.

In 1995, the government passed Small Business Law Number 9. This act led to the National Partnership Programme.

The Sixth Five-Year Plan focused on the development of small enterprises in 2,200 villages. Indonesia amended import duties, effective January 1996. On fish, duty rates ranged from 0 to 25%.

In 1996, the National Agency for Export Development began reporting to a recently enlarged ministry. The agency included centres for export information, promotion and product development.

Provincial Efforts

The provincial governments and the provincial offices of the (federal) Ministry of Industry jointly implement a Small Industries Development Programme, the *Program Pembinaan dan Pengembangan Industri Kecil*, commonly referred to as BIPIK. Unlike the federal credit programmes, BIPIK provides no capital. Instead, it contributes technical assistance.

Under the wing of BIPIK, the Directorate General of Small Industry got involved in the *Bapak Angkat-Mitra Usha* (Foster Father Business Partner) linkage scheme, to assist, finance, train and facilitate marketing for entrepreneurs. This involves a large "Foster Father" firm and a small business partner, both entering in a symbiotic, co-operative agreement. Several thousand large firms have signed co-operation agreements with tens of thousands of small business partners across Indonesia.

Provinces also have their own development programmes. The island province of Bali, for instance, has carefully formulated economic and social objectives, which bridge the gap between village life and commerce. Emphasis is on agriculture and small-scale industries, as well as tourism. Indonesia is the world's principal supplier of vanilla, and 85% of Indonesia's vanilla is grown in Bali. Farmers here also produce cashew nuts, cinnamon, cocoa, and coffee. In addition, women in Bali raise pigs, which are exported live to Singapore. As well, Bali is a regional exporting centre for canned tuna fish. Although Indonesia exports tin, a commercial beef-canning facility closed when it could not obtain tin-plate for its cans.

Exhibit 6.13   Tourism is an Important Sector in Bali; photo ©2006 Leo Paul DANA

International Entrepreneurship

Indonesia has relaxed restrictions on foreign direct investment, allowing a foreign entrepreneur 100% ownership of a firm in the industrial and services sectors. The Capital Investment Co-ordinating Board — locally known as BKPM — oversees such enterprises. Restrictions are published in the Investment Negative List — locally called the DNI — listing businesses for which foreign ownership is restricted. Approved entrepreneurs may be entitled to exemption from import duties and to postponement of Value Added Tax (VAT), in addition to unrestricted international movement of funds.

Non-Governmental Assistance to Entrepreneurs

In Indonesia, not only the state, but also large firms have programmes to assist entrepreneurs. A motivating factor is that once assisted, entrepreneurs often become subcontractors, suppliers and/or distributors for the assisting firm. This results in sophisticated vertical integration.

In 1980, PT Astra International established the Dharma Bhakti Astra Foundation (YDBA) to demonstrate the firm's commitment to the Small to Medium Scale Enterprise and Co-operative Reinforcement Programme. The foundation's mission is to assist entrepreneurs in production techniques, processes, financing, management, and marketing. The YDBA began providing on-the-job training for entrepreneurs, and many of these became subcontractors for PT Astra International. Until the Asian Crisis, 243 foundation-assisted firms were subcontractors, while 224 served as suppliers and vendors for multinationals.

Other non-governmental organisations, which assist entrepreneurship in Indonesia, include the Association for the Promotion of Small Enterprises and the Indonesian Chamber of Commerce and Industry. In addition, the Institute of Management Education and Development provides training for entrepreneurs.

Sentras

Sentras are clusters of similar small-scale enterprises in the same line of business and in geographical proximity of one another. These clusters exist in the rural areas of each province, and also in some urban centres, including Bandung, Jakarta, Semarang and Surabaya. The clusters are based on comparative advantage.

The first clusters occurred naturally. These included the producers of batik in Java and weavers of cloth on several islands. Other clusters were created by government initiatives.

Tambunan (2005) identified different types of clusters in Indonesia:

(i) The first involves low productivity and wages, usually in the context of micro-enterprises. This is the most common in Indonesia, indicating that the process of clustering in this country is still at an infant stage. This type of cluster displays characteristics of the informal sector; the levels of productivity and wages are lower than those of clusters dominated by formal SMEs. Tambunan wrote, "many producers are illiterate (2005, p. 143)." Producers rely on middlemen for sales;

(ii) Active clusters involve better technology and result in successful penetration of domestic and export markets;

(iii) Dynamic networks have extensive international trade networks. The clusters exhibit internal heterogeneity; and

(iv) The modern or advanced cluster is complex in structure, with a high degree of inter-firm co-operation. Networking includes banks and universities.

Sentras facilitate the state's task of providing assistance to entrepreneurs. Machinery and technical support — unaffordable by any one firm — are made available for common use, within a *sentra*. In some cases, participating firms also form *kopinkras* — small-scale craft co-operatives — to facilitate procurement of inputs and access to credit; these also strengthen the marketing programmes of smaller firms.

Such networking and co-operation between entrepreneurs has enhanced performance, and competitiveness. Also, the cluster approach has been cost-effective. From the government's perspective, clusters facilitate logistics of assistance, by the state and by state-owned firms such as the electric utility company, PLN.

Clusters of traditional craftsmen include silversmiths in Sumatra and copper specialists in Java. Clusters of wood carvers exist in Bali. Other clusters group together entrepreneurs in the chemical, food, footwear, leather and textile industries.

Sentras encourage co-operation among different firms in the same industry. Clustering may also facilitate marketing. The geographical proximity of firms — within a cluster — simplifies sub-contracting to firms that require huge quantities of goods.

Toward the Future

When, in 1998, the flight of capital coincided with the exodus of ethnic-Chinese entrepreneurs, this led to economic and social chaos. Chinese entrepreneurs had controlled important distribution channels in Indonesia and these took time to be replaced. Government efforts were needed, in order to create a new class of *pribumi* entrepreneurs. In 1999, populist decision-makers were giving loans based on economic need, rather than on entrepreneurship potential. The return on capital would be low. Critics accused such incidents as attempts to buy votes.

Nonetheless, the *sentra* system and the co-operatives arising there from have been successful means by which to assist entrepreneurs in absorbing technology, developing skills and enhancing their marketing abilities.

A problem, however, is that the recent crisis and riots prompted children to drop out of school, becoming street-wise entrepreneurs with short-term goals, but lacking a knowledge-intensive base. Perhaps members of *sentras* can be encouraged to absorb such youths.

The old-style entrepreneurs in Indonesia usually had two or three sets of accounting books: one for personal use, another for shareholders, and yet another for tax purposes. The next generation includes MBA graduates more open to a Western management style. However, it is very likely that corruption will survive into the future. Corruption, common in business and in government, is a reason for which people aspire to be civil servants. Parnwell and Turner (1998) and Turner (2003a) reported that individuals may pay Rp 5 million to obtain such a job, and then spend a large part of their career trying to obtain bribes to make their money back.

Exhibit 6.14   Street-wise but Not Educated; photo ©2006 Leo Paul DANA

Entrepreneurship in Indonesia is in transition. Each year, the Capital Investment Co-ordinating Board (BKPM) publishes a priority list, which targets areas for growth. Entrepreneurs, in desired sectors, may qualify for tax incentives. In addition, the Bank of Indonesia oversees the implementation of credit facilitation to entrepreneurs, while the Directorate-General of Small-Scale Industry contributes technical assistance. The Ministry of Manpower operates an entrepreneurship-training programme, and the National Agency for Export Development assists entrepreneurs to sell overseas. Yet, many would-be entrepreneurs are below the poverty line and not aware of either development programmes or tax incentives. Another concern is that despite Indonesia's secular constitution, "Nearly 30 local governments have introduced Shariah laws or Shariah-inspired legislation… To many, the new laws represent stealthy movement toward excessive intrusion of Islam into Indonesia's political process (Perlez, 2006, p. 2)."

Chapter 7

Japan[37]

Introduction

Japan is an archipelago of 3,000 islands, covering about 378,000 square kilometres. *The Economist* reported that the self-employed, and their unpaid family workers, account for nearly a third of the labour force in Japan; this corresponds to Japan having more entrepreneurs per capita than any other big industrial economy. The flagship of entrepreneurship, here, is the sector of small and medium enterprises. Of two million enterprises in Japan, only 1% is considered to be large. Over 80% of Japan's two million farms plant rice annually.

The new Small and Medium Enterprise Basic Law defines SMEs as: a sole proprietorship with up to 500 employees; or a service enterprise with up to 100 employees and up to 50 million yen in capital; or a retail operation with up to 50 employees and up to 50 million yen in capital; or a wholesaler with

---

[37]This chapter is based on information obtained from a variety of sources, including: the All Japan Committee of the Association of Small and Medium Sized Enterprises; the Association for the Promotion of Traditional Craft Products of Japan; the Central Federation of Societies of Commerce and Industry; the Institute of Small Business Research and Business Administration at the Osaka University of Economics; the Japan Chamber of Commerce and Industry; the Japan Federation of Smaller Enterprise Organisations; the Japan Small Business Firm Foundation; the Ministry of Economy, Trade and Industry; the Ministry of Foreign Affairs; the National Association for Subcontracting Enterprise Promotion; the National Federation of Merchant and Industrial Organisation; the National Federation of Small Business Associations; the National Small Business Information Promotion Centre; the New Business Investment Co. Ltd; the Organisation for Small and Medium Enterprises and Regional Innovation; the Small and Medium Enterprise Agency; the Small Business Information Gathering Promotion Association; the Small Business Investment Company Limited; and the Traditional Craft Industry Council. Travel to Japan was provided by the University of Pittsburgh. The chapter includes material that first appeared in Dana (1999b).

Exhibit 7.1   Rice Fields; photo ©2006 Leo Paul DANA

Exhibit 7.2   After the Harvest; photo ©2006 Leo Paul DANA

Exhibit 7.3   Small Scale Retailers; photo ©2006 Leo Paul DANA

up to 100 employees and up to 100 million yen in capital; or a manufacturer or other enterprise, with up to 300 employees and 300 million yen in capital. Small enterprises are defined as those with 20 or fewer employees; in commerce and in the service sector, a firm must not have more than five employees in order to qualify as being small. In the die and mould industry, a firm with 100 employees is considered to be a major producer.

An old proverb teaches, *"When seeking a shelter, look for a big tree."* Rather than compete with large firms, entrepreneurs in Japan co-operate with them, serving as suppliers and assemblers, in an intricate relationship revolving around cultural beliefs. Japan has an ancient and intricate cultural tradition, founded on legends, myths and rituals.

Central to the Japanese belief system are the concepts of mutual obligation, indebtedness, hard work, self-sacrifice and loyalty, all of which reinforce the very important notion of harmony for the common good. In Japan, the individual is always conscious of belonging to a group, and enterprises also tend to form associations. The concepts of obligation, indebtedness and loyalty contribute to the unity and success within each partnership, and to the harmony among groups.

Exhibit 7.4   Harmony; photo ©2006 Leo Paul DANA

Historical Overview

External influences were often responsible for major changes in Japan. Until the 9th century BC, the Japanese archipelago was home to a gathering society who fished and hunted for subsistence. Approximately in the 3rd century BC, the Yayoi era started, and people cultivated rice. The art of farming was introduced from the mainland. Metal tools, such as ploughshares, arrived from Korea, and the development of agriculture led to community life. Hence, villages were settled. Eventually, with the collapse of the Han dynasty in China, a huge wave of migration was observed all over the archipelago. The 7th century was typically characterised by the whole range of movements that took place. As the number of Chinese refugees increased, there was a wave of people moving down the Korean Peninsula and up to those that are now considered the Japanese islands.

As movements of people, together with mixes, borrowings and exchanges, increased all through the archipelago and as writing and the Buddhist religion were introduced, inequalities became accentuated and some clans began to enjoy much more power than did others. Out of this situation emerged the Yamato clan, which seemed the most powerful because of its close ties with the Korean court. The latter, in turn, had the closest links with the powerful lineage that ruled China from 618 to 907 — the Tangs. Thus, as time went on, a trend toward private land ownership, by nobility links to the Yamato clan, became increasingly accentuated, especially during the Heian Period. The year 894 AD marked the beginning of Japan's cultural independence from China and Korea. In 940, the Naritasan Shinshoji Temple was founded by the monk Kancho-sojo; it is the heart of the Shijan sect of Buddhism.

For the several centuries between 1185 and 1868, Japan continued to have an emperor, but the shogun was the powerful head of the samurai (mercenaries). During the 14th century, a civil war was fought over two lines of emperors.

In 1467, the destruction of Kyoto — the capital of Japan, at the time — was an important turning point in history. During the Momoyama Period, from 1573 to 1603, manufacturing and commerce were greatly encouraged, and international trade flourished. (Table 7.1 provides a chronology of Japan.) A concern, however, was that contact with foreigners introduced Christianity and Western influence to Japan, beginning around 1600. In response to this,

Exhibit 7.5   Naritasan Shinshoji Temple; photo ©2006 Leo Paul DANA

Table 7.1   Historical Periods in Japan

Ancient or Early Japan	Nara	710–784
	Heian	784–1185
Medieval Japan	Kamakura	1185–1333
	Muromachi	1333–1573
	Momoyama	1573–1603
Early Modern Japan	Tokugawa (Edo)	1603–1868
Modern Japan	Meiji	1868–1912
	Taishô	1912–1926
	Shôwa	1926–1989
	Heisei	1989–date

the principal characteristic of the Edo Period (1603 to 1868) was a severe policy of seclusion.

The Japanese were divided, according to the Confucian model, into four distinct social classes: (i) samurai, including bureaucrats as well as warriors; (ii) farmers, a class comprised of entrepreneurs who owned their own land as well as peasants who did not; (iii) craftsmen; and (iv) merchants. This, coupled with efficient government personified by the shogunate, maintained harmony in Japan.

In an effort to end a period of war, the Tokugawa leaders came up with the Confucius-inspired *Baku-han* policies that divided the empire into various little groups called *han*. The fact that all of these autonomous regions reported directly to the shogun resulted in a total lack of lateral contacts between various *hans*, and in the formation of many dialects. This very totalitarian top-down political system led to the isolation of the archipelago from other countries, because of bureaucratic law. However, it is important to realise that the insulation of the shogunate did not imply ignorance of what was going on in the rest of the world. Rather, information was tightly controlled. For instance, while a group of people was sent abroad to study Dutch medicine, Christian missionaries were crucified because they represented a threat to the shogunate. Consequently, contact with the outside world was to be avoided — in order to limit European impact and influence — and was strictly restricted to the port of Nagasaki, where a limited amount of trade was permitted.

Japan's self-imposed isolation ended when Commodore Perry of the US Navy penetrated Tokyo Bay on July 8, 1853, thus ending Japan's 250 years of seclusion, and asking for the opening up of Japan to trade with Westerners. In 1868, power was returned from the shogun to the emperor. This was referred to as the Meiji Restoration.

The end of a policy of seclusion, coupled with the Meiji Restoration, would lead to rapid industrialisation, as Japan was faced with the dilemma to form a modern nation or to surrender to colonialism. The government opted to invest heavily in infrastructure and in the establishment of pilot industrial plants in various sectors. These sectors included bricks, cement, glass, machine tools, military needs and mining.

In order to avoid being engulfed by industrialised powers of the West, Japan would need to master the fundamentals of Occidental economics, while rejecting Western culture. The Japanese government hired several prominent Jews to help modernise Japan.

The 1860s were typically characterised by the "opening of Japan" as various revolutions to dismantle the shogunate and its overarching power structure took place. Afterwards, during the first decade of the Meiji era, the doctrine of *bunmei kaika* (civilisation and enlightenment) prevailed. This was characterised by a collective effort to eradicate the past and to modernise, in order to "look" Western. Consequently, not only was Tokyo entirely rebuilt and literally unrecognisable by the end of the 1870s, but the Japanese adopted Western fashions, read Shakespeare and Tolstoy, and some rejected their own language for the sake of adopting English. At the heart of all this was a firm and optimistic belief that enlightenment, science and modernisation would solve everything. Thus, Japan adopted standardised mass production along with imported economic models, but modified them in order to incorporate Japanese cultural values. The motto was *wakon yosai*, which is roughly translated as "Japanese spirit and Western knowledge." However, the *sai* is more than knowledge; it also incorporates skills and wisdom.

The 1880s arrived with a financial crisis, to which the government reacted by privatising some industries. In 1884, the Ministry of Agriculture and Commerce promulgated the Trade Association Regulations, the purpose of which was two-fold: to protect traditional industries and to prevent the mass-production of poor quality goods.

In 1897, the government passed the Law on the Trade Association Dealing with Major Export Products, establishing an association of exporters. However, three years later, this law was repealed, and replaced by the broader Law Regarding the Trade Association Dealing with Major Products. This new law shifted the focus of policy from exporters to manufacturers and marketers of domestic products.

The co-operative association system was launched in 1900, with the Industry Co-operatives Law. In 1904, Japan imposed a tariff on rice imports. In 1914, the Japanese Commerce and Industry Association was established. An account of Japan at the time appears in Scidmore (1914).

In 1920, Japan had only thirty large firms in the machinery sector. In contrast, there were 6,450 small firms (with between five and 30 employees), that produced lower quality goods. There was a large gap between the large and the small firms. The preponderance of small, low-precision, engineering firms gave Japan a reputation of being backward in the machinery industry.

The Law on the Chamber of Commerce and Industry was passed in 1927. The Japan Chamber of Commerce and Industry was established in 1928.

Castle (1932) and Griffis (1933) described Tokyo and Japan, respectively, during the early 1930s. In 1931, Japan enacted the Industrial Co-operatives Law and in 1932, the Commercial Co-operatives Law legalised the commercial co-operative system. The year 1934 saw the introduction of the Unfair Competition Prevention Law. Patric described his experience in Japan, "Often I saw cans and packages whose shape, color, and familiar American labels made me think of home. But always, though almost identical with an American in appearance, it turned out to be an imitation (1936, p. 479)."

During the 1930s, a petition of signatures was collected from people protesting the establishment of department store branches and the spread of department stores in city-centres. As a result, in 1936, the Retail Industry Improvement Investigation Committee resolved "Matters Regarding the Relationship between Department Stores and Smaller Retailers." This led to the Department Store Law, in 1937. The Commercial Retail Store Law followed in 1938. In 1942, the cabinet announced a policy to improve the retail industry.

Respecting a Samurai maxim from the Bushido code of ethics — "Even a hunter is not allowed to kill a bird who comes to him for refuge" — Japan was a haven for thousands of Jews during WWII. By 1941, Kobe was home

Exhibit 7.6   Traditional Retailers; photo ©2006 Leo Paul DANA

to 2,000 Jews. Among the prominent Jewish entrepreneurs of Kobe was real estate magnate David Sassoon.

"After World War II… the majority of retailers were on a small scale, serving local markets (Sanghavi, 2002, p. 270)." The Fair Trade Commission was established in 1947. The Small and Medium Enterprise Agency and the Small and Medium Enterprise League of Japan were both established in 1948. That same year, the National Federation Headquarters established the Committee on Promotion Measures for Small and Medium Industries. The Small and Medium Enterprise Agency recommended that local organisations set up counselling offices for entrepreneurs.

In 1949, the yen was fixed at 360¥ per dollar. Also in 1949, the Small and Medium Enterprise Agency launched a monthly journal entitled, *Information on Small and Medium Enterprises*. The following year the agency launched a semi-monthly newsletter.

In 1952, the Small and Medium Enterprise League of Japan became the Small Business Associations League of Japan. In 1956, the Small and Medium Enterprise Promotion Council was established.

The Small and Medium Enterprise Basic Policy Council was established in 1962. In 1963, the Institute of Small Business Research was created, at

CENTER
JEWISH COMMUNITY of KANSAI
NO 66/1 Kitano-cho 4-chome
Ikuta-ku. KOBE

関西ユダヤ教団

神戸市生田区北野町四丁目六六ノ一

Exhibit 7.7   Jewish Community Centre; photo ©2006 Leo Paul DANA

Exhibit 7.8   Kobe Synagogue; photo ©2006 Leo Paul DANA

the Osaka University of Economics. Also in 1963, production began on the original Shinkansen bullet train, which began operating in 1964. In 1967, the Small Business Promotion Corporation was launched.

In 1971, McDonald's expanded its franchise operation to Japan. In 1981, the Small and Medium Enterprise Agency established the Small and Medium Enterprises' Overseas Investment Advisory Programme. The purpose was to provide advice for entrepreneurs expanding overseas.

The Plaza Accord of October 1985 led to a 50% revaluation of the yen against the dollar. Rather than increase American exports, this action spurred Japan's export performance. In 1988, Japan's per capita GNP exceeded that of the United States for the first time. In April 1989, the Institute of Small Business Research of the Osaka University of Economics was enlarged to become the Institute of Small Business Research and Business Administration.

In 1991, the Subcontracting Small and Medium Enterprise Working Group of the Small and Medium Enterprise Modernisation Council announced a plan to revise the Subcontracting Small and Medium Enterprise Promotion Law. The so-called bubble economy is said to have burst around that time. Nevertheless, very low interest rates helped the economy recover in 1996.

Exhibit 7.9   Shinkansen Bullet Train; photo ©2006 Leo Paul DANA

Exhibit 7.10   Franchise; photo ©2006 Leo Paul DANA

In April 1997, Japan raised its consumption tax. Immediately, household consumption decreased. Later that year, crisis in Asia spread to Japan. Unemployment rose from 3.5% in 1997 to 4.3% in 1998 — the highest since such data was first compiled in 1953. Real GDP growth declined in the fiscal year ending March 1998. This was the first incident of negative growth since March 1994.

The economy entered a period of recovery in 2002. The number of bankruptcies in Japan fell, in 2004, to 13,697 — the lowest figure since 1981.[38]

The Influence of Japanese Culture

Since the Edo Period, wholesalers have held an important position in Japan, and this nation still has four times more wholesalers per retailer than is the case in the United States. While the United States has 1.9 million retailers, Japan, with

---

[38] Source: Small and Medium Enterprise Agency, Ministry of Economy, Trade and Industry, ed., *The 2005 White Paper on Small and Medium Enterprises in Japan: Structural Change in Japanese Society and the Dynamism of Small and Medium Enterprises*, Tokyo: Japan Small Business Research Institute, 2005.

roughly half the population, has 1.7 million retailers. The average product, in Japan, passes through five layers of distribution — more than double that in the United States. Americans may perceive this as inefficient, but for the Japanese, the maintenance of such established relationships is very important. More direct marketing channels would reduce direct costs, but this would destroy the existing harmony, and the reasons for this existing distribution system extend beyond cultural values. Given that Japan is, geographically, a small island nation covered largely by rugged mountains, 70% of the population lives in an area occupying only 20% of the country. The result is densely populated cities and high real estate prices therein. Consequently, storekeepers save much rent by keeping their shops small. However, such small shops have limited storage space. Similarly, Japanese homes have small kitchens with limited storage space for fresh foods. Therefore, Japanese consumers shop for food on a daily basis. This contributes to high turnover in small neighbourhood shops. To avoid daily stock-outs, these small shops rely on small-scale wholesalers who make frequent deliveries, each involving a small load. Each small-scale wholesaler, in turn, relies on other wholesalers, and the global picture is one of a multi-tiered distribution system, which emerged as a result of complex cultural, political and physical factors.

In 1974, liberalisation strengthened this pattern, with the Large Store Law, stating that no retail outlet larger than 5,400 square feet may be built without the permission of local storekeepers. This barrier to entry helped maintain the status quo, and the complex network of marketing channel survives, with its implicit code of elaborate interpersonal obligations.

Among Japanese cultural obligations is gift-giving. This interaction can increase harmony, and facilitate business transactions. Gift offering is an expected behaviour; in Japan, the art of gift-giving is among one's important interpersonal obligations. There are gifts for all occasions and for many, money is not a concern when presenting an offering. Yet, caution is warranted here, as the wrong gift may be disruptive to harmony. A potted plant must not be presented to a sick patient for fear that an illness may take root. Knowing what is appropriate for every occasion can lessen somewhat embarrassing moments and actually enhance business and personal relationships. Table 7.2 illustrates a gift glossary by identifying the Japanese words associated with the occasion for such offerings.

Table 7.2   Japanese Gift Glossary

Ochugen	These are seasonal gifts presented in July, to those to whom one is indebted throughout the year.
Oiwai	These are gifts which are presented on occasions of personal celebrations, including weddings.
Okaeshi	These are "return" gifts, which are presented by recipients of goodwill presents, such as to acknowledge appreciation. Funeral money is thus returned with a gift worth 50% of the original present. Other gifts are returned with *okaeshi* worth 15 to 20% of the value of the original gift.
Okurimono	These gifts can be very useful when they are presented to individuals from whom one is requesting a favour.
Omimai	These are gifts presented to those who are ill or recovering from disease.
Omiyage	These are souvenirs, which commemorate a particular journey, such as a business trip.
Oseibo	These are seasonal gifts presented in early winter to those to whom one is indebted throughout the year.

Exhibit 7.11   Friends in Harmony; photo ©2006 Leo Paul DANA

Public Policy on Entrepreneurship

Japan has long been interested in its entrepreneurs. In 1930, the Temporary Industrial Council issued a report on public policy for small and medium industries. The League of Small and Medium Commerce and Industry of

Exhibit 7.12   Among Obligations is Sending New Year's cards; photo ©2006 Leo Paul DANA

Japan was established in 1932. Given the then current economic depression, a relief fund was set-up, in the context of a Financial Relief Programme for Small and Medium Commercial and Industrial Enterprises.

In 1938, the Ministry of Commerce and Industry set up its Committee on Unemployment Relief Measures for Small and Medium Commerce and Industries. Also that year, the ministry established basic policies regarding entrepreneurs, and announced the Plan for Small Industrial Enterprises to Co-operate in Performing Shared Activities.

In 1940, the cabinet established Measures for Small and Medium Commerce and Industries. Later that year, the Ministry of Commerce and Industry circulated a document, *Guidance and Counselling to Help Small and Medium Commerce and Industries with Each Other*. As well, the cabinet announced a new economic system in which entrepreneurs were to flourish and streamline themselves voluntarily.

In 1942, the Planning Agency established the Reorganisation Committee for Small and Medium Commerce and Industries. The cabinet announced the Policy Regarding the Improvement of Small and Medium Industries.

After WWII, Division 1 of the Economy Stabilisation Headquarters created the Committee on Measures for Small and Medium Industries. In 1947, new measures prohibited private monopolies and unfair trading. The government established guidelines for small and medium enterprises assistance.

In 1948, the Small and Medium Enterprise Agency Establishment Law was passed. Also that year, the state established guidelines for small and medium enterprises. Meanwhile, the Finance Restoration Committee established procedures for using funds for the financial reconstruction of small and medium enterprises.

In 1952, regulations were established to govern the registration of consultants to entrepreneurs. In 1954, the state created a subsidy programme for the acquisition of modern equipment. This was regulated by the Guidelines Concerning the Granting of Subsidies for Constructing Common Facilities for Small and Medium Enterprise Co-operative Associations.

In 1955, the Small and Medium Enterprise Stabilisation Law was revised, as was the Law Regarding Co-operative Associations of Small and Medium Enterprises. Also, the state established a programme for the granting of subsidies to encourage small and medium enterprises to produce goods for export. A minimum wage law was enacted in 1959.

In 1963, the Small and Medium Enterprise Basic Law created the Small and Medium Enterprise Agency, to safeguard the interests of this sector. In 1964, revisions to the Small Business Association Law imposed restrictions on the advancement of large-scale enterprises into the sectors dominated by small and medium enterprises. In 1967, the Organisation of Small and Medium Enterprise Assistance Law was revised, thereby establishing the joint-business co-operatives system.

In 1970, the government enacted the Law on the Promotion of Subcontracting Small and Medium Enterprise. During the following years, many existing laws were amended. The Small and Medium Enterprise Basic Law was revised in 1973 and again in 1983. In 1993, the state enacted the Law Regarding the Assistance for Small and Medium Enterprises by Societies of Commerce and Industry and the Chamber of Commerce. In 1995, Japan passed the Special Law on Facilitating the Creative Business Activities of the Small and Medium-Sized Enterprise.

Although entrepreneurship in Japan may have acquired Western knowledge, it has retained Japanese spirit, including cultural and traditional values such as the sense of obligation, indebtedness and loyalty within business alliances. Public policies help perpetuate this pattern, and across industries, small businesses in Japan are usually linked to a network of one kind or another. The new Small and Medium Enterprises Basic Law promotes business innovation, as well as training programmes.

Toward the Future

Since WWII, a few small-scale engineering firms in Japan grew into multinationals. These include Honda and Sony. However, these very large firms were exceptions. The majority of Japanese enterprises specialised in niche activities. For many, the niche was to serve as subcontractor for major enterprises.

This complementarity between small and large firms, coupled with a cultural system of harmony, has enhanced the efficiency of the Japanese economy.

Exhibit 7.13   Japanese Spirit; photo ©2006 Leo Paul DANA

Exhibit 7.14   Major Enterprise; photo ©2006 Leo Paul DANA

Small-scale entrepreneurs have helped large corporations to prosper, while the latter gave entrepreneurs a raison-d'être as well as a livelihood.

Cultural values helped propagate the inter-firm linkages. Dana (1998b) described the business alliances in Japan. These include: the *keiretsu*[39] (a diversified enterprise group); the *sanchi* (a group of small firms in a similar line of business); the *kyodo-kumiai* (a co-operative of small businesses); and the *shita-uke gyosha* (subcontractors) of the *shita-uke seido* (subcontract system). Such alliance systems can serve as de-facto trade barriers, because loyalty within a network makes it harder for outsiders to penetrate. In difficult economic times, however, financial constraints may strain relationships within alliances.

For the future, the Ministry of Economy, Trade and Industry is committed to provide support for start-ups; for SMEs entering new activities; for the development and use of human resources at SMEs; for revitalisation of SMEs; and for the revitalisation of shopping districts, including city centres.

---

[39] See also Lasserre and Schütte (1995).

Chapter 8

Korea[40]

Introduction

The Republic of Korea — popularly known as South Korea — shares the Korean Peninsula with the Democratic People's Republic of Korea (North Korea). The two Koreas are separated by the Demilitarised Zone (DMZ), a four kilometre-wide strip at the 38th parallel.

Prior to the 1945 division of Korea, industry was concentrated in the north, and agriculture in the south. During the three and a half decades during which the Japanese occupied Korea, they built factories, railroads and hydroelectric plants in the north of the country, i.e., the area which became North Korea. In the territory that eventually became known as South Korea, the principal industries were farming and fishing. Given its abundant coal and iron reserves, North Korea was expected to prosper more than its counterpart to the south.[41]

Until the financial crisis of the late 20th century, South Korea prospered with a growth-oriented model. Although President Roh Moo-hyun pledged to nurture economic conditions favourable to enterprise, the 21st century ushered in discussion of a "drastic shift in industrial structure (Yang, 2005, p. 12)." In June 2005, data from the National Statistical Office "showed that the number of people preparing to look for jobs in May hit a record high

---

[40]This chapter is based on information obtained from a variety of sources, including: the Bank of Korea; the Economic Planning Board; the Federation of Korean Industries; the Korea Development Institute; and the Ministry of Trade and Industry. Travel to Korea was provided by Air Canada. The chapter includes material that first appeared in Dana (1999b).
[41]See Hwang (1993).

Exhibit 8.1   Harvest from Korean Waters; photo ©2006 Leo Paul DANA

Exhibit 8.2   Growth-oriented Seoul; photo ©2006 Leo Paul DANA

(Soh-jung, 2005, p. 5). Meanwhile, the government decided to relocate 176 public organisations out of Seoul,[42] in an attempt to promote development in the provinces (So-young and Hae-in, 2005).

Historical Overview

Korea was first unified during the 7th century, and the nation prospered under Buddhist culture.[43] The Yi dynasty, started by General Yi Song-gye in 1392, ruled Korea until Japan abolished the Korean monarchy in 1910. Under the Yi dynasty, Korea maintained a tributary relationship with China. There was little market activity in Korea. Until the 18th century, monopoly rights protected Korean merchants.

In 1876, Japan made Korea accept a one-sided commercial treaty. China and others did the same. Investment flowed to Korea, from Britain, France, Germany, Russia and the United States, but Japanese entrepreneurs dominated the business realm in Korea.

As foreign traders controlled the Korean economy, the Yi dynasty instituted reforms, but these were not enough, and in 1894 Korean peasants revolted. Military intervention suppressed the revolt, but this led to substantial Japanese military presence in Korea.

Following its victory in the Sino-Japanese War (1894–1895) and the Russo-Japanese War (1905), Japan annexed Korea in 1910 and the Japanese yen replaced the Korean barter system. From 1910 to 1945, the Japanese treated Korea as a colony. Japan separated the monarchy from the state, codified civil law, outlawed discrimination against commoners and monetised the economic system. The colonisers appropriated 40% of Korea's area, monopolised natural resources, took control of public services and took command of finances.

The educational system was designed to assimilate the Koreans as lower elements in Japanese society. Japanese firms discriminated against

---

[42] During the Japanese colonial period, which lasted until 1945, Seoul was referred to as Keijo (Deering, 1933).

[43] For a discussion, of Buddhism in Korea, see Curzon-of-Kedleston (1924).

Exhibit 8.3   Rural Korea; photo ©2006 Leo Paul DANA

Korean employees, and Korean entrepreneurs were unable to compete with Japanese entrepreneurs. This prompted two million Koreans to revolt in 1919. Nevertheless, the harsh military rule obligated the Korean people to produce more and more rice for the Japanese, and to serve as a market for goods manufactured in Japan.

New technologies were introduced as the Japanese invested in irrigation. While the Japanese were countering a rice shortage in their archipelago, Korean farmers starved to death because their entire rice harvest was shipped to the colonising country.

Eventually, Japan moved from an "agriculture first" policy to one of manufacturing in Korea. The Japanese owned virtually all large-scale firms in Korea, while Koreans had some smaller factories. The number of Japanese companies increased from 109 in 1911, to 1,237 in 1929. In contrast, Korean entrepreneurs owned 27 firms in 1911, and 361 in 1929.

Japan implemented a policy to eradicate Korean national identity. The Koreans were forbidden to speak their language and Korean families were forced to replace Korean names with Japanese names. Japan censored the press, and despoiled Korea's resources.

Beginning in 1930, Japan focused on preparing for war. That year, almost one quarter of Korean factory products went to Japan. Northern Korea was used as a manufacturing base for Japan, while the south provided fish and agricultural produce.

Following the Manchurian Incident (1931–1937), the Japanese decided to industrialise Korea in order to fully take advantage of its mineral resources in the north and of its rice supply. The Japanese needed to build factories, hydroelectric plants and railroads. They needed capital (90% of which came from Japanese conglomerates known as *zaibatsu*), technology (100% of which came from *zaibatsu*), and labour (100% of which was provided by poorly paid Korean workers). Consequently, the ratio of light to heavy goods in Korea (which was 80:20 in 1930) became 50:50 during WWII. By 1940, half of Korean factory products went to Japan. This process resulted in the growth of small and medium scale capitalists, the increase of skilled male workers, migration, urbanisation, and the loss of the black and white nationalist outlook which had characterised the Korean people ever since the arrival of the Japanese.

At the end of WWII, Soviet forces took control of northern Korea, while American troops occupied the south. In August 1948, the Republic of Korea (South Korea) was proclaimed. To the north of the 38th parallel, the Soviets created the Democratic People's Republic of Korea (North Korea).

In 1950, North Korea invaded the south, with the aspiration of creating a united communist Korea. An armistice was signed in 1953.

In 1963, Park Chung Hee became the president of South Korea. His policy was to develop the economy of his country. The next section shall examine his policy for economic development and its impact on entrepreneurship in the Republic of Korea.

Public Policy

From 1953 to 1961, South Korea received about two thirds of its total investment in the form of rehabilitation aid from the United States. These investments were used to implement an import substitution policy.

A military coup in 1961 initiated a policy of rapid industrialisation. As South Korea accelerated its industrialisation, legislation was introduced to protect entrepreneurs and to help them be productive contributors to the economy. In 1961, the Small and Medium Industry Bank Act designated a financial institution — the Industrial Bank of Korea — to make loans only to small-scale entrepreneurs. Similarly, the Kukmin Bank was mandated to give loans only to enterprises with fewer than 200 employees.

In 1962, when South Korea adopted its first Economic Development Plan (1962–1966), per capita GNP was $82. President Park Chung Hee subsequently created a command economy with wages and interest rates at his order. With the objective of maximising growth and export volume, he set wages low and subsidised interest rates.

Several economic development plans helped the president guide the economy. The Second Five-Year Plan (1967–1971) and Third Five-Year Plan (1972–1976) allowed him to encourage exports rather than import substitution. The won was devalued, and financial support was channelled to high performers. Given that market demand interest rates may cause a heavy debt burden on entrepreneurs, and hence decrease the pace of new venture formation while increasing the bankruptcy rate, selected firms in South Korea were granted subsidised interest rates well below the market-clearing point. The low cost of borrowing allowed for the development of capital intensive methods of production over labour-intensive ones, and the excess supply of labour kept wages low, a competitive advantage for exporting. Thus, instead of helping entrepreneurs at large, President Park Chung Hee specifically used his control over bank credit to channel subsidised loans to export-oriented borrowers. These few exporters soon grew into the debt-based mega-conglomerates known as *chaebols* — literally "financial cliques." Small-scale entrepreneurs were squeezed out of many markets, resulting in numerous monopolies and oligopolies.

The economic effects, of South Korea's Vietnam venture during the late 1960s and early 1970s, went far beyond the simple acquisition of foreign exchange. Many South Korean firms, including Hanjin and Hyundai, got their first big economic boost from the Vietnam War (known in Vietnam as the American War). Korean firms became contractors for the United States army in South Vietnam and later made use of their Vietnamese contacts and experience to expand into the international construction business, most notably in the

Middle East. Between 1974 and 1979, South Korea's top ten *chaebols* took home nearly $22 billion in Middle East construction sales, of which Hyundai's share alone was over $6 billion.

In 1974, the Credit Guarantee Funds Act provided guarantees for liabilities of entrepreneurs. In 1975, the Sub-Contracting System Promotion Act promoted co-operation between large firms and smaller ones. The Fourth Five-Year Plan (1977–1981) perpetuated a tight credit policy. Consequently, the national economy of South Korea was based on rapid industrialisation of only very few non-integrated industries — heavy industry and chemicals — for the purpose of increasing exports. Hence, the economy was dominated by a small number of highly diversified mega-conglomerates, resulting in various problems.

South Korean industry was largely dependent on foreign suppliers for raw materials and light industry components as well as for machinery and replacement parts which also had to be imported, a drain on the country's financial resources. Therefore, much capital had to be raised in the form of foreign loans, causing a further burden — that of debt service.

As national policy favoured the *chaebols,* these flourished while small business remained small. Although the factories of *chaebols* were efficient, their offices tended to be less so, as considerable time was consumed in meetings as well as bureaucracy. A further problem with *chaebol* administration was the highly hierarchic structure, which makes a manager feel very subordinate to an immediate superior, often causing an employee to serve a superior personally instead of concentrating on innovation.

The Small and Medium Industries Promotion Corporation Act, in 1980, provided financial support, technical assistance and managerial consultancy to entrepreneurs. The following year, the Procurement Facilitating Act specified the conditions of government procurements from entrepreneurs. This allowed smaller enterprises to sell to the state, collectively, via co-operatives.

In 1983, the Policy to Support Promising Small and Medium-scale Enterprises provided low interest loans, technical training and management consulting to promising small and medium enterprises. In 1984, the Mutual Assistance Fund Act provided special loans to entrepreneurs. In 1988, the Production Research Institute Act created an institute to assist entrepreneurs with technology transfers and product development.

Exhibit 8.4   SMEs; photo ©2006 Leo Paul DANA

Prior to the labour unrest of 1989, wages were very low, a factory worker earning as little as the equivalent of roughly $50 for a 72-hour week. Wages were subsequently raised substantially. Salaries were 45% higher in 1989 than in 1987, and those in automotive industry climbed 80% from 1986 to 1989 — contributing to price increases, which were already high due to the lack of competition in many monopolistic and oligopolistic markets. Rationalisation, which followed, led to increased unemployment.

In 1989, the government made available credit guarantee funds for technology development among entrepreneurs. Also that year, several commercial banks were permitted to provide services exclusively to entrepreneurs.

Five *chaebols* were producing more than 50% of Korea's GNP. In consideration of this fact, a government priority during the 1990s was to build up small and medium sized firms and to encourage the development of innovative entrepreneurs, with programmes such as capital assistance including low cost loans for new ventures and R&D incentives to facilitate innovation. Government initiatives were designed to encourage: a general trading company system and the provision of fiscal or commercial advantages; commitment by the constitution to foster small business; special support for small exporters; direct

Exhibit 8.5   Enjoying Government Incentives; photo ©2006 Leo Paul DANA

and indirect financial assistance for small business; commitment by banks to make 35% of their loans to smaller firms; tax concessions for new ventures, particularly those with innovative ideas or using competitive technologies; and facilitation of foreign investment.

In February 1993, a newly elected government issued the 1993–1997 Five-year Plan. This called for reduced government intervention in the economy, lowering of entry barriers and deregulation of business activities. Tariffs were reduced. Many restrictions on the import of capital goods were eliminated. A special depreciation allowance was introduced for fixed assets. High-tech entrepreneurs were allowed to import capital goods duty-free, and their firms were granted a five-year exemption on corporate income tax. Registration qualifications for trading enterprises were abolished effective 1997. Lee (1998) gave an overview of small Korean firms during the 1990s.

In 1998, the government established the Corporate Restructuring Fund, with a value of $1.2 billion, half of which was provided by the Korean Development Bank, and the other half by a consortium of banks, insurance companies and investment houses. Seventy percent of the fund was earmarked for

Exhibit 8.6   Micro-enterprise; photo ©2006 Leo Paul DANA

Exhibit 8.7   Prominent; photo ©2006 Leo Paul DANA

established small and medium firms, especially those focusing on high technology and exports. The top five *chaebols* were banned from borrowing from the fund. Yet, public policy initiatives to promote SMEs have had little success in this country where *chaebols* remain prominent.

During the early years of the 21st century, Korea implemented policy initiatives for the long-term planning of research and innovation. This is discussed by Lee and Kwun (2003).

Pre-crisis Trends

Development of a Domestic Component Industry

The *chaebols* traditionally imported light industry components as well as raw materials. Gradually, foreign suppliers were replaced by the small business sector. The development of one million small and medium-sized businesses in South Korea — diversified in various sectors, including manufacturing, trading, service, transportation, and construction as well as mining — led to increased trade between *chaebols* and small firms providing components.

Exports

The general trading company systems, as initiated by the government, significantly contributed to export volume by small firms. Product and market diversification became prime objectives of the trading companies, resulting not only in short-term profit but also in long-term growth. Small firms began to export labour-intensive light-industry goods, which South Korea previously did not export. Their production also developed component industries within South Korea, thus helping domestic growth and further helping exports indirectly.

Productivity

Until the Asian Crisis, small manufacturers consistently increased their production at a rate higher than that of large manufacturers. Government sources indicate that productivity in South Korea's manufacturing sector improved by an average of 11% per year, while productivity among smaller firms — in the same sector — increased by an annual average of 14%.

The Crisis and Beyond

The post-1993 financial liberalisation in South Korea encouraged entrepreneurs to obtain short-term loans. Some borrowers opted to borrow abroad. In 1996, the country qualified for admission to the Organisation of Economic Corporation and Development (OECD). However, problems soon emerged. Although *chaebols* had an average debt-equity ratio of 400%, the economy was still healthy in 1997. Growth rate was 5.5%, inflation was stable at 4.4% and unemployment at 2%. A foreign exchange crisis, however, led to an economic crisis. Korea's meltdown, in November 1997, led the government to seek an International Monetary Fund (IMF) package. The following month, Korea signed a $58 billion IMF bailout. Financially-fragile entrepreneurs faced the domino effects of bankruptcies.

Before the crisis, Korea's economic sector had been characterised by few fluctuations, indirect financing, and the dominance of *chaebols*. Since 1998, there have been high fluctuations in business conditions, considerable financial restructuring and an increasing influence of foreign enterprises.

Up to the crisis, owners tended to be active managers, and seniority was paramount. More recently, chief executive officers have gained importance, as have ability and outcome.

In the social sector, low levels unemployment before the crisis, and high levels of saving, have given way to rising unemployment, in turn causing growing gaps between the rich and the poor. Lee (2003) pointed out that the

Exhibit 8.8   Business Was Slow; photo ©2006 Leo Paul DANA

crisis laid down favourable conditions for enabling employers to introduce performance-based personnel systems. In 2005, the Anti-Corruption Act was amended henceforth including indirect corruption.

Toward the Future

The South Korean policy approach, subsidising credit to selected export-oriented firms, resulted in a command economy dominated by *chaebols*. From 1961 to 1967, the government supported *chaebols*, and these generated full employment. *Chaebols* could produce mediocre products in a protected environment and Korean consumers bought their products. Then, tariff reductions made South Korea increasingly open to competition from abroad.

The opening of the economy, coupled with the Asian Crisis, necessitated major changes. As the highly diversified *chaebols* were being trimmed, cost reduction measures released skilled personnel with entrepreneurial potential. Also, product restructuring gave rise to new opportunities for

Exhibit 8.9   Growing Gaps; photo ©2006 Leo Paul DANA

Exhibit 8.10   Open to Competition; photo ©2006 Leo Paul DANA

Exhibit 8.11   Toward the Future; photo ©2006 Leo Paul DANA

emerging entrepreneurs. Thus, the restructuring of *chaebol* portfolios provided opportunities for entrepreneurship. However, in 1998, 1,000 Korean entrepreneurs were going bankrupt every month. According to unpublished documents at the Bank of Korea, 18 large companies and 5,221 smaller ones declared bankruptcy during the first five months of 1998, compared with 10 and 2,197 during the same period in 1997. Some communities experienced reverse industrialisation, as entrepreneurs gave up industrial production, in favour of agriculture. Nevertheless, the economy rebounded. In June 2006, the Port of Busan was looking to increase its berths from 22 to 52 by 2011.

Chapter 9

Laos[44]

Introduction

Officially the Lao People's Democratic Republic, Laos is one of Asia's least developed nations, and among the five poorest in the world. Perazic wrote: "Once a great kingdom, 'the Land of the Million Elephants and the White Parasol' faces its struggle for survival (1960, p. 46)." The same is true today. The landlocked country, enclosing 236,800 square kilometres, is nestled between Cambodia, China, Myanmar, Thailand and Vietnam. Laos is sparsely populated. It is among the least urbanised nations in Asia.

Traditionally, business activities in Laos have not been associated with high social status. Cultural values, stemming from religious beliefs, emphasised, instead, the elimination of desire. Commerce, on the other hand, is perceived as a means to satisfy desire. Social forces thus discouraged enterprise, and trade has usually been the role of those with inferior social standing. Where Lao men refrained from doing business, women often succeed (Dana, 1997c). Yet, the communist take-over further discouraged entrepreneurial spirit. As a result, Lao society is generally non-entrepreneurial. The Chinese community is very active in the entrepreneurship sector. Large corporations in Thailand, each earn more than the value of all the goods and services produced in all of Laos.

---

[44]This chapter is based on information obtained from a variety of sources, including: the Ministry of External Economic Relations and the Ministry of Industry and Handicraft, in Vientiane. It also incorporates information obtained during various interviews with entrepreneurs, such as that detailed in Dana (1997c). The chapter includes material that first appeared in Dana (1995b; 1999b; 2002).

Exhibit 9.1   Sparsely Populated; photo ©2006 Leo Paul DANA

Exhibit 9.2   Satisfying Desires; photo ©2006 Leo Paul DANA

Exhibit 9.3   Grey Market; photo ©2006 Leo Paul DANA

O'Driscoll, Holmes and Kirkpatrick (2001) reported a black market in Laos, larger than the formal economy. The popularity of the parallel economy is no surprise, considering the low initial role of legitimate private enterprise, coupled with a high degree of liberalisation, and hindered by the lack of macro-stability in the absence of a sufficiently developed legal framework.

Historical Overview

The Lao people are thought to have arrived from China during the 8th century. During the 1200s, Kublai Khan led the Mongols to seize power in China. This prompted further migration to the region, which would later become Laos. During the following century, a Khmer empire was established here. It was known as *Lan Xang* — literally "Million Elephants." The Lao people organised themselves into Lao principalities.

During the 19th century, France persuaded one of the leaders to accept a French protectorate, as insurance against conquest by China or Siam. France then united all of the Lao principalities into one country. Thus came to be the name Laos, which is the plural of Lao.

France used Laos as a buffer between French Vietnam and British Burma. The French imposed a Vietnamese-staffed civil service in Laos, but they did not contribute to the protectorate. When the Japanese occupied French Indochina in 1941, the Lao people obtained more autonomy than they had experienced under French protection. Following WWII, France tried to take back Laos; in 1949 the latter was declared an independent associate state of the French Union. The United Nations recognised Laos as a separate country, and in 1953 France allowed Laos to become a monarchy. In 1954, communists occupied areas of two Lao provinces, namely Phong Saly and Sam Neua. In 1959, King Savang Vatthana became monarch of the Lao kingdom. By 1960, the communist-led *Pathet Lao* (Lao People's Party) forces made advances, and during a three-day period in December that year, Vientiane was ruled by four successive governments (White, 1961a).

In 1962, the Royal Lao Government and the State of Israel embarked on a joint experimental farm, along the Mekong River. Known as the Vientiane

Exhibit 9.4   French Language; photo ©2006 Leo Paul DANA

Exhibit 9.5   French Taste; photo ©2006 Leo Paul DANA

Exhibit 9.6   French Architecture; photo ©2006 Leo Paul DANA

Pilot Project, this project provided farmers with seed, fertiliser, insecticide and even irrigation. The objective was to transform subsistence farmers into market-oriented entrepreneurs. Participants prospered and by 1968, 250 families participated in the project (White, 1968).

In December 1975, the Lao Patriotic Front — the political arm of the *Pathet Lao* — abolished the monarchy and created a communist[45] entity, the Lao People's Democratic Republic. All Christian seminaries were closed that year. Zasloff and Unger (1990) presented a detailed account of Laos following the revolution.

When the Lao People Revolutionary Party took control of the Lao People's Democratic Republic, in 1975, it implemented a policy of accelerated socialisation. Harsh policies shunned entrepreneurship and co-operatives replaced private initiatives. Former royalists were sent to re-education camps where they were forced to accept communism. In 1977, Laos and Vietnam signed a treaty of friendship and co-operation.

---

[45] For a thorough discussion of the communist movement in Laos, see Brown, Zasloff and Staar (1986).

Exhibit 9.7   From Farm to Market; photo ©2006 Leo Paul DANA

A Radical Model of Transition: The New Economic Mechanism

In 1987, Laos implemented its New Economic Mechanism — a radical shift in public policy. This recognised market forces as legitimate, and began liberalising the centralised economy. The first national election took place in 1989. Inflation reached 76% that year. In 1990, the state launched a drive to attract foreign investment, privatise state enterprises, develop import-substitution industries and promote exports. In 1991, a new constitution ushered in further economic reforms. New laws were subsequently introduced, governing property, labour and foreign investment. New relationships were also developed. Laos signed treaties of friendship and co-operation with Thailand in 1991, with Cambodia in 1992, with China in 1994, and with Myanmar in 1994.

In April 1994, Laos and Vietnam signed an agreement on goods in transit, which allowed these commodities to be transported across either Laos or Vietnam, on the way to the other. The following month, Laos introduced a liberal law governing investments. This streamlined foreign investment regulations and tax structures. Legislation included tax holidays, a 1% import duty on capital goods associated with production, and a flat-rate corporate tax of 20%.

This was to lead to a major influx of foreign capital to create joint ventures, as well as 100% foreign-owned investments in commerce, industry and services. Furthermore, the government committed itself to expedite the business application process. Japanese and Taiwanese investors expressed considerable interest. Until 1996, Laotians needed permission to change residences; then, this requirement was done away with.

On July 23, 1997, Laos joined ASEAN. In 2000, GDP growth was 4.5%. Yet, GDP per capita was a mere $272 that year, and half the nation's budget came from foreign aid. In March 2001, Laotian and Thai officials initialled an agreement to build a second bridge to link the two countries; the geographic position of Laos could help it become an important assembly and trans-shipment centre.

The Traditional Belief System

W. Robert Moore, Chief of Foreign Editorial Staff at *National Geographic*, wrote about Vientiane, the capital of Laos, "Biggest buildings in town, except for a few government offices are the Buddhist temples (1954, p. 666)." Even

Exhibit 9.8   In Transit; photo ©2006 Leo Paul DANA

today, Theravada monasteries, known as wats, dominate every town in Laos; almost every house, shop and office has a private temple. It is even common for boats, cruising along the Mekong River, to dock for the crew to jump ashore, light incense and pray. The Lao wats are architecturally distinct from monasteries elsewhere in Asia. In Laos, wats have large terraces, and flare symbols on the roofs. Religious beliefs are very important in this country, and Laotians are noticeably influenced by folk tales, superstitions, and traditional animist beliefs — in addition to the ancient beliefs of the national religion, Theravada Buddhism. An article in the August 28, 1992 issue of *Asiaweek* explained that it is commonly believed that the Mekong River gets "hungry" for human souls, without which the annual rains will not arrive:

> a little girl (was) swept away by the current while picnicking with her family on a sandbank. Her mother and father made no attempt to save her. Two foreigners snatched the child from the swift water after a desperate effort. The parents were fearful because the river had been thwarted in claiming the child (p. 63).

Exhibit 9.9   Religion Above All; photo ©2006 Leo Paul DANA

Exhibit 9.10   In Exchange for Honour; photo ©2006 Leo Paul DANA

Theravada monks are highly influential in Lao society. They are consulted on virtually all matters, thereby playing a role in a diversity of spheres, ranging from private life to government policy. They have traditionally had a great impact on the educational system; it used to be that the only schools were in wats.

Central to the belief system in Laos is the ultimate goal to extinguish unsatisfied desires. Its doctrine focuses on aspects of existence, including *dukkha* (suffering from unsatisfied desire), and *anicca* (impermanence). Assuming that unsatisfied desires cause suffering, suffering can be eliminated if its cause — desire — is eliminated. A respectable person, then, according to this ideology, should not work towards the satisfaction of materialistic desires, but should, rather, strive to eliminate the desire itself. A monk, for instance, is specifically prohibited by the religion, from tilling fields or raising animals.

Lao folk tales reinforce the belief that a male monk should not labour for material wealth; yet, the same folklore conditions women to accept a heavy burden in exchange for honour, protection and security.

Numerous Lao families who farm during the wet season become self-employed gold-diggers during the dry season. The prospectors camp along the Mekong River, especially in the region of Luang Prabang, the former royal capital, discovered by Henri Mouhot in 1861. The women do the heaviest work, digging for dirt and panning it in wooden trays. The men weigh the gold, up to one gram per day.

The *Far Eastern Economic Review* quoted a London newspaper as saying that "Lao rice farmers have a reputation in this dynamic region for lying down, closing their eyes and listening to their crops grow in fertile paddy fields (1994, p. 60)." Indeed, entrepreneurial spirit is not very prevalent in the traditional Lao belief system. Dana (1995b) addressed this issue in detail.

The official calendar used in Laos is that of the Lao Buddhist era — not to be confused with the Thai calendar; the Christian year 2007, for example, corresponds to 2645 in the Lao calendar, and 2550 in the Thai calendar.

Pluralism

Laos has a diversity of ethnic minorities with a variety of beliefs, attitudes and traditions. White reported: "There's a Thai Dam... They sacrifice dogs to the spirits. They beat them to death before they roast them, so that the meat will be tender. And here's a Kha Koui. They never wash... (1961a, p. 260)."

According to government sources, ethnic minorities in Laos include: Lan Tene; Meo Khao; Meo Lay; Mouseudam; Mouseudeng; and Mien, formally known as Yao. In addition, Laos is home to eight kinds of Kais, and to seven types of Thais. There are also the Hmong people, referred to by the Chinese as *Miao* — literally meaning barbarians; these are the subject of Garrett (1974).

In all, there are 68 recognised ethnic groups in Laos. White (1987) grouped these into three broad segments: the highlanders, known as Lao Theung; the mountain tribes, called Lao Soung; and the valley dwellers, referred to as Lao Lum. According to United Nations sources, the Lao Lum people comprise 60% of the country's population; these people are involved in government, as well as wet-rice agriculture. The Lao Theung people are concentrated in slash-and-burn subsistence agriculture, and they have less contact with consumer culture and the monetised economy. The Lao Soung people are cut off from any legal sector of the monetised economy; some are involved in the smuggling of gems or narcotics.

Given the traditional belief system of Laos, the business sector in this country consists largely of people who are not ethnic Laotians. A significant Chinese minority is prominent in small-scale enterprise. This community consists primarily of people — most of whom are Teochews — who are descendents of migrants from southern China. Vientiane is home to at least 2,500 Chinese entrepreneurs, and these people own a disproportionate percentage of restaurants, movie theatres, hotels, repair shops and jewellery shops in this capital city.

Muslim men are also very active in the small business sector of Laos. Individuals from India and Pakistan are especially active in the garment industry.

In addition, Thai and Australian entrepreneurs have recently created numerous new ventures in Laos. Unlike the Chinese and the Muslims who reside in this country permanently, the Thais and Australians in Laos tend to be sojourners.

Entrepreneurship

Whereas American involvement in Lao business tends to be in the form of large business, Thai investments tend to be in the medium-size category, as are Australian ventures. Even more involved in small business are French entrepreneurs.

One problem encountered by entrepreneurs in the manufacturing sector is the poor infrastructure. Given the generally inadequate conditions of the roads — often flooded during the rainy season — and the lack of a railway, a quarter of all traffic in Laos uses the Mekong River. People and buffalo stand side by side, on boats or barges, for hours. Sometimes, cargo gets damaged. A gift from the people of Australia, the $30 million Friendship Bridge across the Mekong River between Laos and Thailand was opened in 1994.

As for the Lao people, 85% are involved in agricultural sectors. Crops include coffee, corn, rice, tea, tobacco, vegetables and wheat. Given that three fifths of the GNP comes from agricultural output, the government has instituted reforms providing incentives to farmers. The plan introduced preferential tax policies for agriculturalists, and increased investment in the sector,

Exhibit 9.11   Farmer's Home; photo ©2006 Leo Paul DANA

Exhibit 9.12   By the Mekong; photo ©2006 Leo Paul DANA

especially in irrigation. The plan also raised the prices of produce, and linked remuneration with output. Yet, although annual per capita rice output in Laos is 350 kilogrammes. Nevertheless, some provinces experience occasional rice shortages.

Many farming communities are migratory; they deforest land for a crop, and then move elsewhere. There is a constant breeze of smoke and ashes over the Mekong River. Opium is an important crop, of which Laos produces about 300 tons annually.

Toward the Future

Reforms have increased the autonomy of firms, and the state no longer has the monopoly on supply, purchasing and marketing. Yet, O'Driscoll, Holmes and Kirkpatrick (2001) reported that Laos, with its average tariff exceeding 19%, had less economic freedom than any of its neighbours. Furthermore, enterprise is largely limited to women and minorities, as local culture does not encourage it. The local shortage of skilled labour limits manufacturing. The shortage of educated individuals limits the service sector.

Exhibit 9.13   Service-oriented; photo ©2006 Leo Paul DANA

Chapter 10

Malaysia[46]

Introduction

Located between Indonesia, Singapore and Thailand, Malaysia occupies 332,633 square kilometres. It covers the Malay Peninsula and it shares the island of Borneo with Brunei Durussalam and Indonesia.

Under colonial rule, British administrators encouraged Indigenous Malays to work the land, while the ethnic-Chinese dominated the entrepreneurship sector in Malaya. Since independence, government efforts have tried to change this, by formulating an ethnic-based policy to govern entrepreneurship in Malaysia. Schaper and Volery (2004) described specific programmes aimed to help Indigenous entrepreneurs in this country. Nevertheless, the Chinese minority — comprising approximately 30% of the population — still control a disproportionate amount of capital assets in this country. Chinese entrepreneurs own most small firms in Malaysia. Over 93% of manufacturers in Malaysia are SMEs (Schaper and Volery, 2004). In 2006, Malaysia had more than 200,000 SMEs, mostly in the wholesale and retail trade sector.

---

[46]This chapter is based on information obtained from a variety of sources, including: the Agricultural Bank of Malaysia; the Central Bank of Malaysia; the Credit Guarantee Corporation; the Development Bank of Malaysia; the Labuan Offshore Financial Services Authority; the Malaysian Industrial Development Authority; the Ministry of Finance; and the Ministry of Trade and Industry. Travel to Malaysia and within Malaysia was provided by the Malaysian Entrepreneurship Development Centre (MEDEC) at the MARA University of Technology. The chapter includes material that first appeared in Dana (1999b).

Exhibit 10.1   Multilingual Trader; photo ©2006 Leo Paul DANA

Historical Overview

Ancient remains suggest that the original Malays came from south-western China, via Indo-China. These people were invaded by the Sumatran ancestors of today's Malays.

In 1402, Prince Parameswara of Sumatra founded Malacca, on the west coast of the Malay Peninsula. In 1405, Emperor Yung-Yo, of the Ming dynasty created favourable relations between China and Malacca. Chinese traders came to the Malay Peninsula and this attracted merchants from distant places. Malacca thrived as a port-of-call for entrepreneurs from China, India, and Arab lands. The trading centre was home to Bugis, Chettiar, Chinese, Gujerati, Javanese, Mon, and Tagalog Muslim entrepreneurs who prospered in the entrepôt trade. In Malacca, cloves and pepper were exchanged for western textiles. Some entrepreneurs on the Malay Peninsula dealt in minerals, rice and teak in addition to cloves and pepper. In time, these traders developed a sophisticated network, which included entrepreneurs in Burma and Sumatra.

Portugal used its colony on the Indian sub-continent, Goa, as a base from which to set off to Malaya. In 1511, the Portuguese conquered Malacca, but the Dutch defeated them, in 1641. The Dutch introduced monopolistic practices and disrupted the traditional commercial patterns of local entrepreneurs. The Mons abandoned their long distance trade routes. The Indigenous trading networks collapsed, and by 1681 Malay entrepreneurs gave up their trade with China, India, Japan, Persia, the Philippines, Siam and Vietnam. Although the Dutch imposed a 20% duty on Chulia entrepreneurs, the Chulias kept their lead in the textile trade.

Exhibit 10.2   Penang; photo ©2006 Leo Paul DANA

In 1786, in exchange for British protection from raiders and pirates, the Sultan of Kedah granted to the East India Company, a virtually uninhabited island off of the west coast of the Malay Peninsula. It was here, on Prince of Wales Island (Penang) that Georgetown, the first of the British Straits Settlements was established. Its founder was the British captain, Francis Light, whose son later founded Adelaide, Australia, which eventually became a sister city to Georgetown. European entrepreneurs set up spice plantations on the island, but growth was constrained due to a labour shortage. In addition to handling rubber and tin from the Malay Peninsula, Penang became "an important coal- and water-supply station for merchant and war vessels (Simpich, 1926, p. 243)."

In contrast to Penang, that had a policy of free trade, further south along the Malay Peninsula, the Portuguese and the Dutch had monopolistic intentions. In 1795, Malacca was given to the British.

In 1824, the Anglo-Dutch Treaty gave Bencoolen (a British post) and the rest of Indonesia to the Dutch, while the British were allowed to control Malaya and Singapore. In 1826, the British formalised the entity that they named the Straits Settlements, under the jurisdiction of the British East India Company, in Calcutta.

Exhibit 10.3   British Colonial Mansion by Penang Waterfront; photo ©2006 Leo Paul DANA

Exhibit 10.4   Rubber Tree; photo ©2006 Leo Paul DANA

The British East India Company controlled the Straits Settlements until the demise of the company, in 1858. The settlements then came under the control of the India Office, in London. In 1867, they were transferred to the Colonial Office, as the Straits Settlements became a Crown Colony. At the time, the Straits Settlements consisted of Penang, Malacca and Singapore. In 1874, the Islands of the Dindings were added to the colony.

For the convenience of the British, the Cocos Keeling Islands were attached in 1886, followed by Christmas Island in 1900 and the Island of Labuan, off the coast of Borneo, in 1906. For administrative purposes, the colony was divided into four settlements:

(i) The Settlement of Singapore (including the Island of Singapore, the Cocos Islands and Christmas Island);
(ii) The Settlement of Penang, including the Island of Penang, Province Wellesley, and the Territory and Islands of the Dindings;
(iii) The Town and Province of Malacca; and
(iv) The Settlement of Labuan.

Exhibit 10.5   The Free Port Brought Prosperity; photo ©2006 Leo Paul DANA

Small-scale rubber production gained popularity in the early 20th century, as there were virtually no barriers to entry. The industry required minimal capital and this was readily available. According to Drabble (1973), by 1921, 37% of the total rubber acreage in Malaya belonged to small-scale entrepreneurs. This corresponded to one-eighth of the total world production of rubber. Simpich wrote, "three-fourths of all our rubber comes out of Malaya (1926, p. p. 235)." However, many Malay entrepreneurs lost their plantations to Chettair money-lenders from southern India. This led to the Smallholdings Restriction of Sale Enactment, in 1931.

The Straits Settlements were dismantled in 1946, just months after the Japanese surrender. Also in 1946, the British territories on Borneo were re-organised such that North Borneo (Sabah) and Sarawak became two separate colonies. That same year, the British also forged the Malayan Union, consisting of Malacca and Penang, along with the nine existing Malay states. These were Johor, Kedah, Kelantan, Negeri Sembilan, Pahang, Perak, Perlis, Selangor, and Terengganu. The union was dissolved in 1948 when the states of the Malay

Exhibit 10.6   Moorish-style 40-metre-high Clock Tower of Sultan Abdul Samad Building in Kuala Lumpur; photo ©2006 Leo Paul DANA

Exhibit 10.7   Strong Chinese Presence in Malaysia's Commercial Realm; photo ©2006 Leo Paul DANA

Peninsula formed the Federation of Malaya, which became independent in 1957. Having lost its status of free port, Penang's importance as a trade centre declined during the 1960s.

In 1963, Malaya joined Sabah, Sarawak, and Singapore to create a new kingdom, Malaysia, with its capital in Kuala Lumpur. However, tension escalated between the ethnic-Chinese and the Malays.

In 1965, Singapore was separated from the union. Yet, there continued to be Chinese people in Malaysia and they became the victims of racial riots.

Ethnic Minorities

Most Chinese immigrants to Malaya did not come as entrepreneurs. During the 19th century, labourers left China to work in the mines of Malaya. Their passage was usually sponsored by an entrepreneur, who became entitled to be their exclusive employer for a period of one year.

When they docked in Malaya, the newcomers (*sinkeh*) were taken by armed guards, to their place of employment. There, they were locked up at night. The employees were virtual prisoners, until they had paid back their debt, at which time they were promoted from *sinkeh* to *laukheh* — literally "old hand."

Exhibit 10.8 Mizrakhi Mansion; photo ©2006 Leo Paul DANA

"Secret societies" were the principal organisations of Chinese immigrants. Chinese entrepreneurs — *towkays* — were the leaders of these societies and they controlled their employees through these societies.

The dominant society in Kuala Lumpur was the Hai San, led by Hakka entrepreneurs. Hokkien entrepreneurs developed an important rice network, importing rice from Burma and elsewhere, milling it in Malaya and exporting it to Hong Kong and beyond. According to the *Straits Settlements Trade Commission's Report,* rice imports to Penang reached 213,648 tons in 1918. In time, the Straits Chinese, known as the Baba and Nyonya, adopted many Malay traditions.

Today, Chinese entrepreneurs own most small-scale industry in Malaysia. At least a third of them were born in China, and their firms generally have a low level of capitalisation. Expansion is not common, and many firms remain sole proprietorships. The Hokkiens are the largest group of Chinese in Malaysia (one-third of the Chinese population) and the prominent Chinese dialect federation in the country — with 138 affiliated associations — is the Federation of Hokkien Associations of Malaysia. The federation developed its own business arm, with investments in China as well as in Malaysia. Malaysia also has important communities of entrepreneurs of Indian origins.

Exhibit 10.9   The Former *Yahudi Gameh*; photo ©2006 Leo Paul DANA

Although Penang was formerly home to Mizrakhi entrepreneurs from Iraq, this is no longer the case. Their synagogue *Yahudi Gameh,* built at 28 Nagore Road, near Lorang Ceylon, had been leased from the family of Ng Huang Lim, who lives next door and remembers fondly, "When we were small we loved to watch through the swinging doors, especially on Mondays, Thursday and I think on Saturday." The synagogue closed down with the passing of Barookh Ephraim,[47] in 1976. The building was transformed into the medicine factory of entrepreneur Khoo Ching Leng. In 1992, it was converted into a florist shop.

The Evolution of Public Policy

The British colonial administration, in Malaya, encouraged a marked division of economic roles, along ethnic lines. Indians were given jobs in plantations, at the post office and in the police service. While rural Malays remained peasants and urban Malays were offered employment in the public sector, many Chinese

---

[47] His wife and daughter have since moved to Sydney, Australia.

Exhibit 10.10   At the *Yahudi* Cemetery; photo ©2006 Leo Paul DANA

people became entrepreneurs. Income gaps were significant. Even after independence, the Chinese continued to dominate the economic realm and this caused racial friction.

With the objective of fighting poverty among Indigenous Malays, the People's Trustee Council — known by its acronym, MARA — was established in 1966. Its role was to promote Indigenous entrepreneurship; it identified opportunities for Malay *bumiputras* — literally "sons of the soil" — to become entrepreneurs. Throughout the 1960s, Malaysian policy encouraged diversified, import substitution.

Following the ethnic riots of 1969, the government opted to create a policy that would achieve more economic parity between *bumiputras* and ethnic minorities. In 1970, *bumiputras* owned 2.6% of the corporate structure in Malaysia. The government's goal was for *bumiputras* to control 30.0% of the nation's capital within 20 years. The reality remained below target for decades.

In 1971, the New Economic Policy was launched, to fight poverty and to achieve more ethnic parity. *Bumiputras* were granted special privileges to help

Exhibit 10.11   *Bumiputra* Landholding; photo ©2006 Leo Paul DANA

them purchase land, obtain business permits, and improve their economic situation.

The Second Malaysian Five-Year Plan (1971–1975) was designed to create a generation of Malay entrepreneurs. It specified that the objective of entrepreneurship training, in Malaysia, was "to foster the emergence of a full-fledged Malay entrepreneurial community, within one generation." The Ministry of Trade and Industry *Bumiputra* Participation Division was created to assist the Indigenous Malays in particular, and the Export Trade Centre came to assist *bumiputras* to identify opportunities for entrepreneurship.

In 1975, the Industrial Co-ordination Act made it mandatory for all manufacturing establishments with a registered capital above 100,000 ringgits to be authorised by the Ministry of Industry. The threshold was subsequently raised to 250,000 ringgits.

The Institute Teknologi MARA (ITM), in 1975, established the Malaysian Entrepreneurship Development Centre (MEDEC), to help develop *bumiputra* entrepreneurship. The National Productivity Centre prepared a

Exhibit 10.12   Opportunity for Self-employment; photo ©2006 Leo Paul DANA

management-training package, in conjunction with MEDEC and the National Economic Research Development Association. In 1977, MEDEC launched a three-month long, part-time, Entrepreneurship Development Programme (EDP), and in 1981 a full-time programme was introduced. The focus of the EDP was to help potential entrepreneurs, with new venture start-ups. This included a 5-day Achievement Motivation Training (AMT) component, the purpose of which was to overcome the frequent complaint that *bumiputras* suffered because of their attitude.

The Fourth Malaysian Five-Year Plan (1981–1985) provided 318 million ringgits to various agencies responsible for promoting entrepreneurship. This included the Agricultural Bank of Malaysia, and the Development Bank of Malaysia.

Also, the Central Bank of Malaysia set a maximum lending rate on loans to *bumiputras*. In addition, the Credit Guarantee Corporation introduced a credit guarantee scheme.

In 1985, small-scale entrepreneurs, in the manufacturing sector, were exempted from the requirement of applying for a manufacturing permit from the Malaysian Industrial Development Authority. To qualify for the exemption, entrepreneurs were not allowed to have more than 49 full-time employees. As well, equity was restricted to below one million ringgits.

While the Malaysia Industrial Development Berhad introduced assistance to entrepreneurs at large, the Ministry of Finance's New Investment Fund of Malaysia was created, to give priority to export-oriented projects. In addition, the state laid down specific guidelines for banks to allocate a specific proportion of their loans to small-scale entrepreneurs.

In 1986, Malaysia launched its Industrial Master Plan, emphasising the need for local firms to internationalise. In 1988, there were 28,335 manufacturers in Malaysia, of which 92.6% were small or medium industries (SMIs)[48] and four fifths of the SMIs had a capitalisation of less than 50,000 ringgits. In consideration of this bi-modal distribution of very large and very small manufacturers, the state intervened to assist SMIs. This was done with the co-operation of the Malaysian External Trade Development Corporation; the Malaysian Industrial Development Authority; the Ministry of Human Resources; the Ministry of Science, Technology and Environment; and the Prime Minister's Support Department.

The year 1990 saw the introduction of an offshore infrastructure in the Federal Territory of Labuan. This included the Offshore Banking Act, the Offshore Companies Act and the Offshore Insurance Act. As Labuan became an international, offshore financial centre, foreign entrepreneurs paid only 3% tax, or a flat fee. During the Sixth Malaysian Five-Year Plan (1991–1995), private investment in Malaysia increased by an average of 16.6% per annum.

In 1992, the Malaysian Technology Development Corporation Sdn Bhd was incorporated, as a joint venture between government and industry, to increase technology-based entrepreneurship in Malaysia. The institution operates as a venture capital company, and identifies entrepreneurs whose ventures can become high-tech companies.

In May 1996, the Seventh Malaysian Five-Year Plan (1996–2000) emphasised the importance of having an export orientation in the increasingly liberal world trade environment. Also in 1996, the Labuan Offshore Financial Services Authority was established.

---

[48] In Malaysia, an SMI is defined as a manufacturing company with equity not exceeding 2.5 million ringgits.

Until 1998, the law required at least 30% of every company in Malaysia to be owned by *bumiputras*. To cope with this requirement, ethnic-Chinese Malaysians used *bumiputras* to register companies and to pose as majority shareholders, but without powers. Thus, *bumiputras* owned the majority of a firm (on paper), while the Chinese partners kept effective control. This was called the Ali-Baba system, Ali referring to *bumiputras* and Baba to the Chinese. In general, the Chinese disliked the *bumiputra* policy, which they described as a political instrument to limit their entrepreneurial activity. Yet, in some cases, Chinese entrepreneurs benefited by appointing influential *bumiputras* to their firms.

During the Asian Crisis, *bumiputra* entrepreneurs faced financial difficulties. The government consequently relaxed its *bumiputra* equity ownership restriction, allowing non-Malays to provide unlimited capital to some firms. Since then, ethnic-Chinese Malaysians have been allowed to own up to 100% of a local company.

Exhibit 10.13　Self-employed; photo ©2006 Leo Paul DANA

Since August 1998, all new manufacturing projects have been free from equity requirements. Also, entrepreneurs who qualify for "pioneer status" have been entitled to a five-year exemption from income tax. In September 1998, Malaysia pegged its currency at a rate of 3.80 ringgits to the dollar.

Toward the Future

The objective behind entrepreneurship promotion in Malaysia has been to redress economic differences between *bumiputras* and other ethnic groups in the country. Yet, Malaysian Chinese ownership of shares in local companies has risen from 29% in 1969 to 41%; *bumiputra* ownership has been stable between 19% and 21%.

When the Asian Crisis affected enterprises belonging to *bumiputra* entrepreneurs, Malaysia allowed Chinese and foreign entrepreneurs to inject more capital into ailing enterprises. In effect, such relaxation of equity

Exhibit 10.14   88-storey Petronas Twin Towers; photo ©2006 Leo Paul DANA

restrictions allowed Chinese entrepreneurs to buy into enterprises at low, crisis-time prices. This will enable Chinese entrepreneurs to gain greater control of the economy than in the past. However, according to the Selangor Federation of Chinese Guilds and Associations, half of all entrepreneurs in Malaysia wind up their enterprise by the third year of operations.

Abdullah Ahmad Badawi, who became prime minister of Malaysia in October 2003, has introduced the concept of *Islam Hadari*. As discussed in Badawi (2006), this includes the principle of balanced and comprehensive economic development.

Chapter 11

Myanmar[49]

Introduction

Myanmar — formerly the Union of Burma — covers 678,500 square kilometres, bounded by Bangladesh, China, India, Laos, Thailand, the Bay of Bengal and the Andaman Sea. In approximately 1295, Marco Polo described the wonders of Burma with astonishment (Moore, 1963). Kipling (1890) said of Burma, that it was quite unlike any land. Garrett used the words "virtually unknown to the outside world (1971, p. 343)." Hodgson summarised Burma as the "most reclusive country of mainland Southeast Asia (1984, p. 90)." Swerdlow described Myanmar as "the secretive nation (1995, p. 73)." Hirsh and Moreau called it "East Asia's last frontier (1995, p. 10)."

Hagen noted, "the Burmese level of living was higher than that of India or China (1962, p. 436)." Until the 1950s, Burma was the world's foremost rice exporter. After an era of socialism, a market-oriented model was introduced in 1988. Since then, many of Myanmar's social indicators — including the literacy rate, and the doctor: population ratio — have compared favourably with those of its richer neighbours (Thein, 1996). Yet — although the country is generously endowed with hardwood forests, oil, precious gems, silver and other minerals — its people have not prospered.

---

[49]This chapter is based on information obtained from a variety of sources, including: the Ministry of Agriculture and Irrigation; the Ministry of Co-operatives; the Ministry of Commerce; the Ministry of Finance and Economy; the Ministry of Industry; the Ministry of Information; the Ministry of National Planning and Development; the Ministry of Rail Transportation; the Myanmar Timber Enterprise; the Union of Myanmar Chamber of Commerce and Industry; and the University for the Development of the National Races of the Union. The chapter includes material that first appeared in Dana (2002).

Exhibit 11.1   Last Frontier; photo ©2006 Leo Paul DANA

Exhibit 11.2   From the Rich Forests; photo ©2006 Leo Paul DANA

Historical Overview

The Pyu — a people who used the Sanskrit script and observed Buddhism with some elements of Hinduism — are the earliest people known to have flourished in this region. They were defeated by ancestors of today's Burmese. Based in Pagan,[50] King Anawrahta — founder of the Pagan dynasty — ruled from 1044 to 1077, and it is under his rule that Buddhism spread across his unified kingdom.

In 1287, the Mongols — under the leadership of Kublai Khan — arrived from China and destroyed the empire of the Pagan dynasty. The region was then ruled in the form of small states, dominated by three ethnic groups — the Burmese,[51] the Mons,[52] and the Shans.[53] This was so until the 16th century, when King Bayinnaung created a second Burmese empire. In 1752, King Alaungpaya established a third empire, which lasted until the arrival of the English. Traders from England arrived in the 17th century. Border troubles between Burma and British India led to war, which lasted from 1824 to 1826, when the British annexed the Burmese provinces of Arakan and Tenasserim. Following a second war, between 1852 and 1854, the British occupied Lower Burma. During a third war, in 1885, the British took over Upper Burma, making the former Kingdom of Burma a province of British India. While the Tibeto-Burmans and the Thai-Shans became British subjects, the Red Karens retained their special citizenship, in accordance with a treaty signed in 1875 (Christian, 1943). During the 1890s, Burma became an important exporter of oil.

The Young Men's Buddhist Association, established in 1902, promoted the independence of Burma, as did Buddhist monks during the 1920s. A peasant uprising, in 1931, also put pressure on the British. The India Act of 1935 became effective in 1937, separating Burma from India. Outram and Fane (1940) gave an account of pre-war Burma. Swerdlow (1995) noted that Burma's annual rice exports exceeded three million tons, making the nation

---

[50] See Roberts (1931).
[51] The Burmese were in control of Upper Burma since the 9th century.
[52] The Mons had come from the east, taking control of Lower Burma.
[53] Hagen (1962) traced the origins of the Shans to the Yünnan plateau of south-eastern China.

the number 1 exporter of rice in the world. Christian elaborated, "Burma is one of the few countries in Asia that have a considerable exportable surplus of food (1942, p. 3)." In December 1941, the Japanese invaded Burma, and by early 1942, the British withdrew. Burma had been an important base for Allied help to China, and the Japanese occupation of Burma was tragic for China, as the Burma Road was closed (Christian, 1943).

In 1943, Japan declared the independence of Burma, and set up a pro-Japanese government. After a long struggle (Arnold, 1944), Allied troops defeated the Japanese in 1945. On October 17, 1947, a treaty signed in London established the independence of Burma, and the Union of Burma came into existence on January 4, 1948 — a day of good omens, according to Burmese astrologers. The Karens[54] — a largely Baptist Christian minority with Chinese origins — waged war against the new government. Civil war lasted until 1952.

On March 2, 1962, General Ne Win pushed aside Burma's only elected prime minister and introduced military rule, along with the "Burmese way to Socialism," a blend of Buddhism, central planning and isolationism. Also in 1962, English was banned as "representative of a degenerate and decadent culture (Maung, 1991, p. 222)." The Burma Socialist Programme Party became the only legal political party. Banks were nationalised, along with the transportation system, wholesale trade, retail trade, and foreign-owned companies. This led to a progressive breakdown of the formal firm-type sector of the economy. The state-controlled planned sector engulfed the national economy. The lack of foreign capital and technology resulted in limited growth during the 1960s.

In 1974, the Union of Burma became a single-party socialist state, and the one-party constitution renamed the country the Socialist Republic of the Union of Burma. The government confirmed its commitment to self-reliance, state control, isolation, and strict neutrality. In 1979, Burma isolated itself even from the movement of nations professing non-alignment. Steinberg (1982) gave a comprehensive socio-political account of the era.

---

[54] For a detailed discussion of the Karens, as researched by anthropologist Peter Kunstadter, see Kunstadter (1972).

Exhibit 11.3   Limited Growth; photo ©2006 Leo Paul DANA

From 1986 to 1988, declining trade contributed to severe economic recession. Per capita income tumbled while inflation escalated. The author observed that between 1986 and 1987, military personnel quadrupled the price of petrol they were selling in the parallel economy.

By 1987, Burma — formerly among the most prosperous economies of Asia — was designated by the United Nations as one of the least-developed nations in the world. Per capita income — which had been $670 in 1960 — fell to $190 in 1987, according to World Bank figures. In September 1987, people aspiring class mobility lost faith in their currency when the government invalidated all notes of 25, 35 and 75 kyat.[55] Falling living standards, coupled with political frustration, contributed to widespread riots during the first half of 1988. Although 77-year old Ne Win, Chairman of the Burma Socialist Programme Party, resigned in July 1988, his party remained in power (*Herald Tribune*, 1988). In August 1988, tens of thousands of demonstrators toppled the dictatorship. In the absence of an entrepreneurial class, a new leadership arose from the military.

---

[55]The unit of currency, spelled kyat, is pronounced "chat."

Exhibit 11.4 Maymyo Stagecoach Immune from Fuel Price Increases; Photo ©2006 Leo Paul DANA

Following a coup d'état, on September 18, 1988, the State Law and Order Restoration Council took control of the country, and adopted a market-oriented policy, officially discarding central planning. On June 19, 1989 the government changed the English version of the country's name to the Union of Myanmar. During the early 1990s, about 6% of the GDP was accounted for by the manufacturing sector. Exports were encouraged, to obtain foreign exchange, but this resulted to local shortages, pushing domestic prices up. The mid-1990s met rampant inflation. A *pyi* — the local unit of weight equal to two kilogrammes — of rice that cost 11.72 kyat in 1991, was worth 41.11 kyat in 1993, and 60 kyat in 1996.[56]

In April 1997, the United States enacted economic sanctions against new investments Myanmar. A few weeks later, on July 23, 1997, Myanmar joined the Association of South East Asian Nations (ASEAN). As Asia entered its financial crisis, the market rate of Myanmar's currency tumbled in July 1997 and the dollar traded at more than 300 kyat. Meanwhile, the official exchange rate stood at about six kyat per dollar. In March 1998, new import restrictions were imposed. In 1999, approvals for foreign direct investment fell by 96%. Annual inflation during the 1990s averaged 27.13%.

---

[56]In 1996, $1 was worth 5.75 kyat at the official exchange rate, or 125 kyat in the black market.

Toward Centrally Planned Transition

Colonial policy, in Burma, is said to have obstructed the development of local entrepreneurship. "Burmese enterprise was discouraged… the manufacture of mechanical lighters was made illegal, lest it should prejudice the revenue from a tax newly imposed on matches (Furnivall, 1956, pp. 166–167)." The colonial government gave preferential treatment to those it favoured, including the British India Steamship Navigation Company, the British Overseas Airways Corporation (BOAC), the Burma Match Co. Ltd., and the Bombay Burmah Trading Corporation, Ltd. (Furnivall, 1957; Macaulay, 1934). Kyi (1970) also examined the impact of Westerners on the evolution of an Indigenous entrepreneurial class.

Nevertheless, there appears to have been an entrepreneurial spirit, despite colonial policy. "Contrary to the widely accepted assumption that European and Indian immigrants monopolized entrepreneurial roles in Lower Burma, the Burmese displayed considerable entrepreneurship in J. A. Schumpeter's sense that they put into effect new combinations in the means of production and credit (Adas, 1974, p. 210)." In particular, Burmese entrepreneurs were successful in the motion picture industry (Christian, 1943; Sein, 1950), printing (Swe, 1972), and rice milling (Hla, 1975). Burmese financiers were prosperous moneylenders (Wai, 1955), as were the Chettiars, who traced their

Exhibit 11.5   B.O.A.C. Boeing 377 Stratocruiser Double-decker; photo courtesy of British Airways, London

origins to southern India. As well, Christian (1942) and Steinberg (1982) both pointed out that the Burmese were successful middlemen in the rice business. This is noteworthy, because elsewhere in the region it was the Chinese who dominated the middleman occupations.

Post-independence Burma — committed to self-reliance, state control, and isolation — adopted an economic policy that conformed to the import substitution model. In line with this model, the means to national economic development was to produce locally, thereby reducing the need for imports. This approach necessitated the existence of high tariffs, quotas and other regulatory mechanisms to discourage importation of goods. Rather than encourage specialisation in sectors of competitive advantage, this resulted in over-diversification. The model allowed the creation of a highly protected, low quality, high cost, and inefficient industrial sector. Furthermore, exports were biased against, due to a typically overvalued official currency exchange rate.

As Ne Win resigned, in late 1988, the Burmese Socialist Programme Party discussed proposals to reform the economy such that the "state would retain monopoly in commodities, broadcasting, the oil industry and gems and jade mining, but private enterprise would be allowed in transport, all kinds of industry and services, fishing, publishing and trade (*Herald Tribune*, 1988, p. 2)."

Exhibit 11.6   Self-reliance; photo ©2006 Leo Paul DANA

It was the State Law and Order Restoration Council that initiated a centrally-planned market-oriented model, in 1988. Private enterprise was resumed that year. The Foreign Investment Law, enacted in November 1988, allowed foreign investment manufacturing, tourism and transportation. Other important reforms included the State-owned Enterprises Law of 1989.

The 1965 Law for the Establishment of a Socialist Economic System was revoked in March 1989. In 1990, further liberalisation measures were introduced to promote a market economy. As well, the Commercial Tax Law was introduced in 1990. The agricultural sector was stimulated by the reduction of controls and regulations relating to the cultivation, milling, storage, transport, and marketing of agricultural products. Records at the Planning Department of the Ministry of National Planning and Economic Development report that the economy grew by 3.7% and 2.8%, during the 1989–90 and 1990–91 periods respectively.

The Short-term Plan (1992–1996) had as objective to pursue an export drive and to achieve an average annual growth rate of 5.1%. Efforts were made to increase savings and to channel these savings into productive investments. According to San Khup, Director-General of the Planning Department of the Ministry of National Planning and Economic Development, actual growth rates — of 9.7% the first year, 5.9% the second year, and 6.8% the third year — were higher than projected (Khup, 1996). It may be argued, however, that these figures are distorted by the fact that inflation is underestimated.

During 1994 and 1995, government emphasis was focused on foreign investment and trade. Certain price controls were phased out, as were subsidies. Taxes were streamlined, banking was restructured, and international business was facilitated. Yangon (formerly Rangoon) was revitalised.

The Foreign Investment Law welcomed capital into Myanmar. Foreign-owned enterprises were permitted, as were joint ventures with local enterprises. The law provided income tax holidays and further tax relief for exporters. It guaranteed repatriation of profits and stated that investments would not be nationalised. Private traders arrived from Singapore, South Korea and Thailand. Yet, a difficulty that remained was the inability of the state to mobilise domestic capital for investment. Another problem was the exchange constraint; although this encouraged barter, it limited trade.

Exhibit 11.7   Yangon Revitalised; photo ©2006 Leo Paul DANA

In April 1995, the Rangoon City Development Committee made international news, by announcing the ban of the sale of betel in the nation's capital. This chewable nut, a mild stimulant that grows on areca palm trees, had been integral to the social and medicinal history in this country. Street-corner betel stands had provided employment for hundreds of people in Rangoon. In March 1998, new import restrictions were imposed, and this led to a boom in the parallel economy.

Myanmar's economic objectives of the 1990s included the development of agriculture as the base sector of the economy and the evolution of the market-oriented economic system. Yet, it was clearly specified that the initiative to shape the national economy must be kept in the "hands of the State and the national peoples."

The Bazaar

Christian described bazaars in Burma, "Rubies, spinels, garnets… are bought and sold in open market… next to a bazaar selling potatoes, garlic, and Chinese radishes (1943, pp. 501–502)."

Typical of the bazaar, shops are clustered according to products or services sold. Jewellery shops stand adjacent to other jewellery shops; each offers jade and fresh water pearls along with gold earrings and rings sold by weight. Likewise fruit-sellers are clustered with other fruit-sellers. There are bananas and coconuts in abundance. Some vendors sell only tomatoes, while others specialise only in onions. Garlic is sold alongside ginger. Straw baskets contain different varieties of dry seeds. Rice comes in many varieties and different grades; some is damaged from poorly maintained husking machines. Cleaning, sorting and packing rice is for some women a social activity. Citrus fruits are not far from the tea specialist. A man is bargaining with a pharmacist as to the fair price of antibiotics. Ampicillin and tetracycline are available, as is penicillin solution for injection. None of these require a prescription.

Food is plentiful. Palmyra palms are sold along with fresh apples, carrots, cauliflowers, coffee beans, cucumbers, grapes, jackfruits, lotus fruits, mangoes, mangosteens, papayas, peanuts, plums, strawberries, sugarcane, and sunflower seeds. There are also dried fruits, and baked goods. As well, one finds pineapple jam, and mango jam, along with glass bottles of beverages. Lemon-barley is a favourite, as is green-coloured cream soda. Beasts of burden — cattle and water-buffalo — watch as chickens, ducks, goats, hogs, quail and sheep are sold alive. Lined up in a row, children are selling dry fish carefully laid out on the pavement. Lizards and stray dogs — friendly toward people, but at times territorial amongst themselves — scrounge for scraps. As the animals sense the oncoming storm, merchants act fast to pack up. Shoppers put their groceries on their head and make their way carefully to the waiting oxcart. The wind can be violent and bicycles can be sent flying. After the storm, the umbrella repairmen will have more business.

As is the case with traditional merchandise, modern items are also clustered. Perhaps most notable are the moneychangers, who use identical exchange rates. They trade currency as a commodity. Nobody has any competitive advantage. There is no product differentiation. The author observed several moneychangers clustered together: Ein Phyusi; 704; Bonton; Win; Yuzana; Crown; Forex; Gonshein Myint; User Friendly Stag; and May Flower — side by side. Although it is seemingly not possible to differentiate among them, each has own, loyal clientele. The focus here is not merely on transactions, but on the relationship between buyers and sellers.

Exhibit 11.8   Artisan; photo ©2006 Leo Paul DANA

Handicrafts

In 1857, King Mindon moved his capital to Mandalay and its Zegyo Bazaar became a principal distribution centre for beans, betel nuts, citrus fruit, cotton, nuts, onions, rice, tobacco, and wheat. The town prospered and artisans made it the handicraft centre of Myanmar.

Among the crafts developed in Mandalay is *shwe saing* — the making of gold leaf. This is occupation is concentrated in the Myatpa Yat Quarter, and found nowhere else in Myanmar (May, 1996). The skills are propagated from father to son, and non-family members are kept away from this occupation. The making of gold leaf is thus restricted to few families. Rather than compete with one another, about forty entrepreneurs join forces to produce and sell gold leaf in a symbiotic manner. The co-ordination of activities, among the firms, facilitates an otherwise complicated process of production and marketing.

The first stage involves melting gold blocks; five households are involved in this initial phase of production, each with three or four skilled employees. Thirty households — each with about two-dozen workers are involved in the later stages of production. The molten gold is poured into a conical vessel, producing finger-shaped bullions. Rollers flatten these bullions, which are subsequently beaten by skilled craftsmen resulting in thin sheets of gold, referred to as *shwe-let* — literally "golden fingers." Each sheet — about $2^1/_2$ cm wide and over one metre long — takes about $4^1/_2$ hours to flatten. These are then sent to another household for further processing. The golden is further cut up, into pieces about $2^1/_2$ cm by 5mm. These are placed between *shwekhat setku* — sheets of bamboo paper made for the purpose of producing gold leaf. The artisans then wrap layers of this deer-hide, and the golden is beaten again, to become film-thin. Once this is done, the strips of gold are joined with one another, to form quadrangles — each about 25 square centimetres. The final product is stored in *shwehlaung setku*, a paper made in Amarapura, from straw. Much of the gold leaf is used by religious people, to gild pagodas and images of Buddha. As is the production of gold leaf, stone carving is also a heredi-tary occupation. This activity is clustered in the Kyauk Sit Tan Yat Quarter of Mandalay. As is the case with the production of gold leaf, this industry is also intertwined with Buddhism and much of the carving — in marble and in wood[57] — involves making images of Buddha.

Images of Buddha are also cast in bronze, and bronze casting is impor-tant in Myanmar. In Amarapura is an area called the Bronze Village, where bronze casting works are clustered. Bronze and copperware are often produced by trained silversmiths who are lacking silver, a scarce metal in Myanmar. Silversmiths are clustered in Ywataung, not far from Sagaing.

Silver and gold are used to make embroidery in Myanmar. In contrast to gold leaf, which is produced for consumption by local people, embroidery — containing gold and silver thread — is used to make tapestries, fabrics and cushion covers, for sale to tourists visiting Myanmar.

Another craft that thrives in Mandalay is silk weaving. Silk — mostly imported from the PRC — is spun into thread, which is boiled in dyes to get coloured. It takes about ten days to weave a metre of cloth. Firms active in this industry are clustered east of the royal palace, in a neighbourhood of Mandalay called Nan Shay.

---

[57] Puppets are also carved in wood.

Covert Economic Activity

According to sources at the United Nations Office for Drug Control and Crime Prevention (UNODCCP), Myanmar is the source of 23.4% of the 4,653 tonnes of opium produced around the world each year. It is from these opium poppies that heroin is made. The wholesale price per kilogramme of heroin, in New York, is $80,000, according to sources at *The Economist*, and at 40% purity, the retail price is $290,000. Production is inexpensive, and the profit margin is immense. Its profitability makes it hard to control, because the hefty contribution margins make it easy to bribe poorly paid law enforcement officials.

Pluralism

According to the Ministry of Information, there are 135 national groups in Myanmar, with the Bamar being the majority; these different ethnicities are classified according to distinct ethno-linguistic groups. While the majority of the people are Tibeto-Burman, the country is also home to Mon-Khmers, and Thai-Shans, as well as Karen people. The Tibeto-Burmans speak a Sino-Tibetan language, as do the Karens. In contrast, the language of the Mon-Khmers belongs to the Austro-Asiatic family, while the Thai-Shans comprise one of the Thai groups.

In addition, there are Chinese and Indian minorities in Myanmar. It was the British who encouraged the immigration of Indians to Burma. Some became moneylenders, and others were given government positions. By the 1930s, the immigrant Indian community in British Burma numbered 600,000, amounting to less than 10% of the population; yet these people held over half the government jobs.

Ethnic consciousness is notable. Dunung noted, "Burmese having West-ernized attitudes are looked down upon. The Burmese also consider themselves to be superior to Indians, Chinese, and Eurasians (1995, p. 528)."

Elephant Labour

Smith described the elephant as a supermachine in Burma's logging industry, and argued, "Efforts have been made to make machinery do elephants' work

Exhibit 11.9   Elephant on the Way to Work; photo ©2006 Leo Paul DANA

in the forest, but without success. Machines cannot think (1930, p. 256)." Although machinery has improved, elephants are still very useful today, and their working life is 50 years.

Myanmar is home to as many as 6,000 wild elephants, and up to 7,000[58] domesticated ones (Gray, 2001). The Myanmar Timber Enterprise — which has a monopoly on teak extraction — employs 2,700 elephants. These are very useful in areas where vehicles cannot penetrate without causing major ecological damage.

A 30-year cycle is used to harvest teak, and only trees of a designated girth are felled within a given area. Given this selection process, trained elephants do a neater job than would be possible if using machinery.

An elephant starts school at the age of three. Students can learn one command every two days. Classes alternate with recess for bathing and resting. Once on the job, a bull elephant can work five to eight hours per day, depending

---

[58]This is a significant number, given that there is a total of 15,000 Asian elephants in captivity (Chadwick, 2005).

on the temperature. The animals use their husks, forehead and trunks to push literally tons of logs at a time. As well, these intelligent workers are made to drag trees estimated to be 150 years old. Retirement age, for the elephants, is 55.

Toward the Future

Since 1988, steps have been taken to liberalise the agriculture sector, legalise trans-border trade, and encourage foreign investment. Firms in Myanmar are involved in agricultural processing, light manufacturing, and the production of footwear, pharmaceuticals and textiles. Their export markets include China, India, Singapore and Thailand.

Yet, as reported by Speece and Sann (1998), managers complain about labour shortages and the lack of loyalty among employees. Not surprisingly, most large companies have a minimal presence in Yangon, and much investment is small scale.

Many local enterprises operate at the subsistence level. A self-employed individual sells air for vehicle tyres. Another fixes umbrellas on a street corner, and on the same broken sidewalk, a barber has set up an impromptu stall. A tourist is being shaven for the price of a coconut, the equivalent of 20 cents. Nearby, a micro-scale merchant sells flashlights and lighters. Another vendor is weighing nails. A woman walks by on her way to the station; she has prepared food to sell to passengers on the train.

At a pagoda, a woman sells sparrows to worshippers who will free them for good luck. As soon as they are let loose, she catches them again, as her inventory is fixed. Meanwhile, the parallel economy is thriving with consumer goods and pirated intellectual property. Near an outlet called Mister donut — the sign of which uses the font of Dunkin' Donuts, a merchant sells photocopies of the book *Burmese Days* (Orwell, 1930). Not far, a Ronald McDonald look-alike promotes Mac Burger, a fast-food outlet serving MacHam, MacChicken, and MacBurgers. A client takes out his "Solem" cigarettes from a pack that looks like that of Salem. An ambulant vendor heads for a bus on which she hopes to sell quail eggs; she is careful not to step on the mangoes being laid on the sidewalk by a micro-scale vendor. What is consistent, throughout all this, is the absence of tension.

Exhibit 11.10   Coconut Sales; photo ©2006 Leo Paul DANA

While the government has focused on improving agricultural output, thus increasing the production of land, Myanmar remains among the less developed countries. Yet, the extent of absolute poverty is limited due to the abundance of inexpensive food and other essentials.

Chapter 12

Nepal[59]

Introduction

Rosenbloom and K.C. noted that Nepal is often overlooked, "Numerous examples exist of Nepal's 'invisibility' in the academic and professional business/management literature (2005, p. 69)." Indeed, there is relatively little literature available about entrepreneurship in this country.

The Kingdom of Nepal covers 147,181 square kilometres, landlocked between China and India. Nepal time is five hours and 45 minutes ahead of GMT, i.e., 15 minutes ahead of Indian standard time. Nepal has always been independent. Nepalese people belong to two distinct groups, namely the Indo-Aryans and the Tibeto-Burman Mongoloids. As noted by Rosenbloom and K.C. (2005), Nepal is the only country in the world to officially declare itself a Hindu state. Christian missions are permitted but conversions prohibited. Nepali is written in Devanagari script. Ngudup, Chen, and Lin (2005), described Nepal as an underdeveloped country. Most people here are subsistence farmers.[60] Roth noted, "In Nepal, 7 percent of girls are wed before they turn 10 (2006, p. 26)."

The model of the Small Business Promotion Project was developed and pioneered in Nepal. Its success prompted the German Agency for Technical

---

[59]This chapter is based on information obtained from a variety of sources, including: the Association of Cottage and Small Industries; the Federation of Nepalese Cottage and Small Industries; the Industrial Enterprise Development Institute; the Ministry of Commerce; the Ministry of Finance and Economy; the Ministry of Industry, Commerce and Supplies; and the Trade Promotion Centre, Kathmandu.

[60]For a discussion, see Henker (1999).

Exhibit 12.1   Indigenous Nepali; photo ©2006 Leo Paul DANA

Exhibit 12.2   Hindu State; photo ©2006 Leo Paul DANA

Exhibit 12.3   Subsistence Farming; photo ©2006 Leo Paul DANA

Exhibit 12.4   Engaged Young; photo ©2006 Leo Paul DANA

Exhibit 12.5   A Wedding; photo ©2006 Leo Paul DANA

Cooperation to market this model internationally, using the brand name Creation of Enterprises, Formation of Entrepreneurs. Pioneered in Nepal, this model has been implemented in over 70 countries.

Historical Overview

Ancient Nepal was composed of small principalities. In 1769, these were unified into one nation, by King Prithivi Narayan Shah, who lived from 1722 to 1775.

Prior to 1846, Nepal was ruled by a hereditary king. Beginning in 1846 and until 1951, the kingdom was ruled by hereditary prime ministers, members of the Rana family. Chetwode (1935) provided an account of Nepal at the time. In 1951, the monarchy was restored under King Tribhuvan, after whom Kathmandu's airport is named. Tribhuvan's son Mahendra succeeded him in 1955.

Nepal's first economic development plan was launched in 1956; it was known as the First Five-Year Plan (1956–1961). The Export and Import Control Act was introduced in 1957. A 1959 parliamentary constitution was replaced by a constitution based on the Panchayat system — a model of traditional village councils.

Hagen (1960) suggested that the cheese industry was a path to prosperity in Nepal. Following his suggestion, the government of Nepal, with the help

Exhibit 12.6   Tribhuvan International Airport; photo ©2006 Leo Paul DANA

of Swiss experts and the United Nations' Food and Agriculture Organisation, established the nation's first cheese factory, in the Lanting Valley. The success of the first stone factory led to the construction of three others, ultimately boosting exports to India.

Following the 1959 rebellion in Tibet, 10,000 Tibetans migrated to Nepal; a discussion appears in Chadwick (1987). In April 1961, Nepal's 15 feudal chieftainships were integrated into the kingdom. The Customs Act was enacted in 1962. The royal constitution was implemented on December 16, 1962, and the national flag was officially adopted.

The Second Plan (1963–1965) focused on infrastructure development and on institutional reform. The Federation of Nepalese Chambers of Commerce and Industry was established in 1965. The Third Plan (1965–1970) emphasised infrastructure development in order to accelerate the pace of economic development.

Agriculture and transport were central to the Fourth Plan (1970–1975). Introduced in 1971, the New Education System Plan attempted to establish vocational education in every secondary school throughout Nepal. The Trade Promotion Centre was also established in 1971. King Mahendra was succeeded by his son Birendra in 1972.

Exhibit 12.7   Slow Times; photo ©2006 Leo Paul DANA

Exhibit 12.8   Agriculture; photo ©2006 Leo Paul DANA

Exhibit 12.9   Favourable Climate; photo ©2006 Leo Paul DANA

The Handicraft Association of Nepal was formed in 1972, as a non-profit organisation. Its purpose is to improve the productivity of the member artisans and to promote their handicrafts in various foreign markets.

Liberalisation of the financial sector began in 1984.[61] The Seventh Plan (1985–1990) emphasised industrial and commercial sectors. This plan encouraged the private sector to take lead role in the promotion of industries, in order to accelerate import substitution and export promotion. In 1989, the National Science and Technology Policy was enacted to create a favourable climate for scholars, scientists and entrepreneurs to work together.

In 1990, Nepal became a constitutional monarchy. In 1992, the Federation of Nepalese Chambers of Commerce and Industry became actively involved in SME promotion. The Industrial Policy of 1992 stressed privatisation, market oriented pricing, determining wages on the basis of productivity and protecting industries through custom duties. The Labour Act of 1992 established the framework governing employers; small-scale enterprises were made exempt from obligation of this act.

---

[61] See Rothenberger (1999).

The Eighth Plan (1992-1997) was implemented beginning in July 1992; its objective was to promote import substitution and improve cottage and small-scale industries using locally available resources to meet internal demand. The plan highlighted sustainable economic growth, poverty alleviation, rural development, regional balance, and the promotion of cottage industries. The plan included:

(i) Development of import substituting and export promoting industries;
(ii) Giving priority to private participation;
(iii) Emphasis on the development and expansion of cottage and small-scale and agro-based industries;
(iv) Institutional arrangements to familiarise cottage and small-scale industries with market, technology, and skills; and
(v) Strengthening existing financial institutions and establishing new ones to assist cottage and small-scale industries.

Exhibit 12.10   Central Kathmandu; photo ©2006 Leo Paul DANA

Exhibit 12.11 Development in Kathmandu; photo ©2006 Leo Paul DANA

Exhibit 12.12 Keen to Be Trained; photo ©2006 Leo Paul DANA

Exhibit 12.13   Improved Road; photo ©2006 Leo Paul DANA

In 1993, the Ministry of Industry reorganised its Department of Cottage and Small Industries. The Cottage and Small Industry Development Board was established that year. In January 1994, the Nepal Stock Exchange began trading in Kathmandu.

In 1996, Nepal's Information Technology Park was placed under the umbrella of the Industrial Enterprise Development Institute. The objective of developing the park was to create favourable environment by providing basic infrastructure to attract entrepreneurs

The Ninth Plan (1998–2002) aimed to train people in order to develop, expand and integrate necessary technical and support services required for cottage and small industries; rural entrepreneurship development programmes were created to encourage the establishment of industries in rural areas.

During the late 1990s Nepal experienced a communist insurgency. In 1999 the National Policy on Technical Education and Vocational Training, recognised the need for a nation-wide coordinated effort to develop human

Exhibit 12.14   Artisans; photo ©2006 Leo Paul DANA

resources such as to enable people to get employment or become self-employed, and thus contribute to economic development.

In 2001, two of Nepal's leading banks were declared insolvent (Rosenbloom and K.C., 2005). Although infrastructure was improved and taxation reformed, Khatiwada (2002) suggested that banking reform was urgently needed.

Kathmandu's Seventh Handicraft Fair took place in February 2006. Organised by the Handicraft Association of Nepal, the fairs aim to develop stronger understanding, in Europe, of Nepalese micro-enterprises and their products. At the fairs, Nepalese entrepreneurs in the artisan sector link up with European buyers.

The Economy and Entrepreneurship Promotion

Rosenbloom and K.C. wrote, "Consistent with an economy that is agriculturally based, Nepal has a low unemployment rate (2005, p. 70)." As the economy shifts away from a dependence on agriculture, entrepreneurship and small business is being promoted via a variety of schemes.

An offshoot of the Economic Promotion Unit of the Nepal-German Bhaktapur Development Project, the Small Business Promotion Project was initiated in 1984. It was assisted by the German Agency for Technical Cooperation. In 1989, the Project was brought under the Ministry of Industry.

The objective of the Small Business Promotion Project was to contribute to the economic and social development of Nepal. Specifically, the Small Business Promotion Project offered training and consulting for entrepreneurs, as a means to attaining poverty alleviation. It is a decentralised organisation with several branches; its approach has been to co-operate with people and empower them to make decisions for their enterprises. Core programmes of the Small Business Promotion Project have included:

(i) New Business Creation;
(ii) Small Business Consultancy;
(iii) Services to Institutions;
(iv) Planning and Business Information; and
(v) The Complementary Credit Scheme.

The New Business Creation programme developed knowledge, skills and motivation among prospective entrepreneurs. Business schemes were then presented to fellow participants for constructive criticism and to the banking community. It is estimated that this programme led to the creation of about 1,000 jobs annually.

The Small Business Consultancy focused largely on assisting newly established small-scale industries with promotional activities. The programme offered technical consultancy, in addition to accounting, marketing and production management expertise.

The Services to Institutions programme involved co-operation with organisations, in the implementation of effective income-generation and entrepreneurship programmes for various target groups. This included the training of rural trainers in methods of income generation.

The Planning and Business Information office made available a well-stocked library and provided information to other programmes of the Small Business Promotion Project. This included technical consultants who visit clients on a cost sharing basis.

Exhibit 12.15   In Need of Poverty Alleviation; photo ©2006 Leo Paul DANA

Exhibit 12.16   Rural Nepal; photo ©2006 Leo Paul DANA

Exhibit 12.17   Managed with Available Resources; photo ©2006 Leo Paul DANA

The Complementary Credit Scheme maintained a revolving fund for credits to entrepreneurs. The fund was administered by the Agricultural Development Bank of Nepal. Loans were secured with collateral from entrepreneurs.

Participants of training programmes were required to pay a non-refundable deposit which was forfeited if they failed to complete the training. The experience of the Small Business Promotion Project suggested that:

(i) only clients who possess observable potential should receive assistance;

(ii) a target group must be identified before services are designed, as opposed to designing a service and then seeking a target group;

(iii) the only services that should be delivered are those which can be adequately managed with available resources;

(iv) transparency benefits all parties;

(v) services must last a limited time, as entrepreneurs must eventually be able to operate without assistance from a programme; and

(vi) services should be cost-effective.

Exhibit 12.18   Operating Without Assistance; photo ©2006 Leo Paul DANA

Exhibit 12.19   Keen for a Bright Future; photo ©2006 Leo Paul DANA

In 1995, the Small Business Promotion Project was transformed into the Industrial Enterprise Development Centre. The following year, this was institutionalised as the Industrial Enterprise Development Institute. With branch offices across Nepal, this institute is actively involved in training the trainers of SME programmes.

In order for entrepreneurs to benefit from clustering, the government has set up several industrial districts. The Industrial Enterprises Development Institution has established a technology park.

Toward the Future

Nepal plans to limit the role of its public sector, such that the role of the state simply be that of serving as a catalyst to expand the role of the private sector. As well, the taxation system is to be simplified. Nevertheless, factors hindering entrepreneurship include corruption, deficiencies of the infrastructure, a weak base of human resources, and inadequate awareness of entrepreneurs.

Chapter 13

The Philippines[62]

Introduction

The Republic of the Philippines is an archipelago of over 7,000 islands, with a total land-mass of almost 300,000 square kilometres. The national animal is the water buffalo.

While the national Filipino tongue is Tagalog-based, English is the language commonly used in commerce. In terms of population, the Philippines is the world's third largest English-speaking country (although not all are conversant in English).

Numerous studies have investigated entrepreneurship in the Philippines. Moser discussed "sidewalk entrepreneurs (1977, p. 361)." Sharma (1979) found that entrepreneurs in the Philippines were independent and highly motivated to take risks, with a great desire to maximise their potential. The same study also asserted that the "Filipino entrepreneur is college educated and hails from a business-oriented family (p. 223)." Almost a decade later, El-Namaki (1988) reported a declining level of small business self-employment in the Philippines. According to Swierczek and Jatusripatak (1994), who examined cultural features of entrepreneurship in the Philippines, entrepreneurs in this country appear to have had greater advantages than elsewhere in

---

[62]This chapter is based on information obtained from a variety of sources, including: the Bureau of Labour and Employment; the Department of Trade and Industry Bureau of Small and Medium Business Development; the Institute for Small Scale Industries; the Philippines Chamber of Commerce and Industry; the Philippines Institute for Development Studies; and the Small Enterprise Research and Development Foundation, in Quezon City. Travel to the Philippines was provided by the Philippine Small and Medium Business Development Foundation. The chapter includes material that first appeared in Dana (1999b).

Exhibit 13.1   Water Buffalo; photo ©2006 Leo Paul DANA

south-east Asia; the authors described their sample as technically skilled, innovative and opportunistic. Chen (1997) focused on small-scale retailers in the Philippines.

While the ethnic-Chinese, in the Philippines, have been very active in small business development, Indigenous Filipinos have tended to exhibit a lesser incidence of entrepreneurship. Since the 1980s, several measures have been taken to broaden the appeal of enterprise and to assist Filipino entrepreneurs.

Despite efforts to promote and to finance business ventures, several constraints have hindered small enterprise development in the Philippines. Furthermore, the nation has encountered fiscal problems during the 21st century. In 2004, the government deficit hit 4.6% of GDP. Inflation was 5.5% at the time of writing in 2006. This chapter gives an overview of entrepreneurship development in this archipelago.

Historical Overview

The first Westerner to discover this archipelago was Ferdinand Magellan, in 1521. The islands were already thriving with commerce, as Arab, Chinese and Indian merchants had come to trade here. King Philip II of Spain took interest

Exhibit 13.2   Pineapple Plant; photo ©2006 Leo Paul DANA

Exhibit 13.3   Landholding; photo ©2006 Leo Paul DANA

in the area, and sent later expeditions; it is after him that the name Philippines was coined.

The Spanish introduced the pineapple — a native of South America — to the Philippines. In time, the Philippines became one of the world's leading pineapple producers.

Over three centuries of Spanish rule came to an end in 1898, when independence was declared. In 1900, the United States took control, followed by the Japanese in 1942. The Americans returned during WWII, and a second republic was created in 1946.

Ferdinand Marcos acquired power in 1965 and declared martial law in 1972. He was ousted in 1986, when Corazon Aquino (widow of his assassinated opponent) took over. One of her major plans was to implement the Comprehensive Agrarian Reform Programme, which was meant to redistribute vast holdings from the elite to the rural poor; however, this programme was less successful than she had planned.

Meanwhile, local entrepreneurs lobbied aggressively for an increase in protective trade barriers. Mrs. Aquino survived seven attempted coups and a struggle with the New People's Army, the aim of which was a communist take-over. In 1992, Fidel Ramos succeeded her with a platform to create jobs, revitalise the economy, reduce foreign debt and fight corruption.

Affected by the Asian Crisis, growth slowed down and unemployment rose. The government lifted exchange controls and reformed the tariff structure. In May 1998, the central bank reduced the reserve requirement for banks, from

Exhibit 13.4   Filipino Currency; photo ©2006 Leo Paul DANA

10% to 8%. This led to the lowering of the prime lending rate. By June, one could obtain a loan for 16% (compared to 30%, six months earlier).

When Joseph Estrada became president, on June 30, 1998, he promised to continue market reforms. Nevertheless, as the effects of the Asian Crisis affected the economy, the jobless rate rose to its highest level in seven years and the budget deficit continued to grow.

The People

The population of the Philippines is heavily concentrated (more than 50%) on Luzon and Mindanao, the two largest islands. The Indigenous Filipinos are of Malayo-Polynesian origin. The Chinese minority is an important one. About one million people in the Philippines have some Chinese ancestry and they tend to be quite visible in the realm of business. During the late 20th century, *The Economist*[63] reported that although less than 1% of the population in the Philippines was of pure Chinese descent, firms owned by ethnic-Chinese accounted for two-thirds of the 67 biggest commercial outfits. The same essay added that the Chinese dominated the small business sector to an even greater degree.

Today, it is perhaps on the island of Cebu that one best sees Chinese entrepreneurship in the Philippines. Most of the entrepreneurs on this island are ethnic-Chinese and real economic growth, here, is consistently higher than is the national average.

A Tradition of Chinese Entrepreneurship

Although Spain was very successful in its efforts to convert the Filipinos to Christianity, it failed in its attempt to displace the economic prominence of Chinese entrepreneurs in the Philippines. The Spanish restricted the Chinese and often threatened violence. Between 1603 and 1762, there were constant massacres of Chinese people in the Philippines. Nevertheless, Chinese entrepreneurs continued to thrive in commerce and they mastered the Spanish language. A new class emerged — multilingual Chinese entrepreneurs.

---

[63]"The Overseas Chinese," July 18, 1992, p. 21.

Descendants of marriages between Christianised Chinese men and Indigenous Filipinas resulted in Christian Chinese-mestizos. Both the Spanish Church and the authorities gave greater privileges to these people than to pure (non-Christian) Chinese. As a class, the Christian Chinese-mestizos were considered higher than the Chinese. Their descendants are quite different than the Peranakans in Malaysia, in the sense that the Chinese-mestizos identify themselves as Christians rather than Chinese.

During the 1700s, the largest landholdings in the Philippines were those of Christian religious orders. Wealthy Chinese entrepreneurs subsequently purchased estates from the clergy, and time widened the gap between the per capita income of economic elites and that of the masses. Among wealthy Chinese parents, a priority was to provide their young with educational opportunities beyond those available to the masses. The emerging educated class of elites acquired the name *ilustrados*, Spanish for "those who are enlightened."

The 19th century brought a new wave of immigrants from China's Fujian Province. These also prospered in commerce, and in money-lending as well as in agriculture. However, they had a lower social standing than the more educated, established Chinese.

Today, the ethnic-Chinese in the Philippines comprise 2% of the population; yet, they control more than half of market capitalisation. Most of them (85%) are Hokkien.

Facilitating Entrepreneurship

Considerable effort has focused on broadening the appeal of entrepreneurship, and entrepreneurs in the Philippines have long been assisted by foreign donors as well as by local sources.

In 1974, the Canadian International Development Agency (CIDA) sponsored the Cagayon Valley Co-operative Development Programme, to develop farmers' co-operatives in the Philippines. In 1978, the same agency launched the Industrial Co-operation Programme (ICP) which soon became involved in matching Filipino entrepreneurs with counterparts overseas. In 1981, another CIDA project was designed to assist small-scale Filipino fishermen. Additional Canadian funds were allocated to help micro-enterprises and small business development. During the late 1980s, CIDA planned an Enterprise Development Project to promote increased entrepreneurial capability in the Philippines. Support was geared to cottage industries as well as to micro-enterprises and small businesses.

The Philippine Development Assistance Programme (PDAP) is yet another project of CIDA. This project was funded by the National Initiatives Programme — of the federal government of Canada — but implemented by a non-governmental organisation. In order to maximise the input of the PDAP fund, small-scale projects were given priority, with the aim of helping self-employed tenant farmers, and fishermen among others. The initial success of the initiative led to its later enlargement.

The international organisation, Approtech Asia — based in the Philippines and financially supported by CIDA — undertook projects to help women entrepreneurs in the Philippines. Likewise, Singapore-based Technonet Asia initiated a project to assist technology transfers to the Philippines.

Meanwhile, the World Bank approved several billion dollars of loans, through the International Bank for Reconstruction and Development. Some of these funds were channelled to half a million family-farms in the Philippines. Also, the Asian Development Bank and Fund approved significant loans to provide credit to micro-enterprises and cottage industries.

Another important player, in the small business sector of the Philippines, is the International Fund for Agriculture Development, which channels aid to small-scale farmers. One of its technical assistance grants, to the International Rice Research Institute in Los Banos, led to research about a training programme to encourage the cultivation of azolla, which is a low-cost, natural fertiliser. Because azolla is labour-intensive, as opposed to capital-intensive, it is ideal for small-scale farmers.

Foreign aid has also contributed to the significant improvement of the telecommunication infrastructure, especially since the 1980s, when most communities in the Philippines had inadequate access to telecommunications. The situation improved during the 1990s, when the Department of Transportation and Communication received technical assistance and training from the Philippines Telecommunications Technical Assistance Project, funded by CIDA. The same Canadian agency also sponsored a project to provide a public toll call facility in each of several communities. Today, most communications services belong to the private sector.

The Philippines traditionally practised an import-substitution policy supported by high customs duties. As a result of high duties, only 20% of components in the local garment industry were sourced in the domestic market; this was true until the early 1990s. Foreign exchange controls were lifted in 1992, and the tariff structure was subsequently reformed. The Philippine Small and Medium Business Development Foundation was established in 1992, and has since been improving managerial and technical skills in small firms.

The government also planned several incentives to enhance entrepreneurial spirit. Among these are industrial estates (see Table 13.1), export processing zones (in Baguio City, Bataan, Cavite, and Mactan) and special development programmes (see Table 13.2). As well, the state created tax holidays and credits to lure entrepreneurs from overseas, especially those creating labour-intensive activity in the Philippines.

In September 1999, a joint effort organised by the Philippine Small & Medium Business Development Foundation (PHILSMED), the Philippine Exporters Confederation, the Trade and Investment Policy Analysis Advocacy

Table 13.1   Industrial Estates in the Philippines

Batangas City
  Tabangao
Bulacan
  First Bulacan Industrial Estate
Cavite
  First Cavite Industrial Estate
  Gateway Business Industrial Estate
Isabela
  Leyte
Laguna Province
  Carmelary Industrial Estate
  Laguna International Industrial Estate
  Laguna Technopark
  Light Industry and Science Industrial Estate
Tarlac
  Luisita Industrial Estate

Table 13.2   Special Development Programmes in the Philippines

- Calabarzon Programme
- Iligan — Cayagan de Oro Programme
- Panay — Negros Agro-Industrial Programme
- Samar Island Special Development Programme
- South Cotabato — General Santos City Area Programme

Exhibit 13.5   PHILSMED Speaker from Canada; photo ©2006 Leo Paul DANA

Support Project, the Ayala Corporation, the Center for Asia Pacific Trade Development Corporation, the Philippine Chamber of Commerce & Industry, the International Labour Organisation, the Small Business Guarantee & Finance Corporation, and the Development Bank of the Philippines, promoted SMEs in the Philippines.

In August 2005, a dragon fruit harvest festival was held in the Tugbok District of Davao City. This promoted local farmers and encouraged future efforts.

Exhibit 13.6   Dragon Fruit; photo ©2006 Leo Paul DANA

The Small Enterprises Research and Development Foundation of the Philippines (SERDEF) was established by the private sector to initiate, sponsor, promote, assist and conduct research, training and development of micro-enterprises, cottage industries, and small and medium sized firms in the Philippines. The foundation works with a variety of organisations, forging linkages with government agencies, industry associations and educational institutions, such as the University of the Philippines Institute for Small Scale Industries. SERDEF has funded several publications, including: *Introduction to Entrepreneurship; Credit Manual for Small and Medium Enterprises; Filipino Women in Business: A Case Book;* and *You, Too, Can Start Your Own Business.*

The Institute for Small Scale Industries offers dozens of training courses to assist entrepreneurs. These include Financial Management; Young Entrepreneurs' Programme; Strategic Marketing; Total Quality Management; Production Management; Business Franchising; Entrepreneurial Career Development; and Appreciation Course on Entrepreneurship. The institute also offers a small business-consulting course. In addition, a trainer's course on entrepreneurship development is given. This course explains entrepreneurship strategies, and teaches participants to design, implement, monitor and evaluate entrepreneurship development programmes. An advanced course, offered by the institute, is the Project Appraisal, Evaluation and Monitoring Course for Small and Medium Enterprise Projects. This course upgrades skills in appraising, monitoring and evaluating small and medium scale enterprise projects. A specialised course offering is entitled Designing and Implementing Entrepreneurship Programmes for Women. This course focuses on cultural, social, legal and other barriers to female entrepreneurship and how to overcome them.

Finally, yet another player in the promotion of entrepreneurship in the Philippines is the Philippine Foundation for Resources Management. Among its projects is the Programme on Women's Involvement in Entrepreneurship.

With a more limited scope is the Business Action Centre of the Naga City Chamber of Commerce, on the island of Luzon. It provides a variety of accounting and legal assistance as well as physical facilities, secretarial support, desktop publishing and courier services.

Constraints on Entrepreneurship

As is evident from the above, many efforts have focused on financing entrepreneurs and on developing an efficient infrastructure for them. Yet, despite efforts by governmental and non-governmental bodies to foster development in the Philippines, the national economy — except Chinese-dominated Cebu — is still characterised by inflation, underdevelopment and slow growth. According to interviews conducted by the author in the Philippines, causal variables include corruption and until recently, power shortages were a problem.

Personal relationships are very important in the Filipino business sphere, and much time is spent on *pakikisama* — the development of inter-personal ties. Among the most important ties in business are those between entrepreneurs and the government, especially a practice known as *lagay* (a polite word for "buying personal ties"). Officials expect bribes in return for allowing entrepreneurship to flourish. Some entrepreneurs have long-established channels of bribery, and these are used to create barriers to entry. This effectively inhibits potential new entrants, and limits competition.

Entrepreneurs are often approached by individuals offering "protection" for small firms, in exchange for special payments, locally known as *tong*. This is effectively a bribe without which an entrepreneur's business can be put in jeopardy.

Finally, an adequate supply of affordable energy is essential for economic development, and for a healthy entrepreneurship sector. Beginning in 1983, the Petro-Canada International Assistance Corporation began a programme of co-operation with the Bureau of Energy and Development. Also, loans were extended to the Philippines National Oil Company and to the National Power Corporation. The objective was to exploit an existing geothermal steam field, construct a power station and improve power transmission lines. Yet, the nation is still dependent on imported petrol. A setback occurred during the Asian Crisis, when the national currency tumbled, raising the effective price of imports sold in dollars.

The Entrepreneurship Sector Today

The economy of the Philippines is a blend of agriculture, fishing and light industry; small enterprises are major players. On family farms, important crops include bananas, coconuts, coffee, copra, corn, hemp, nuts, pineapples, rice, sugarcane, tapioca, tobacco, vegetables, yams, and abaca (a fibre related to the banana plant). Both subsistence farming and subsistence fishing are common to this day.

Although the nation could have been self-sufficient in food, it is not. The low yields can be traced to a tradition of absentee landlords in a peasant society.

Clothing and food-processing are the most developed industries, along with the light manufacturing of home appliances. Sectors showing growth include aquaculture, furniture assembly and microcircuit production. Most exports are manufactured goods such as electrical microcircuits and semi-conductors.

Some literature (Halloran 1991; Kinyanjui, 1993) has suggested that for some countries the growth of the entrepreneurship sector is constrained by the lack of easy access to financing. This is *not* the case in the Philippines. During the early 20th century, missionaries introduced to these islands the concept of co-operatives. Basing these co-operatives on the rural credit unions of the United States, the missionaries launched a movement that eventually gained considerable popularity. Today, several hundred credit unions provide low-cost capital to entrepreneurs who lack collateral. Chinese entrepreneurs have their own credit circles. In addition, foreign entrepreneurs provide financing to informal enterprises sometimes without collateral.

Toward the Future

It has been shown that entrepreneurs in the Philippines have a great deal going for them. Several programmes were created to help small enterprises and cottage industries. Entrepreneurship is even fostered at the Iwahig Penal Colony (on Palawan Island), where prisoners are required to make and sell handicrafts.

Unlike the situation described in other countries, neither financing nor infrastructure is problematic here. In the case of the Philippines, entrepreneurship is limited mostly by corruption and by the insufficient access to affordable energy.

Exhibit 13.7   Many Successful Entrepreneurs Reside in Makati; photo ©2006 Leo Paul DANA

Chapter 14

Singapore[64]

Introduction

At the tip of peninsular Malaysia lies Singapore, a city-republic covering one main island (23 kilometres from north to south and 42 kilometres wide), and some tiny islets, the latter mostly uninhabited. Its area totals 646 square kilometres, and it is home to almost 100,000 small and medium-size enterprises. The island republic is multicultural with each ethnic group having its set of traditional belief systems, and living in harmony with people from other groups.

Since its early years, the Singapore Government created a positive investment climate, attracting multinational corporations to a free port with a business-friendly environment. Foreign firms responded; they brought their technologies, created employment, and contributed to economic development. As foreign firms began to shift operations to lower-cost locations, the Singapore Government began encouraging its own entrepreneurs to thrive. However, market saturation in Singapore soon threatened the survival of many local entrepreneurs; internationalisation of entrepreneurship became a necessity.

---

[64]This chapter is based on information obtained from a variety of sources, including: the Construction Industry Development Board; the Economic Development Board; the Enterprise Promotion Centres Pte Ltd; the National Science and Technology Board; the Singapore Productivity and Standards Board; the Singapore Tourism Board; and the Trade Development Board. The author is also grateful to Deputy Prime Minister Dr. Tony Tan Keng Yan, and to Professor Tommy Koh for personally sharing some thoughts. Travel to Singapore was provided by Nanyang Technological University. The chapter includes material that first appeared in Dana (1999b).

Exhibit 14.1   Respecting Ancestors; photo ©2006 Leo Paul DANA

Exhibit 14.2   Little India; photo ©2006 Leo Paul DANA

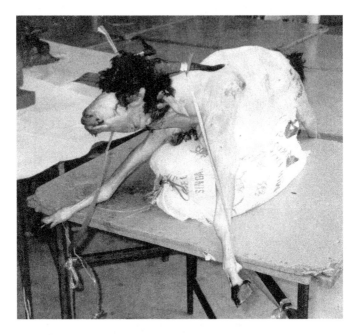

Exhibit 14.3   Belief Systems Are Respected; photo ©2006 Leo Paul DANA

Exhibit 14.4   Survival Threatened; photo ©2006 Leo Paul DANA

Exhibit 14.5   Motivated by Opportunity; photo ©2006 Leo Paul DANA

To assist with communications, Singapore launched a national broadband project called Singapore One.

Wong, Wong, Lee, and Ho (2005) identified the trend that the total entrepreneurial activity index for Singapore has been on the rise, and opportunity entrepreneurship accounts for the majority of entrepreneurial activity. Comparing early-stage entrepreneurship, in Singapore and Thailand, Minniti, Bygrave, and Autio (2006) pointed out that opportunity motives — as opposed to necessity motives — explain entrepreneurship in Singapore more so than is the case in Thailand.

Historical Overview

A Chinese document from the 3rd century referred to Singapore as *Pu Luo Chung*, literally meaning, "island at the tip of a peninsula." Because of its location, at the tip of a peninsula between China and India, traders already knew this island.

While Marco Polo referred to Singapore as *Malayur* (Tamil for "Hill Town"), the Javanese called it *Temasek*, meaning "Sea Town." The harbour made it attractive to Arab, Chinese, and Indian merchants, who came to trade with entrepreneurs from Java, Malaya and Siam — as Thailand was then known. The Sumatra-based Srivijaya Empire ruled the region, including the Malay Peninsula and the islands of Java and Sumatra.

In 1299, on the island of *Temasek*, a prince from Sumatra saw an animal that he could not identify. An elder said it might be a lion. It was probably a tiger, as lions have never been indigenous to this area. Nevertheless, the island came to be known as *Singapura*, meaning "Lion City" in Sanskrit. Later, the name was anglicised to its present form, Singapore.

Merchants from Arab lands, and others from India, frequently passed by Singapore. These entrepreneurs were the middlemen in the spice trade between Indonesia and Europe. During the early 1500s, Europeans began coming to this part of the world, to obtain spices directly. In the sub-continent, the British established the British East India Company. An increase in demand for Chinese tea, silk and pottery, among European consumers, prompted the company to send expeditions from India to China.

In 1781, Thomas Stamford Raffles was born at sea, into a poor family from London. At the time, the British were interested in India for its tea, and their trading arm was the British East India Company. The firm had trading posts in Bombay (today's Mumbai), Calcutta (today's Kolkata), and Madras (today's Chennai). From India, the company sent ships to China, to obtain pottery and silk. Since the journey between India and China was a lengthy one, it was therefore decided to set up a node along the way, where British ships could stop for water, food and repairs. Accordingly, in 1786, the British East India Company set up a base in Penang.

In 1795, 14-year old Thomas began working for the British East India Company, in London. Ten years later, the company sent him to Penang, where he learned Malay. In 1811, he was put in charge of Java, where he abolished slavery. In 1818, he was transferred to Bencoolen, a British trading post on the island of Sumatra. This was before Sumatra became Dutch.

Exhibit 14.6 David Elias Was a Prominent Entrepreneur of Iraqi Descent; photo ©2006 Leo Paul DANA

In 1819, Sir Thomas Stamford Raffles, Lieutenant-Governor of Bencoolen, selected Singapore as the location for a new port for the British East India Company.[65] The local population was estimated to be 150 people (Djamour, 1959). Raffles paid the local leaders for permission to set up a free port, and this attracted thousands of entrepreneurs. Raffles segregated different ethnic groups into assigned neighbourhoods.

When the British took full control of Singapore, in 1824, the settlement had 10,683 people, of whom 31% were Chinese. In 1826, Singapore became part of the British Straits Settlements, along with Malacca and Penang. That year, a famine in China prompted 4,000 men to come to Singapore. When Chinese men had children with Malay women, the offspring were known as Baba Chinese or Straits Chinese. Their descendants are known as Peranakans. By the late 19th century, more than 70% of Singapore's population was Chinese (Freedman, 1961).

---

[65] See Turnbull (1977).

Exhibit 14.7   Not Industrialists; photo ©2006 Leo Paul DANA

In 1830, a group of Jewish entrepreneurs came to Singapore from Iraq, to work in the spice trade. Many followed, and Singapore became home to a thriving community of Jewish entrepreneurs, among them Baghdad-born Menasseh Meyer, reputed to be the richest Jew in the Far East.

In 1867, the Straits Settlements became a Crown Colony. The inauguration of the Suez Canal, in 1869, made Singapore an important node along the route from England to Australia. This helped the growth of Singapore as a centre of international trade. As well, Mizrakhi Jews from Iraq made Singapore an important node in their international network of international business. Entrepreneurs set up go-downs (warehouses) and trading houses. Singapore became a centre for entrepôt trade.

The British were interested in the development of modern capitalism in Singapore. They promoted trade and commerce, in an environment of minimal regulation. This attracted entrepreneurs from countries such as Burma, Iraq, Syria, and of course China.

Many migrants from China were sojourners who intended to eventually return to their homeland. Since these people had no long-term commitment

Exhibit 14.8   The Straits Clinic Stood on Middle Road; photo ©2006 Leo Paul DANA

to the British colony, they usually avoided capital-intensive industries, which required long pay-back periods. Thus, the ethnic-Chinese in Singapore were largely concentrated in commerce, an activity in which gains were more immediate.

Simpich wrote, "Nearly all of the trades and the retail commerce of Singapore are in the hands of the Chinese (1926, p. 268)." Gasse (1982) cited the pre-war Chinese community in Singapore as cultivating entrepreneurs more easily than others. It should be noted, however, that these entrepreneurs were mostly merchants, not industrialists.

On February 15, 1942, the Japanese took control of Singapore, renaming it *Syonan-to*, Japanese for "Light of the South." Although the British returned after the Japanese surrender, an independence movement began to grow. The year 1946 saw the break-up of the Straits Settlements, as Malacca and Penang joined the Malayan Union.

Under British colonial rule, the Jews of Singapore were denied full access into British society. A Jew by the name of David Marshall — president of the Maghain Aboth Synagogue on Waterloo Street — led the movement for

Exhibit 14.9   Former Shopping District; photo ©2006 Leo Paul DANA

Singapore's independence and became the Chief Minister of Singapore. In April 1956, he led a delegation to London and asked for internal self-government; on April 23, 1956, David Marshall showed Herbert Morrison signatures of 167,000 people requesting independence for Singapore. In 1959, when self-government was granted, Lee Kuan Yew became the nation's prime minister. David Marshall later served as Singapore's ambassador in France, Spain, Portugal and Switzerland.

Singapore's Economic Development Board was formed in August 1961. In 1963, Singapore joined Malaya, Sabah and Sarawak to form Malaysia but was expelled. Turnbull wrote, "Singapore's expulsion from Malaysia destroyed the basis on which responsible Singapore politicians had considered the state viable. She was unique among colonial countries in having independence thrust upon her unilaterally (1977, p. 297)."

On August 9, 1965, Singapore became an independent republic. Until 1985, the city-state relied on foreign multinational corporations to industrialise the nation and to develop the economy. At the time, there was no perceived need

Exhibit 14.10   The Victoria Building; photo ©2006 Leo Paul DANA

Exhibit 14.11   Old and New; photo ©2006 Leo Paul DANA

to encourage local entrepreneurs. However, a global recession that year led the government to realise the vulnerability of a domestic economy that relied very heavily on foreign capital and overseas markets. At that time, focus shifted to entrepreneurship and more recently to technopreneurship, as Singapore rushed to become a regional technology hub. To make way for the new, old buildings were demolished; among these was the Victoria Building, last renovated during the 1990s.

In 2005, Singapore accepted a proposal to establish a youth enterprise academy. As discussed by Zainol, the purpose was to "provide experiential programmes that focus on entrepreneurship and leadership (2005, p. 1)."

A Multicultural Society

Singapore was built by people of numerous cultural backgrounds, including Malays, Tamils, and ethnic-Chinese from different provinces of China. From Fujian Province came Foochows, speaking Fuzhouhua; Henghuas, speaking Xinghuahua; Hokchias, speaking Fuquinhua; and Hokkiens, speaking Minnanhua. Cantonese people speaking Guangzhouhua, and Teochews speaking Chaozhouhua, came from Guang Dong. Hainanese immigrants, speaking Hainanhua, came from Hainan Island. Hakkas, speaking Kehua, came from Fujian and Guang Dong. The Hokkiens are the largest ethno-cultural group in Singapore.

For linguistic reasons, people tended to live among, and to work with others, who spoke the same dialect. This led to considerable occupational clustering. The Hokkiens — who had political contacts with the colonial government — became very involved in entrepôt trade. Many traded along Chulia Street. Other Hokkien entrepreneurs lived on China Street, where they sold sundry items as well as fresh greens. Telok Ayer Street was home to larger-scale Hokkien entrepreneurs who imported goods from neighbouring countries.

The Teochews dominated the rice trade across south-east Asia. In Singapore, Teochews could be found along Circular Road, not far from the Singapore River. On Chin Chew Street, they traded spices. On Chulia Street, Teochew dealers sold bird's nest and shark's fin.

Under the leadership of Mr. Aw Boon Haw, producer of Tiger Balm, Hakka entrepreneurs dominated Singapore's medicine halls. The Cantonese were regarded as a lower class. They were clustered in the district around Kreta Ayer. Many sold cloth. Some sold furniture, musical instruments, tobacco and silk, which they imported from China. They had shop-houses on Pagoda Street and on Temple Street. Others were artisans, goldsmiths, tailors and restaurant-owners.

To foster co-operation among people sharing the same dialect, and to promote commercial and industrial development, entrepreneurs established and joined clan associations. Mingling with other members helped individuals understand trends in product development as well as price fluctuations. Here, entrepreneurs could discuss partnerships and obtain financing. Clan associations provided social contacts, training, business ideas, market information, business concepts, start-up capital and technical assistance. This web of networking played an important role in the development of entrepreneurship in Singapore.

The Hokkien Hui Kuan (Hokkien Clan Association) donated land to build Nanyang University, which opened in 1958. This was the first Chinese-language university outside China. After independence, nationalism transcended clan loyalties, and clan associations lost their dominance.

Singapore society, today, is quite heterogeneous. Buddhists comprise 28% of the population, while 19% are Christian, 16% are Muslim, 13% are Tao and 5% are Hindu.

The behaviours and values of the Chinese in Singapore are deep-rooted in Confucian dynamism, which includes the virtues of perseverance and thrift. Both of these factors tend to facilitate entrepreneurship. Singaporeans have been discouraged from believing in extreme individualism. Instead, they have been conditioned to feel a loyalty to the nuclear and extended family. They accept that the family is the building block of society. Divorce rates are low. All these factors may be said to have contributed to the success of family business in Singapore.

Singaporeans are also taught the importance of saving, frugality and hard work. These factors, when coupled with compulsory Central Providence Fund (CPF) contributions, have made Singapore's savings equal to 46% of

Exhibit 14.12   Informal; photo ©2006 Leo Paul DANA

GNP — the highest in the world. When entrepreneurs need capital for new ventures or to expand existing firms, informal financing is often available.

Confucian values have served as guidelines for social norms, which may help entrepreneurship. However, research has not found ethnic-Chinese cultural values to emphasise initiative. Although the Singapore Government once relied on foreign investors for economic growth, since 1985 there has been emphasis on encouraging Singaporeans to develop initiatives in the realm of entrepreneurship.

The Singaporean Model

In 1985, BG Lee Hsien Loong, the Acting Minister of Trade and Industry and Chairman of the Committee on Small Enterprise Policy, stated: "We must have our own entrepreneurs… We need a focal point for small business, a single agency to co-ordinate these schemes, work out new ones, and provide one-stop service for small enterprises." He was introducing the Small Enterprise Bureau of Singapore, with programmes to help entrepreneurs. The Singapore Government allocated S$100 million to this end, and the Small Enterprise

Bureau was established as a division of the Singapore Development Board, for the purpose of helping promising entrepreneurs.

Until 1995, the Economic Development Board was in charge of small and medium-size enterprise development. Its Small and Medium Enterprise (SME) Master Plan emphasised local entrepreneurship. That year, the Singapore Productivity and Standards Board was created. The new agency's mission was to raise productivity such as to enhance Singapore's competitiveness and economic growth for a better quality of life. It also took the responsibility to promote entrepreneurship in Singapore.

The Singapore Productivity and Standards Board developed a three-pronged strategy to promote entrepreneurship: (i) broad-based assistance to small and medium size firms; (ii) focused assistance to selected, promising entrepreneurs; and (iii) industry-wide assistance.

During 1996 — its first year of operations — the Singapore Productivity and Standards Board provided broad-based assistance to more than 2,500 small and medium enterprises. This assistance was implemented through its Local Enterprise Upgrading Centre. The Board helped entrepreneurs to participate in a variety of Government Development Assistance Programmes. Under the industry-wide assistance scheme, it facilitated the creation of new franchises. The Board also helped entrepreneurs to harness information technology. For instance, Shopnet linked small-scale retailers with suppliers, and financial assistance was offered to entrepreneurs who wished to adopt the system. Funding came from the Local Enterprise Technical Assistance Scheme. Additional money to train entrepreneurs how to use Shopnet was available from the Skills Development Fund.

Various agencies are responsible for the different government assistance programmes. For example, there are two capital loan programmes. There are also business development grants. The Trade Development Board administers grants to assist entrepreneurs in developing their brand names. The Economic Development Board has a Local Industry Upgrading Programme to foster ties between multinational corporations and smaller-scale suppliers of parts and services in Singapore.

Other programmes include the Partners-in-Training Scheme, the Research and Development Incubator Programme, and the SME Manager

Scheme. The first of these encourages wholesalers and franchisers to train their small and medium-sized enterprise partners, such as retailers and franchisees, for mutual gain. The Research and Development Incubator Programme facilitates research and development by Singaporean entrepreneurs, by offering laboratory space in the Science Park.

In addition, there are business innovation grants such as the Innovator's Assistance Scheme, administered by the National Science and Technology Board. The objective of this programme is to assist innovators and investors to develop their concepts into commercially viable processes and products.

As well, there are Information Technology Application Grants. For instance, the Innovation Development scheme encourages and assists entrepreneurs to engage in the innovation of processes, products, applications and services. The Local Enterprise Accounting Programme introduces and implements systematic and effective financial reporting and management systems to small and medium enterprises. In 1999, the Supreme Court unveiled a new scheme, offering contractual manufacturers a waiver of the Goods and Services Tax (GST).[66]

Leong discussed Government Development Assistance Schemes:

> Several government bodies have been tasked to support and promote SME growth. Efforts include well-structured departments able to provide assistance in all areas of operations such as monetary assistance… a month-long promotional event to create awareness of the programmes for SMEs, etc. The Economic Development Board (EDB) is the government's primary agency that plans and executes strategies to make Singapore a compelling global hub for business and investment. It aims to develop and help multinationals and Singapore-based companies thrive and upgrade to higher value-creating operations. The Singapore Productivity and Standards Board (PSB) champions the raising of Singapore's Total Factor Productivity (TFP), promotes innovation, enhances market access, and upgrades the domestic sectors. The Trade and

---

[66]For a discussion about the nature of GST, see Dana (1993).

Development Board (TDB) enhances Singapore's economic competitiveness by helping Singapore companies globalize through trade and investments. TDB also plays a key role in promoting e-commerce, and is shifting its focus toward helping companies develop and export high value-added knowledge services.

PSB is now renamed SPRING Singapore, which stands for Standards, Productivity and Innovation for Growth. SPRING Singapore will take over the responsibilities of PSB to spearhead the National Productivity Movement and play a lead role in raising the productivity of the domestic sector. Similarly, TDB is renamed International Enterprise Singapore (I.E. Singapore), which signifies the importance of developing local enterprises into world-class operations. It proposes to help local companies grow and internationalize by shortening their learning curve and helping them to make the right connections. The main provider of GDAPs is PSB, which administers the Enterprise Development Fund (EDF) comprising of the Local Enterprise Finance Scheme (LEFS) and the umbrella of schemes under Local Enterprise Technical Assistance Scheme (LETAS). Some of the broad-based programmes and schemes that SMEs and new start-ups in Singapore common apply are SME 21, ProAct 21, Promising Local Enterprises Programme (PLEs), and Start-up Enterprise Development Schemes (SEEDs). In addition, there are new programmes and schemes such as Technopreneurship 21, Business Angel Fund, and Technopreneurship Investment Fund (TIF), which are targeted specifically at high tech startups in knowledge-based and emerging sectors.

There are more than 60 assistance schemes available to SMEs through various statutory boards, and they come in the form of grants or loans. These schemes cover all areas of business needs in operations, working capital, management, human resources and even expenses incurred in the course of developing business overseas. A total numbers of 1,626 and 2,645 approvals of LEFS and LETAS, respectively, were made in 1999. So far, more than 6000 companies have benefited from both schemes. LEFS aids SMEs in acquiring fixed productive assets and working capital loans to upgrade and automate their businesses and expand their productive capacity, LETAS aids SMEs in paying for the costs of engaging external consultants to upgrade their operations. Both schemes work hand-in-hand in assisting SMEs to develop and expand operationally (Leong, 2004, pp. 130–131).

This section has illustrated that various loans, grants and tax incentives are available for entrepreneurs in Singapore. The wide range of programmes covers financing, business development, management, productivity improvement, manpower training, marketing, exporting, technology transfer, information technology and automation. Some programmes are for new venture start-ups, and others for expansion or internationalisation. The next section shall address government attempts to internationalise entrepreneurship from Singapore.

Exhibit 14.13   Incentives Available; photo ©2006 Leo Paul DANA

Internationalising Singaporean Entrepreneurs

In the late 1980s, the Singapore Government began promoting the "Growth Triangle," giving incentives for Singaporean entrepreneurs to relocate manufacturing activities to Indonesia and Malaysia. However, internationalisation was limited.

It was in 1993 that Senior Minister Lee Kuan Yew declared, "We can enthuse a younger generation with the thrill and the rewards of building an external dimension to Singapore. We can and we will spread our wings into the region and then into the wider world."

Notwithstanding Singapore's attractiveness to foreign multinational corporations, Singaporean entrepreneurs can also play a role in international business. Given the limited size of Singapore's domestic market, internationalisation would help Singaporean entrepreneurs to achieve economies of scale. Thus, internationalisation can improve local production.

Hence, the Singapore Government has been promoting the internationalisation of Singaporean entrepreneurship. Among the incentives are a variety of Going Regional Grants, some of which are administered by the Economic Development Board. Examples include the Malaysia-Singapore Third Country Investment Feasibility Study Fund. The purpose of this programme is to encourage Singaporean firms to undertake, jointly with their Malaysian counterparts, feasibility studies on pursuing joint investment and business projects in third countries. Another programme administered by the Economic Development Board is the Singapore-Australia Business Alliance Forum Joint Feasibility Study Fund. This programme encourages Singaporean entrepreneurs to set up joint ventures with Australians, again in third countries. The Economic Development Board also has a Business Development Scheme, which assists Singaporean entrepreneurs to identify opportunities abroad. The Trade Development Board has a Franchise Development Assistance Scheme, the purpose of which is to encourage Singaporean entrepreneurs to develop a franchise package and to market the concept overseas.

The Association of Small and Medium Enterprises has also been promoting the internationalisation of Singaporean small and medium enterprises. In 1998, it launched SME Day, with networking events for entrepreneurs, under the theme Towards Globalisation.

In September 1998, the first conference on international entrepreneurship brought together leading academics from around the world. It was decided that Singapore's Nanyang Technological University would sponsor the second conference, at the Goodwood Park Hotel, in Singapore, August 15–18, 1999, and the Proceedings were published as Dana (1999c). As the domestic market in Singapore became increasingly saturated, it became increasingly important for Singaporean entrepreneurs to look beyond Singapore.

Technopreneurship 21

During a parliamentary debate, in November 1998, it was announced to have a special committee to promote technology-based entrepreneurship, in Singapore. Deputy Prime Minister Dr. Tony Tan saw the Asian Crisis as an opportunity to accelerate the transition of the island republic to a knowledge-based economy, and a high-powered panel was organised to create a climate conducive to boosting high-tech entrepreneurship. Technological entrepreneurship was termed "technopreneurship" and ingredients were identified to promote it. These included: the availability of creative talent (foreign and local); low barriers to entry; easy access to capital; easy access to markets; tolerance of failure; and high gains. Dr. Tony Tan, chairman of the Technopreneurship 21 Ministerial Committee, explained, "Technopreneurs serve as the critical interface between ideas and markets, translating creative ideas into vehicles to serve market demand."

Toward the Future

Prior to independence, entrepreneurs in Singapore thrived as merchants. The colony was an important hub of entrepôt trade, but it had few industrialists. During the 1950s, the Khong Guan Biscuit Factory produced biscuits in Indonesia. Similarly, Ho Rih Hua opened a manufacturing plant in Thailand. Yet, Singapore's entrepreneurship sector was lacking in industrialists, and was limited by a distinctly local orientation. Singaporean entrepreneurs had few foreign direct investments.

After independence, the government designed an enterprise-friendly environment to attract foreign direct investment from abroad. Multinational corporations were handed the task of industrialising Singapore. More recently, the state has been encouraging both entrepreneurship and the internationalisation of entrepreneurs.

Singapore, at the turn of the millennium, has two types of entrepreneurs. One set is comprised of elder individuals who became entrepreneurs because they lacked formal education and could not compete in educated Singapore. These people were motivated by money. Failure would bring shame to their families, and so they worked very diligently to succeed. They attribute their success to hard work, patience, persistence and luck. Although successful in their home market, they tend not to venture abroad.

In contrast, the other set of entrepreneurs consists of young, educated individuals. Power and fulfilment motivate them in addition to money. Most importantly, they are expansion-oriented. Yet, they are not many in number.

In the future, according to Senior Minister Lee, "How well we do depends on how many entrepreneurs or wealth creators we have in our

Exhibit 14.14   Corporate Offices Tower over Singapore; photo ©2006 Leo Paul DANA

midst."[67] However, given the high salaries provided by multinational corporations, many Singaporeans identify a huge opportunity cost with becoming entrepreneurs. Unlike the poor Chinese migrants who lacked alternatives in colonial Singapore, non-enterprising Singaporeans can become very successful in corporate life, without becoming entrepreneurs.

---

[67] Source: *The Straits Times*, July 11, 1996.

Chapter 15

Taiwan[68]

Introduction

Taiwan is an island with an area of 35,751 square kilometres, off the coast of China. While Taiwan is home to several high-mountain Indigenous peoples, such as the Tsou,[69] the majority of the people here are Han Chinese. Many are descendants of people whose migration was encouraged by Qing emperors. Han immigrants often originated along China's southern coast, and consequently Taiwanese dialects resemble those along China's southern coast.

Each country has its mix of large businesses and smaller firms. The ratio depends on a variety of factors. Environmental forces, such as a government's credit policy, may greatly influence the ratio and relative importance of small enterprises to large ones. Credit policy in Taiwan has traditionally been tight; loans have been expensive and difficult to secure. Most firms in Taiwan are small, and tightly held. Entrepreneurs typically exert an over-riding influence on their enterprises. Even large companies tend to be owned by families, with a senior family member being the central decision-maker. Lin (1998) reported that of 935,000 entrepreneurs in Taiwan, 96.5% are small or medium enterprises, collectively employing 78.6% of the workforce. Taiwan has more entrepreneurs per capita than does any other nation in south-east Asia. Taiwanese entrepreneurs are "major players in international business (Ali, Lee,

---

[68]This chapter is based on information obtained from a variety of sources, including: the Board of Foreign Trade; the Directorate-General, Accounting and Statistics; and the Ministry of Economic Affairs. Travel to Taiwan was provided by a grant from the University of Oxford; in Taipei, the author was hosted by Academia Sinica. The chapter includes material that first appeared in Dana (1999b).

[69]For accounts, see Hipwell (2005), Kirjassoff (1920), and Simon (2005).

Exhibit 15.1   From Taiwanese Waters; photo ©2006 Leo Paul DANA

and Camp, 2002, p. 29)." Aw (2002) explained that productivity gains have been high in Taiwan, as a result of low barriers to entry and exit.

As noted by Schive and Hu, "Whilst taking advantage of… the infrastructure inherited from the era of the Japanese rule, and the aid provided by the US during the early phase of Taiwan's modern industrial development, the government undertook an active role… through the adoption of market-oriented policies. This gave rise to the emergence of SMEs in the private sector (2001, p. 248)." Taiwan's cottage industries then played a significant part in the development of the national economy.

Historical Overview[70]

The island today known as Taiwan was settled during the 14th century, by Han Chinese from southern China. The Portuguese arrived in 1517, and named it *Ilha Formosa*, literally "the island of beauty."

In 1624, the island was claimed by the Dutch East India Company. Under Dutch rule, the island became a trans-shipping hub for international

---

[70] See also Roy (2003).

Exhibit 15.2   Entrepreneur; photo ©2006 Leo Paul DANA

commerce. Its economic importance increased Chinese interest in the island, and by 1662 the Dutch were defeated and Formosa was Chinese.

In 1858, the Chinese allowed the British and the French to establish trading facilities on the island. Eventually, the French occupied a piece of Formosa.

In 1895, the Qing dynasty ceded this island to Japan, but on May 12, 1895 Taiwan declared its independence as the Republic of Formosa. A Japanese expedition landed on the new republic on May 28, 1895 and made Taiwan a Japanese colony. For fifty years, Japan ruled Formosa as a colony. Fiscal incentives encouraged the establishment of firms which were owned by Japanese entrepreneurs and which in turn, produced for the Japanese market.

At the end of WWII, Formosa was returned to China. When the communists took-over China, Chiang Kai-shek and almost two million followers fled to Taiwan. In 1950, Chiang Kai-shek became president of Taiwan.

When Taiwan declared itself as its own country, it was largely agricultural, and manufacturing was limited to light industries, such as sugar refining and the

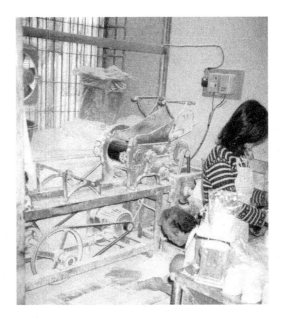

Exhibit 15.3   Cottage Industry; photo ©2006 Leo Paul DANA

production of fibres. The state nationalised assets that had been controlled by the Japanese, and the government set out to develop a comprehensive economic policy suitable for the nation's situation.

Taiwan's first national policy was known as the Four Year Economic Construction Plan. At the time, it seemed reasonable to produce for the national market. Thus, in 1953, Taiwan adopted a policy of import substitution. This boosted local, small-scale enterprise. However, the size of the Taiwanese market limited local growth. Therefore, in 1958, the government adopted a new model of export promotion.

Taiwanese entrepreneurs began to produce electric machinery for export. To facilitate export-development, a free access zone was established in Kaohsiung. The government developed export-processing zones in Nantze (an area in Kaohsiung) and in Taichung. The purpose of these zones was to encourage industrial development, to facilitate technology transfer, and to promote exports. This new policy proved very successful, and the zones still offer several incentives, such as exemptions from duties and taxes. In addition, the high success rate of industrial parks led to the establishment of others.

Exhibit 15.4   Traditional Agriculture; photo ©2006 Leo Paul DANA

During the 1980s, the Taiwanese economy shifted to a service orientation. This was facilitated by the government's relaxation of laws.

Beginning in 1987, entrepreneurs in Taiwan realised that their small
businesses could not survive by simply undertaking local labour-intensive production. Along with economic and political factors, this contributed to the
internationalisation of Taiwanese entrepreneurs to its ASEAN neighbours.

Schive and Hu wrote, "Since the mid-1990s, when Taiwan's economy
entered a period of medium growth (at a rate of approximately 6% a year), the
relative proportion of SMEs has continued to ascend (2001, p. 255)." Schive
and Hu also noted, "the extent to which Taiwan's SMEs are achieving success
in overseas markets might be said to be quite unique (2001, p. 270)."

By 1996, Taiwanese firms had 241 projects in Vietnam, representing
$3.6 billion. This was a larger investment in Vietnam than any other single
country made. Taiwanese entrepreneurs also made significant investments in
other countries across East Asia.

Taiwanese entrepreneurs have also been active in China. The average
Taiwanese investment in China is $800,000. Indeed, Taiwanese entrepreneurs
have been contributing significantly to economic development in Asia.

Exhibit 15.5   World Class Service; photo ©2006 Leo Paul DANA

In recent years, the Taiwanese government has promoted venture capital, innovation incubators, an open laboratory system, and e-commerce. This is discussed by Lee and Wang (2003).

Credit Policy and Entrepreneurship

Two models can be used to describe the credit policy framework of nations:

Model I

In consideration of the fact that high interest rates may cause a heavy debt burden on entrepreneurs, while decreasing the rate of new venture formation and increasing the rate of bankruptcies, the government intervenes with subsidised interest rates, helping a few favoured borrowers. Subsidised interest rates, below the market-clearing rate, help few privileged entrepreneurs, while creating jobs for the masses. This is the model which was adopted by South Korea, and which led to the growth of the *chaebols*, very diversified and powerful mega-conglomerates.

Model II

Subsidised rates are considered unjust, as low-cost money encourages capital intensive methods of production, consequently limiting employment growth. Therefore, interest rates rise with market demand. High real interest rates encourage savings and keep inflation under control by reducing demand. The formal financial systems have rigid financing regulations. This is the model adopted by Taiwan.

The Taiwanese Model

Since 1950, the economy of Taiwan has followed the path of Model II, letting its interest rates rise to high market levels. This policy resulted in the world's highest rates of savings, and efficient investment in atomised industrial structures. Savings per capita, in Taiwan, have been traditionally high. Taiwan bloomed largely because of the efforts of small-scale entrepreneurs, with thousands of entrepreneurial small businesses. Each firm had minimal debt, and entrepreneurs strive to be efficient. *The Economist* of July 14, 1990 estimated that 80% of the firms in Taiwan had fewer than 20 employees (p. 20).

Taiwan's experience with a Model II approach gave rise to a multitude of successful small businesses thriving in a healthy economy. The typical firm in Taiwan is small and equity-based. The selection of such an approach has allowed policy to remain stable with no major corrections necessary along the path to prosperity. Entrepreneurs often boast that their firms have no debt.

A shortcoming which may be attributed to a Model II approach is that small firms may lack economies of scale. However, Taiwan's low overheads, good infrastructure, and excellent network of local suppliers all help compensate for any disadvantage due to size. Local suppliers being small, a firm may be required to deal with several of them. This reduces risks, as compared to dealing with only one supplier overseas. Taiwanese SMES often link up with firms abroad, thus gaining access to marketing expertise specific to foreign markets.

Whereas South Korea's implementation of Model I has necessitated many corrections, Taiwan's success with Model II has necessitated fewer corrections. Other countries might learn from the experience of these two tigers and their contrasting styles. In both cases, a healthy small business sector comes into existence, sooner (as in Taiwan) or later (as in South Korea after corrections). However, the Asian Crisis has shown that Model II is more sustainable. In contrast to the situation arising in states where subsidised credit is available, entrepreneurs in Taiwan borrow principally from the informal market, and at higher rates. This encourages them to focus on labour-intensive activities while optimising the use of capital.

Today, small industries are the backbone of Taiwan, and these small industries have become internationally competitive; 300 have become large, without government assistance.

Flexible Entrepreneurs

Entrepreneurs in Taiwan tend to combine management and ownership into one function. They like to have power over their firms, and they often prefer a sole proprietorship to other forms of enterprise. They also have a higher self-funded proportion of capital than do large-scale enterprises.

As a consequence of a Model II type policy in Taiwan, Taiwanese entrepreneurs have relied relatively little on loans. Consequently, they have coped with the Asian Crisis better than have their neighbouring counterparts. By limiting external sources of income, Taiwanese entrepreneurs have reduced their risks. On the other hand, limited capital has also limited their opportunities for economies of scale.

To compensate for the lack of scale, economies of scope have been emerging. Entrepreneurs in Taiwan are willing to produce a large variety of similar products, albeit in relatively small quantities. For example, the process of production is similar for steel car-plates and machinery-shells. Therefore, one firm can easily make both items. Nevertheless, entrepreneurs usually do so only after receiving specific orders.

In contrast to large corporations, which have heavy capital investments, entrepreneurs in Taiwan have relatively less fixed production equipment. This makes it easy to adapt facilities in order to modify products or to produce different items, as necessary. This allows Taiwanese entrepreneurs to adapt rapidly to changing needs.

Exhibit 15.6   Adapting with Ease; photo ©2006 Leo Paul DANA

Entrepreneurs in Taiwan also respond quickly to changes in purchasing power. Owner-managers are often involved in sales as well as in production. They know their costs, and can rapidly adjust prices according to market demand. This ability is very helpful during crises.

Large-scale enterprises, which tend to be more formal in their organisational structure, have depth and breadth. In contrast, entrepreneurs in Taiwan tend to have few employees outside family members and friends. Furthermore, in a traditional Taiwanese firm, the founder is generally the role model for employees. These factors allow entrepreneurs to lean toward emotion for the smooth operation of their firms. Emphasis is on team-work.

The situation in Taiwan is such that manufacturing processes are flexibly organised among entrepreneurs, each optimising on efficiency brought about by the division of labour among firms. Although the division of work among firms is clear, the division of labour within a small firm is vague. Employees are often asked to do more than required by their respective job descriptions, and

Exhibit 15.7   Team-work; photo ©2006 Leo Paul DANA

they usually comply. This includes personal sacrifice, when the entrepreneurs need extra input. In turn, this reduces costs and contributes to the profitability of entrepreneurship in Taiwan. During the crisis, employees have been asked to make due with less.

As discussed by Lin (1998), successful entrepreneurs in Taiwan have focused on people-related issues rather than structure or technology, and there has been more concern with attitudes and skills than with equipment. Entrepreneurs, here, do not perceive a need to be the vanguard of technological innovation. As long as there is a demand for existing goods, made with existing technology, entrepreneurs are not hasty to change production methods.

Toward the Future

Taiwanese entrepreneurs often prefer to have a small family business than to lose control and obtain growth via delegation to professional outsiders. The tendency is to seek a niche, and entrepreneurs in Taiwan seldom produce a complete product from start to finish; most have prospered as suppliers of parts. Many have concentrated on the manufacturing of consigned components; in

Exhibit 15.8   Good People Skills; photo ©2006 Leo Paul DANA

these cases, mass marketing has not been an important concern, because an entrepreneur needed few clients.

Growth-oriented entrepreneurs in Taiwan often expect to encounter challenges. Banks are reluctant to lend capital to SMEs in Taiwan, especially those lacking a sound accounting system.

As discussed by Luo (1997), entrepreneurs, in Taiwan, rely very much on personal networks, for market information, for suppliers, for clients and for employees. This approach combines the economic and social activities of entrepreneurs. One very important economic and social activity is gift-giving. Gifts are very symbolic in Taiwan, and neglecting an opportunity for gift-giving may be perceived as poor conduct. Similarly, an inappropriate gift — such as clocks, knives, handkerchiefs, scissors and watches — may sever relations.

Although small — by world standards — Taiwanese firms serve their purpose. Neither government nor financing is central to entrepreneurship in here. Nor are technological innovations perceived as crucial. The focus is on people. The establishment of a new venture creates jobs for the entrepreneur's

Exhibit 15.9   No Need for Growth; photo ©2006 Leo Paul DANA

family, and sometimes for strangers who become adopted as family members of the firm. The small size of most firms facilitates communications. A friendly, teacher-apprentice relationship is superimposed on the entrepreneur-employee relation. As job descriptions are vague, employees fill in for one another. People develop a width of professional knowledge, but often lack depth. The work environment is friendly. Yet, non-family members have few opportunities for promotion. Therefore, turnover is high.

Better be the head of a chicken than the tail of an ox.

— Chinese proverb

Chapter 16

Thailand[71]

Introduction

Neighbouring Cambodia, Laos, Myanmar and Malaysia, the Kingdom of Thailand covers 514,000 square kilometres. An independent, sovereign state for over seven centuries, Thailand is the only country in south-east Asia that has never been colonised. During the latter half of the 20th century, the nation's industrial structure was transformed from that of a primary product producer to a major manufacturer. Under the Ministry of Commerce, the Department of Export Promotion was established to promote Thai exports overseas. In 1984, devaluation helped boost Thai exports. Textile exports have since surpassed rice exports. In 1997, however, the fall of the baht initiated the Asian Crisis.

Compared to their counterparts elsewhere, entrepreneurs in Thailand have been given greater leeway, and this has resulted in a vibrant entrepreneurial verve, reinforced by the Thai interpretation of Buddhist values. Thailand has long had a free-market culture, and entrepreneurs, along with their efficient work force, have contributed greatly to the Thai economy. Yet, while multi-nationals have been in the limelight, the potential of entrepreneurs has been

---

[71]This chapter is based on information obtained from a variety of sources, including: the Bangkok Bank Limited; the Board of Trade of Thailand; the Department of Industrial Promotion; the Department of Information; the Department of Technical and Economic Co-operation; the Federation of Thai Industries; the Industrial Finance Corporation of Thailand; Khon Kaen University; the Ministry of Commerce (especially the Department of Business Economics and the Department of Export Promotion); the National Economic and Social Development Board; the Office of the Board of Investment; the Siam Commercial Bank; the Thai Bankers Association; and the Thailand Development Research Institute. Travel to Thailand was provided by the Asian Institute of Technology (AIT). The chapter includes material that first appeared in Dana (1999b).

Exhibit 16.1   Affected by the Crisis; photo ©2006 Leo Paul DANA

underestimated. The Global Entrepreneurship Monitor study revealed that in 2005, Thailand had an exceptionally high score in the Established Business Index, when compared to Singapore and the United States. "With respect to early-stage entrepreneurial activity, countries such as… Thailand (20.7%)… exhibit very high rates of individual involvement compared to other countries such as… Japan (2.2%)… (Minniti, Bygrave, and Autio, 2006, p. 10)."

Historical Overview

The original Thai kingdom came into existence in 1220, as a result of a Thai rebellion against the Khmers. King Ramkhamhaeng, who reigned from 1278 to 1318, adapted the Khmer alphabet to the Thai language. Monks from Ceylon were brought in to form a different form of Buddhism than that practised by the Khmers. The Thais subsequently adopted the Hinayana School of Orthodox Buddhism. When Ayutthaya was the national capital of the Thais (1358-1767), it was known as the Baghdad of the East — a thriving area for trade. Merchants reported that it was larger than was London at the time.

Exhibit 16.2   Buddhist Influence; photo ©2006 Leo Paul DANA

During the 19th century, the Thai kingdom — known as Siam, at the time — ceded some land to Britain (currently the north of peninsular Malaysia) and to France (currently part of Cambodia and Laos). Nevertheless, Siam succeeded in being the only country in the region to escape European colonial rule.

The country became a constitutional monarchy in 1932. In 1939, Siam changed its name to Thailand. During the next several decades, Thailand received considerable assistance from the United States. In 1991, Thailand embarked on a programme of economic deregulation and liberalisation.

The Asian Crisis caused growth to slow down during the latter years of the decade. By 2006, the economy had picked up and $1 traded in the range of 40 baht.

Influence of the Hinayana School of Orthodox Buddhism

Buddhism is more than a religion in the Western sense; it is also a philosophical system. With 94% of Thais being Buddhist, this way of life dominates culture and society in Thailand. Yet, since tolerance is central to Buddhist beliefs, Buddhism has never led to fanaticism or religious war.

Buddhism's tolerance has also allowed the survival of ancient Thai beliefs. Thus, Buddhism, as it is practised in Thailand, coexists with beliefs in omens. Stars and spirits are principal forces in daily life. Entrepreneurs consult astrologers — many of them self-employed Chinese — to determine the most auspicious time to expand their firms. Similar to the eye in Arab countries, or to garlic in Greece or Turkey, amulets are said to protect the Thais from misfortune.

Every factory, every store and every office in Thailand is expected to have a spirit house. This is an ornate, miniature temple, where spirits can be comfortable. This applies to all business enterprises — even brothels. In contrast to Christianity, which links sensual pleasure to sin, Buddhism involves a partnership of piety and pleasure. While good spirits do no harm, entrepreneurs often fear that bad spirits may hurt their business. To counter this, tattoos are used to keep away bad spirits.

The same philosophical system contributes greatly to entrepreneurship in Thailand, as it instils values that appear to encourage entrepreneurial spirit. The importance of tolerance extends beyond religion, to a respect for business competition.

Likewise, the prevalent philosophy in Thailand discourages abuse and envy. Buddhism in Thailand encourages: (i) asceticism; (ii) self-reliance; (iii) taking initiative; (iv) love of work; (v) diligence; (vi) patience; (vii) frugality; and (viii) efficiency. These qualities are very compatible with entrepreneurship:

(i) Since a young age, Thais are taught that Buddha left the comforts of his home to live a life of asceticism. The importance of asceticism is not unique to Buddhism. Weber (1904–1905) linked entrepreneurship to asceticism.

(ii) Self-reliance is emphasised through Buddha's teaching, "Make of yourself a light. Rely upon yourself. Do not depend upon anyone else." Indeed, many Thais become self-employed, not to depend on others for employment. Bandura (1982) and Bandura and Adams (1977) reported a correlation between self-efficacy and subsequent task performance.

(iii) Buddha noted that people believing that everything happens by chance consequently lose hope and neglect to act wisely. Likewise, teachings discourage the belief in destiny, as the existence of destiny would imply that human plans and efforts for improvement and innovation would be in vain. Thais are taught not to rely on chance or fate. Instead, it is important to take initiative. There is an emphasis on an internal locus-of-control. Hull, Bosley, and Udell (1980) found a correlation between an internal locus-of-control and entrepreneurial activity. Brockhaus (1982) and Begley and Boyd (1987) contended that entrepreneurs have a more internally oriented locus-of-control, than do non-entrepreneurs.

(iv) The teachings of Buddha specify that foolish people are avaricious for good results, but are too timid to go after them, and therefore fail. This is interpreted as emphasising the importance of a strong work ethic. Like asceticism, Weber (1904–1905) linked work ethic to entrepreneurship.

(v) It is said that a man, who is satisfied with the progress he has made by little effort, relaxes his effort and becomes proud and conceited, falling into idleness and failure. This teaches people the importance of continuous efforts and determination. Hornaday (1982) noted that perseverance and determination are among the entrepreneurial characteristics most reported in academic surveys.

(vi) It is explained that a farmer cannot expect to see buds today, plants tomorrow and harvest the day after. The Thais learn that patience is a virtue.

(vii) King Udayana once asked Ananda what he was going to do with 500 garments he had just received. Ananda replied:

I am going to distribute them among my brothers in rags.
What will you do with the old garments?
We will make bed covers out of them.
What will you do with the old bed covers?
We will make pillowcases.
What will you do with the old pillowcases?
We will make floor covers out of them.
What will you do with the old floor covers?
Use them for foot towels.
And the old foot towels?
Use them for floor mats.
And the old ones?

Tear them into pieces, and mix them with mud and plaster the house-walls.

The moral of the parable is that frugality is desirable. Again, frugality is a quality that Weber (1904–1905) linked to entrepreneurship.

(viii) Buddhism, as it is taught in Thailand, also teaches the importance of efficiency. A parable recounts the story of a traveller who came across an obstacle to his journey: a river. He therefore built a raft and safely crossed the river. Upon reaching the other bank, the man decided that despite its weight, he would keep the raft, "I will not abandon it to rot, but will carry it with me." Buddha explained that this was not efficient. Even a valuable asset should be discarded, when the cost of keeping it is greater than the benefit it provides.

The Visible Hand

The National Committee for the Hill Tribes

In 1951, Thailand launched an initiative to reach isolated hill-tribes. In 1959, the government established the National Committee for the Hill Tribes, to formulate policy focusing on the development of hill-tribes.

The government's intention has been, and continues to be, to integrate hill-tribe people into mainstream society, thereby discouraging traditional subsistence self-employment. There are six major hill-tribes in Thailand:

(i) The Akha people — also known as Ikaw — are of Tibetan origin. They practise slash-and-burn subsistence agriculture. Other subsistence activities include spinning cotton into thread using a hand spindle.

(ii) The Hmong groups — called Miao by the Thai people — originated in China. Until recently they supported themselves by cultivating opium. Today, they cultivate beans, corn and rice. Women use cotton or hemp to make richly-decorated clothes.

(iii) The Karen people — known as Kaliang or Yang in Thai — came to Thailand from Burma. They raise animals and they use tame elephants to clear land for agriculture. They also hunt.

Exhibit 16.3   Ascetic; photo ©2006 Leo Paul DANA

(iv) The Lahu — or Mussur — people speak a Sino-Tibetan language. They practise hunting and trapping to supplement their slash-and-burn subsistence agriculture.

(v) The Lisu clans are originally from Tibet. They trap animals and practise subsistence agriculture. Some grow opium, and others sell crafts.

(vi) The Yao people — also referred to as Mien — are of Chinese origin. They are skilled at working metal, and they have long been making paper.

Other hill-tribes in Thailand include the Khamu people who first arrived from Laos seeking paid employment; nowadays they are self-employed farmers, fishermen, hunters and traders. The Mlabri people, originally from Laos, were hunter-gatherers until recently. The Thins people are well-known for cultivating glutinous rice. The Lawa people are indigenous to Thailand; they are self-employed, engaged in subsistence agriculture, and selling hand-woven cloth and silver jewellery via the Internet.

Early Economic Development Plans

The first National Economic Development Plan of Thailand (1961–1966) was greatly biased in favour of large enterprises. Its goal was to stimulate economic

Exhibit 16.4   Self-reliant; photo ©2006 Leo Paul DANA

Exhibit 16.5   Determined; photo ©2006 Leo Paul DANA

Exhibit 16.6   Environmentally-friendly; photo ©2006 Leo Paul DANA

growth by providing large-scale investments via the Board of Investment and the Industrial Finance Corporation of Thailand.

Small-scale enterprises were given limited encouragement. The governor of Udorn helped small-scale farmers by introducing sorghum to them. While rice sold for 100 baht ($5 at the time) per acre and required 210 days to mature, sorghum needed only 90 days to yield 200 baht per acre.

Eventually, policy-makers identified the need to upgrade existing small-scale enterprises, and in 1966, the Small Industry Service Institute was formed. Supported by the United Nations Development Programme (UNDP), its purpose was to provide technical assistance in order to modernise small-scale industries in Thailand.

Thailand's second economic development plan (1967–1971) largely replicated the first. Industrial estates were provided for small-scale industries, outside Bangkok. However, no assistance was provided to entrepreneurs.

The third economic development plan (1972–1976) perpetuated the concern with the importance of relocating industries outside the capital city. Incentives were promised. However, the oil crisis and the recession, which it caused, both contributed to delays.

The Board of Investment

The year 1977 witnessed the Investment Promotion Act, which developed the legal foundation for Thailand's Board of Investment. This government agency was empowered to grant preferential status to enterprises engaged in a variety of designated activities which were singled out including agriculture (see Table 16.1); mining and related industries; heavy industry; manufacturing; and services.

Projects attracting the most generous incentive packages include: those expected to generate substantial employment; those located outside Bangkok; those which conserved energy; those which involved substitutes for imported fuel; those with the potential for foreign exchange earnings; and those deemed complementary to the development of basic industries. Qualifying entrepreneurs may be granted exemptions from import duties, from withholding taxes and from income tax. In addition, the Investment Promotion Act empowered the Board of Investment to provide guarantees against competition from new state enterprises. Finally, tariff protection may be introduced, and in some cases, the products of foreign competitors may be banned.

The Board of Investment evolved over time. In its early years, it served as an incentive-granting agency, dedicating much of its resources to monitoring

Table 16.1   Agricultural Products and Commodities Eligible for Special Status in Thailand[72]

• Animal feed	• Oil production from agricultural produce
• Animal products	• Processing of agricultural produce
• Corn produce	• Processing or preservation of food
• Cultivation of mulberry trees	• Production of milk powder
• Deep-sea and off-shore fishing	• Production of soybeans and complete refinement of oil
• Large-scale cultivation	• Products from stick lac
• Livestock raising	• Rabbit raising and processing, for export
• Manufacture of products made from bamboo, for export	• Rubber products
• Manufacture of products made from rattan, for export	• Silk reeling and/or spinning
• Manufacture of products made from palm leaf, for export	• Silk worm farming
• Multiplication of vegetable seeds	• Slaughter of cattle

[72]Source: Board of Investment, Bangkok, Thailand.

Exhibit 16.7   Efficient; photo ©2006 Leo Paul DANA

Exhibit 16.8   Outside Bangkok; photo ©2006 Leo Paul DANA

the tax incentives granted to enterprises. Eventually, it established a "One Stop Centre" and took on the role of business advisor, providing technical expertise to entrepreneurs.

Changing Priorities

Like its predecessor, Thailand's fourth economic development plan (1977–1981) was also concerned with the importance of relocating industries outside

Bangkok. However, the facilities in the estates continued to be minimal, and operating costs were high. This situation prompted a shift in priorities.

The fifth economic development plan (1982–1986) ushered in a new era for Thailand, marking a shift in policy direction. This time, the government emphasised the need to promote small-scale industry as the pillar of industrial development in Thailand. Policy-makers expected that providing specific incentives to small-scale enterprises would result in these firms growing faster than the rate of growth among large corporations. Also, if small firms were concentrated outside the nation's capital, then growth would be decentralised outside Bangkok. This new approach was consistent with the state's long-term objective of narrowing the gap between Bangkok and the less developed regions of the country.

The state-owned Transport Company, Ltd. controlled 10% of the total traffic on buses linking Bangkok and the provinces. In a bold move, this company gave franchises to local entrepreneurs. This turned out to be highly profitable for the franchiser, as well as for the franchisees.

Exhibit 16.9   State-owned; photo ©2006 Leo Paul DANA

During the mid-1980s, large enterprises achieved unexpected success in expanding their export performance. This prompted policy-makers to change their strategy again. Rather than providing policies to promote small industries, it was decided to focus on promoting exports. Consequently, Thailand's sixth economic development plan (1987–1991) was not concerned with small firms.

Major Reform

In September 1990, the Royal Thai Government reduced tariffs on machinery, from 20% to 5%. This stimulated latent demand among price-elastic entrepreneurs, thereby facilitating the transfer of technology.

In January 1991, the Royal Thai Government agreed to create a free trade area and to reduce tariffs among the members of the Association of South East Asian Nations (ASEAN), at the time consisting of Brunei, Indonesia, Malaysia, the Philippines, Singapore and Thailand. Later that year, Prime Minister Anand Panyarachun introduced economic reforms, and streamlined several government bureaus, in order to open Thailand to competition.

Of particular concern to entrepreneurs was the structure of the tax system at the time. Personal income tax rates were very high, especially compared to those in neighbouring Malaysia. Furthermore, the cascading nature of the business tax discouraged backward linkages. Consequently, a Value Added Tax (VAT) was introduced in January 1992, replacing the old system of business taxes. In April 1992, Thailand announced that it wanted to slow down tariff cuts to which it had agreed the previous year.

Making Entrepreneurship Central to the Economy

Propelled by manufactured exports, Thailand became the world's fastest growing economy. A problem, however, was that the manufacturing sector became top heavy, i.e., strong in final assembly but less so in supply industries. This led to a bottleneck, as firms developed a dependence on imported raw materials and machinery. Supply and support industries have a major impact on a nation's industrial sector, because their role is to feed manufacturing operations.

Thailand's seventh economic development plan (1992–1996) explicitly emphasised a commitment to the rapid development of key support industries,

Exhibit 16.10   Rural Thailand; photo ©2006 Leo Paul DANA

and this was of special interest to entrepreneurs. Countless small firms are the core of the domestic support industries in Thailand. Yet, they often suffered from a lack of economy of scale or the lack of technology to be globally competitive. Although components could be produced in Thailand, local firms lacked the resources to produce the quantities for which demand existed. Therefore, the Board of Investment implemented a special programme to promote the growth of small and medium scale Thai companies in the area of support industries. The Board of Investment Unit for Industrial Linkage Development (BUILD) devised a scheme to market the concept of backward linkages to smaller firms, whereby small firms acquire technology from multinationals, in order to supply them with components.

In recent years, the Bank of Thailand and also the Industrial Finance Corporation of Thailand have given preferential financial assistance to entrepreneurs. Priority has been focused on rural entrepreneurs using local raw materials to produce exports.

The Financial Crisis

In early 1996, the baht was showing signs of weakness. In July 1997, it collapsed, prompting a domino effect across the Far East. Almost two million people lost their jobs and unemployment surged from almost nil, to 6%.

In November 1997, a new coalition government was elected, headed by Prime Minister Chuan Leekpai. He proved himself an honest man, eager to implement economic reforms proposed by the International Monetary Fund, along with a $17.2 billion package.

Within a few months, the Royal Thai Government closed over 50 finance companies, nationalised four failing banks, and opened the financial industry to foreigners. These government actions were followed by an announcement that Bangchak Petroleum, Thai Airways International and the Electricity Generating Authority of Thailand were scheduled to be at least partially privatised. Not surprisingly, this led to opposition from labour. Meanwhile, the Asian Development Bank led a consortium of banks which lent $1 billion to Thai exporters.

In 1998, the Royal Thai Cabinet approved the Industrial Restructuring Master Plan, prepared by the Ministry of Industry. This involved strategies to: (i) move towards production of higher value-added products for middle-to-higher markets with higher quality standards by upgrading technology and quality management and developing product designs in line with market

Exhibit 16.11   Distribution Channels; photo ©2006 Leo Paul DANA

Exhibit 16.12   A Promising Future; photo ©2006 Leo Paul DANA

preferences; (ii) improve efficiency in terms of production costs, streamline production processes and improve delivery and quick response, (iii) create production and trading alliances to enhance technology transfer and expand marketing channels; (iv) reduce industrial pollution; (v) disperse industrial employment to regional and rural areas; and (vi) upgrade the knowledge and skills of the industrial workforce.[73]

The National Economic and Social Development Bureau, which is the economic planning body of Thailand, prepared a privatisation plan, to shift economic functions from the state to private enterprises. The Council of Economic Ministers of the Royal Thai Government endorsed this plan, promising a bright future for entrepreneurs in Thailand.

To help farmers earn supplementary income during economic downturns, the Bangsai Arts and Crafts Centre brings together local volunteers and individuals from various educational institutions to teach artistic skills. The objective is for Thai farmers to have a secondary occupation to fall back on, in case of need.

---

[73] Source: Mr. Manu Leopairote, Director-General, Department of Industrial Promotion, Ministry of Industry, Royal Thai Government.

Foreign Assistance for Entrepreneurs

In addition to enjoying an enterprise-friendly public policy, which has been supportive of entrepreneurship, Thai entrepreneurs have long benefited from a variety of foreign aid programmes. It was mentioned earlier that the Small Industry Service Institute was founded in 1966.

With financial assistance from the International Labour Organisation and from the United Nations Special Fund, the Small Industries Service Institute evolved into the Industrial Services Division of the Ministry of Industry's Department of Industrial Promotion. Initially, its scope was to modernise small-scale industries across the board; by the 1990s its mandate was to focus on enterprises in specific sectors, regardless of firm size.

The Industrial Services Division was organised into three sub-divisions, namely (i) the Furniture Industry Sub-Division; (ii) the Miscellaneous Industries Sub-Division; and (iii) the Design Promotion Sub-Division. This allowed the Division to allocate its resources across six industrial sectors: (i) furniture; (ii) agro-industry; (iii) jewellery; (iv) packaging; (v) toys; and (vi) industrial design. These sectors were selected because they were "particularly beneficial" to the industrial and economic development of the nation.

Entrepreneurs and potential entrepreneurs interested in the above sectors are entitled to a wide range of services from the Industrial Services Division. These include training courses, seminars, exhibitions, technology, acquisition, product testing, analysis, design promotion, consultancy and industrial studies.

Another important contributor has been the International Fund for Agricultural Development, which began making loans and giving grants to self-employed small-scale farmers in Thailand, in 1978. Earning its reputation as the "rice bowl" of Asia, Thailand has become an important exporter of food. Principal crops include cassava, kenaf, maize, rice and rubber.

Individual nations have also made contributions. The Canadian International Development Assistance (CIDA) programme, for example, established the Small and Medium Enterprise (SME) Project to support the growth of SMEs in north-eastern Thailand. This programme has included the provision of credit as well as advisory services. The SME Project has been administered through the Royal Thai Department of Industrial Promotion.

CIDA also designed the Northeast Fisheries Project, to assist small-scale fishing operations. In addition, CIDA funded a community-based Integrated Rural Development project, helping small-scale farmers and cottage industries. Finally, CIDA launched the Enterprise Collaboration Project, aimed to support joint ventures between Canadian and Thai entrepreneurs.

Chinese Entrepreneurs

Chinese traders have long been active in Thailand. This is especially so in Bangkok, the nation's main port. Two groups of ethnic-Chinese became prominent — the Hokkiens and the Teochews. The former spoke Minnanhua — a dialect from Fujian Province — while the latter spoke Chaozhouhua — a dialect from Guang Dong Province. Hokkiens found employment as tax collectors for the royal family, during the 18th century. Teochews became entrepreneurs.

Throughout the 20th century, more ethnic-Chinese entrepreneurs migrated to Thailand, and became prominent in business. Whereas religious and cultural differences prevented the Chinese from assimilating smoothly into Muslim countries, this was not the case in Thailand. A common religion (Buddhism) and the lack of discrimination helped them blend into Thai society. Unlike Burma, Indonesia, Malaysia and Vietnam, Thailand never favoured its Indigenous people at the expense of the ethnic-Chinese community. As explained by respondents interviewed by the author, "We don't feel any different whether they are Thai or Chinese." Thailand's tolerance of entrepreneurship, in its Chinese community, contributed to a healthy national economy. In 1999, 14% of Thailand's population was Chinese, and ethnic-Chinese entrepreneurs controlled 90% of manufacturing in Thailand (Yeung, 1999).

Through marriage to Thai women, Chinese men integrated well into their host society, and it became fashionable to adopt Thai names. Barth (1981) argued that when two groups interact, they begin sharing values. In the case of Thailand, although the government limited the number of Chinese schools, the community preserved its cultural values, a desire for education and its diligent work ethic. Silcock (1967) described the Chinese of Thailand as the "Jews of the East." Thailand also has a community of Jews, many of them entrepreneurs.

The most powerful Chinese family used to be the Tejapaibul family, owners of a banking, distilling and real estate empire. Chin Sophonpanich, owner of hospitals and plantations and father of the Bangkok Bank, was a prominent leader of the Chinese community in Bangkok, until his death in 1988. Also among the prominent ethnic-Chinese entrepreneurs, in Thailand, is Chan Ratanarak.

Chan Ratanarak was born in China in 1920, and was brought to Thailand by his parents, in 1926. In 1945, he was still a wage-worker at the port of Bangkok. He then established his own firm, loading sea vessels. In time, he progressed to banking and manufacturing, as did numerous ethnic-Chinese entrepreneurs in Thailand. By the 1990s, he controlled the Bank of Ayudhya and Siam City Cement.

Other important families of Chinese entrepreneurs in Thailand include the Chearavanonts, the Chokwatanas and the Shinawatras. The Chearavanonts established the Charoen Pokphand (CP) group. This involved animal feed, petrochemicals and a joint venture with British Telecom. Thiam Chokwatana started out with one shop in 1942. This evolved into the Saha Pathana group, including 60 companies producing a variety of goods from clothing to detergents. Although a third of these came to be listed on the stock market, each of Chokwatana's sons has kept control of at least one listed corporation. The family business proved to be very successful, despite competition from Colgate, Procter & Gamble, and Unilever. Thaksin Shinawatra, an ethnic-Chinese from Chiang Mai, started out as a distributor of IBM computers. He later set up a cable-television network and then decided to establish his own cellular telephone operation.

More than half of Bangkok's seven million people have Chinese blood, and they tend to be active in entrepreneurship. They are involved in a wide range of activities, from manufacturing to retailing. Some are bakers. Others are self-employed astrologers and palmists, respected occupations in this superstitious society. Entrepreneurs in Bangkok's Chinatown sell cloth, gold and noodles.

In addition, hundreds of entrepreneurs from Taiwan have been contributing to foreign direct investment across Thailand. There are about eight million ethnic-Chinese in Thailand. Although they comprise only 14% of Thailand's population, they control four fifths of the market capital in Thailand. Fifty-six percent of them are Teochew.

Women Entrepreneurs

Although Thai women are often portrayed as being subservient to men, Thai culture fosters a relatively egalitarian status for men and women. According to the culture, both genders are equally important.

Traditionally, Thai women have had leadership roles in community health, education and earning family income. More recently, women have become very visible in Thailand's entrepreneurship sector. Many are owner-managers of small firms; others own enterprises which have grown into larger-scale businesses.

One woman entrepreneur owns a golf course. Another — this one from Chiang Mai — operates a large antique business. Women operate a bus company in Bangkok, along with a fleet of ferryboats.

Toward the Future

Several development plans have recognised the potential of entrepreneurs; yet, programmes to foster entrepreneurship have been over-shadowed by politics encouraging multinationals. In some cases, this has been at the expense of local entrepreneurship.

During the latter decades of the 20th century, Thailand became an export base for multinationals, which enjoyed low labour costs in an open economy. However, little was done to supply these corporations from within Thailand. Therefore, much production activity was little more than assembly work.

The Thai government's vision is to make Thailand a knowledge-based society through entrepreneurship and innovation by 2010. In the 21st century, the use of local suppliers will increase cost-effectiveness for multinationals, while allowing local entrepreneurship to play an increasingly vital role in the Thai economy. The regional economy will also contribute to entrepreneurship in Thailand. Already, Thai entrepreneurs have been engaging in business with Laos and Myanmar. To further shape an enterprising culture, the state should increase emphasis on entrepreneurship education.

Chapter 17

Vietnam[74]

Introduction

The Socialist Republic of Vietnam covers 329,560 square kilometres. With shores on the Eastern Sea — also known as the South China Sea — the country borders Cambodia, Laos and China.

Until the 1980s, Vietnam had an economic policy that conformed to the command system. Leaders at the national level made centralised decisions about local production, often without knowledge of local conditions. Produce raised or goods manufactured in one locality were shipped to the central level and then distributed back to the localities, creating huge inefficiencies and losses, due to mould, rats and slippage. Manufacturing was very limited because the French colonialists had concentrated on extracting raw materials and emphasised neither industry nor infrastructure. Manufacturing equipment was old and rusty. In addition, the US-led embargo that started in 1964, prevented people and firms in Vietnam from legally replacing industrial parts patented in the United States. In late 1986, Vietnam launched its *Doi-Moi* Model — literally meaning "renovation" — laying the path to a free-market economy.

---

[74]This chapter is based on information obtained from a variety of sources, including: the Central Bureau of Statistics; the Committee of Foreign Economic Affairs; the Export Development Trading Corporation; the Foreign Trade Development Centre; the Ministry of Commerce; the Ministry of Industry; and the Planning and Trading Department of Artex-Saigon. Travel to Vietnam was provided by McGill University. The chapter includes material that first appeared in Dana (1994a; 1994b; 1994c; 1999b; 2002), and benefited greatly from the personal assistance of Lady Borton, Field Director, American Friends Service Committee, in Hanoi.

Exhibit 17.1   Near the Border with China; photo ©2006 Leo Paul DANA

Exhibit 17.2   French Colonial Architecture; photo ©2006 Leo Paul DANA

Under the command economy, farming had been done through farm co-operatives. These were privatised in 1988, with the land divided among families of the community. The result was a stunning surge in productivity; farmers who had once lolled about on their production teams worked their own fields from "dew to dew." Within a year, Vietnam began to export rice; by 1989, villagers and city people were no longer gaunt. Up to 1990, most trade was with socialist block countries. Until the late 1980s, the state-supported currency differed widely with the real market value, and this led to a parallel rate.

Since Vietnam had never been an industrial country, the government concentrated its efforts on agricultural development, the rural economy and the domestic market. Thus, the great changes of *Doi-Moi* took place first in the agricultural sector.

Economic policy in Vietnam has been aimed at creating a market economy. In the attempt to ensure domestic growth, the Socialist Republic of Vietnam implemented a drastic programme of economic reform. Those regulations, which formerly limited the private sector, have been substantially

Exhibit 17.3   Training on the Job; photo ©2006 Leo Paul DANA

reduced and Vietnam has moved away from being a very highly centralised command economy. By the end of July 1995, Vietnam had joined ASEAN, signed a treaty with the European Union, and established normalised diplomatic relations with the United States. Smith-Hunter (2006) noted that only 20% of women entrepreneurs in Vietnam receive training, compared to nearly a half of their male counterparts.

Historical Overview

Tonkin, the northern part of today's Vietnam, was originally inhabited by different ethnic groups with the Viet predominating. It was conquered by the Chinese in 111 BC and became a province of the Chinese Empire. Further south was the Kingdom of Champa, founded in the 3rd century. It eventually came to be under the control of the Viet peoples, as they expanded from the north. After a lengthy civil war, the Vietnamese kingdom was split into two in 1660, when the Nguyen family established their own separate kingdom. The extreme south of Vietnam, known as Cochin-China, remained under Khmer rule until a century later. Finally, the whole of Vietnam was unified in 1802, by the Nguyen dynasty. Its capital was Hué.

The people of the north are of a Sino-Tibetan race that has strong Han influences, from many years of Chinese domination; the people of the south tend to have been exposed to slightly more Dionysian and fewer Promethean values. While the people of the north adopted a northern sect of Buddhism, those of Cochin-China included followers of a southern sect, with some Hindu influence.

In 1859, in order to protect persecuted Catholic missionaries and their economic interests in the region, France invaded the south. In 1867, Cochin-China became a colony. In 1885, France established a protectorate over Tonkin and to the south. Hence, France controlled all of today's Vietnam, which it grouped with Cambodia and Laos to create a new entity called *Indochine française* — French Indochina. In 1887, Hanoi became the seat of the French colonial government. Many resented French rule, and Confucian scholars led some of the earliest revolutionary movements. Particularly famous is Phan Boi Chau, whose "Go East Movement" sent young revolutionaries to study in

Exhibit 17.4   Proud to Be Vietnamese; photo ©2006 Leo Paul DANA

Japan. One candidate decided to go west instead; Nguyen Tat Thanh, later known as Ho Chi Minh — Ho the Enlightened — left Sai Gon (later Saigon) in 1911 on a French steamer, on which he worked as a cook's assistant. In February 1930, using the name Nguyen Ai Quoc, i.e., Nguyen the Patriot, he got together with other revolutionaries in Hong Kong, where they established the Indochinese Communist Party, with the hope of overthrowing the French colonial administration. In the fall of 1940, Japan invaded, but the Japanese kept the French administration in place.

Ho Chi Minh returned to the region in early 1941, and lived in a cave in Pac Bo, in Cao Pang Province, on the Vietnamese side of the Chinese border. In 1941, he drew together competing nationalist factions to form the *Viet Nam Doc Loc Dong Minh Hoi* (League for the Independence of Viet Nam), known as the Viet Minh. When the Japanese army confiscated rice from Vietnamese peasants, two million Vietnamese people starved to death (Dinh, 1989).

On August 16, 1945, within days of the Nagasaki bombing, Viet Minh gathered at Tan Trao, in the northern highlands, where they planned the August

Revolution; on August 19, they seized key buildings. On August 25, Emperor Bao Dai yielded to the Viet Minh in Hué. After the revolution, Ho Chi Minh entered Hanoi and wrote the *Declaration of Independence* while hidden in the second floor of an import-export company. The declaration was read before 500,000 people in Hanoi, on September 2, 1945. Ho Chi Minh declared himself president of a newly independent country, but his government faced huge challenges. Only 5% of the population was literate. In accordance with the Potsdam Conference Agreements, Nationalist Chinese occupied Hanoi along with French troops.

Less than three weeks after the declaration of independence, the French landed again in the south, taking over Saigon and regaining control of its former colony of Cochin-China. The Associated States of Viet Nam — formerly Tonkin, Annam, and Cochin-China — became a member of the French Union. The spirit of entrepreneurship thrived, and the nation welcomed refugees from communist China. Long described the sidewalks of Saigon:

> Barbers hang mirrors on trees, unfold stools, and are ready for business. Dentists pull teeth and fit gold replacements before admiring audiences. Physicians cup and massage their patients. Herbalists hawk bottled cure-alls, and fortune-tellers feel heads, measure palms, and divine the future. Squatting vendors sell anything from American cigarettes to lottery tickets and incense sticks (1952, p. 289).

Following their defeat at Dien Bien Phu, in 1954, the French were expelled from the region. The cease-fire of July 22, 1954 led to an armistice agreement, in Geneva, creating the Democratic Republic of Vietnam — North Vietnam — north of the Ben Hai River, and the Republic of Vietnam — South Vietnam — to its south. Small-scale land-owners and Catholics fled from the north to the south. Samuels (1955) reported that about forty civilians moved from the south to the north; interviewees suggest that there were many more who went north for regrouping, expecting to return home after elections that were scheduled to take place in 1956. However, according to Eisenhower's memoirs, the United States disallowed the elections, for fear that Ho Chi Minh would win.

According to the Geneva Agreement, the Viet Minh took control of Hanoi on October 10, 1954, and of Hai Duong on October 30. Hanoi, formerly the administrative capital of Indochina, became the capital of North Vietnam. Saigon became the capital of South Vietnam. At the suggestion of Cardinal Spellman, Ngo Dinh Diem — who had been living in the United States for over three years — was brought back to Saigon to lead the government of the South. In North Vietnam, the government — led by Ho Chi Minh — instituted a programme of land reform. The First Five-Year Plan, 1961-1965, put emphasis on basic heavy industries.

Only in South Vietnam could the spirit of entrepreneurship survive — but not for long. The Viet Cong — South Vietnamese who sympathised with the North — fought a civil war, with weapons and leadership from communist North Vietnam and "their inspiration from Peking or Moscow... From dusk to dawn, the Viet Cong ruled nearly half of Viet Nam (White, 1961b, p. 447)." During the war, Sochurek reported, "Despite 30 guards to a train, Viet Cong guerrillas take a fearful toll: Mines and ambushes have killed or

Exhibit 17.5   Coal; photo ©2006 Leo Paul DANA

injured hundreds of passengers, railroad employees, and soldiers, and have wrecked scores of cars and engines (1964, p. 414)." By 1967, more Americans had died in Vietnam than in the American Revolution of 1776 (White, 1967).

By 1975, South Vietnam, which had formerly been a rice exporter, was living off daily airlifts of rice from Louisiana. This major source of food ceased in April 1975, when the communists took over. The United States extended its embargo to the entire country. The following year saw the creation of the Socialist Republic of Vietnam. With the new regime came a shortage of foreign exchange, resulting in a shortage of imported inputs, new materials and spare parts. This led to under-utilisation of capacity, while domestic supply could not satisfy consumer demand. Further constraints in capacity utilisation were brought about by shortages in energy production and a weak transportation network, which received minimal maintenance and had seen virtually no improvements since the departure of the French. Furthermore, state firms in Vietnam lacked access to modern technology. Their costs of production were high, relative to the quality of products, which tended to be low by international standards. All firms were nationalised. Government newspapers replaced the existing dailies. Private homes were raided and "decadent" literature was burned. Schools of bourgeois learning were closed, as Hanoi spread its Marxist ideology.

With reunification, all bank accounts in former South Vietnam were frozen, and its people were told they had twelve hours to take their cash to the banks, as the South Vietnamese currency would become valueless. Henceforth, all of Vietnam would have one currency, but each family was limited to a maximum saving, the equivalent of approximately $200.

Chinh gave his rendition of the fourth national congress of the Communist Party of Vietnam:

> The State of the Socialist Republic of Vietnam is a proletarian dictatorship state. On the one hand, it represses counter-revolutionaries, eliminates the comprador capitalist class and the remnants of the feudal landlord class, carries out socialist transformation of the. . . private capitalist economic element; at the same time it effects the socialist transformation of the private economic section. . . (1977, p. 1).

Toward the Doi-Moi *Model*

The Second Five-Year Plan (1976–1980) set a 16–18% targeted annual growth rate for industrial production; actual outcome was 0.6%. In 1978, the Sino-Vietnamese War prompted an exodus of ethnic Chinese from Vietnam. In 1979 and 1980 there were shortages of basic consumer goods including food, as well as shortages of inputs to the industrial sector.

It was liberalisation, in 1981, which helped industrial output to grow an average in excess of 9% during the period of the Third Five-Year Plan (1981–1985). Growth was primarily generated by small and medium-sized enterprises, some in the private sector. The Three-Plan System, introduced in 1981, made this possible:

(i) Plan A: Enterprises operating under this scheme were required to produce using state-supplied inputs and to sell their outputs to the state at low command prices.

(ii) Plan B: This scheme permitted firms to acquire inputs on their own, and to sell their outputs independently, provided that the profits were used to purchase additional inputs.

(iii) Plan C: This scheme permitted entrepreneurs to diversify and to sell "minor" products with no centrally planned external control.

In 1982, the Fifth Party Congress officially adopted its new economic orientation, recognising the need to: shift emphasis from heavy to light industry; transfer resources to the agricultural sector; and promote exports. As production activities were partially deregulated, individual enterprises were granted some autonomy. In 1984, the government further relaxed restrictions.

When a new currency was introduced, in 1985, old dong were exchanged at a rate of 10:1, but only up to a set quantity. Also in 1985, consumer price subsidies were replaced by wage adjustments. Most prices remained under central control, determined by an average cost-plus formula; however, some costs were not accurately assessed.

The nation's economic development followed an import substitution model. Industrial policy in Vietnam was influenced by that of the former Soviet Union. Centrally planned industrialisation was aimed at the domestic

Exhibit 17.6   Self-sufficient; photo ©2006 Leo Paul DANA

production of heavy industry such as capital goods. The state supplied the input and capital requirements of enterprises and set quantitative output targets. Policy typically leaned towards achieving self-sufficiency, but neglected opportunities for international trade.

Coupled with fighting and the embargo, the command economy led to desperate poverty. The attempt to be self-sufficient had led to insufficient specialisation. Investment had been scattered over too many projects, in a haphazard fashion. Despite vertical integration, there was a lack of horizontal integration. Entrepreneurship was restricted by regulation coupled with excessive bureaucratic centralisation. Innovation and creativity were stifled. Research, science and technology for industry were weak. Energy supplies were lacking. Export-oriented activities were not being given enough attention and there were insufficient links between foreign markets and Vietnamese producers, the latter lacking awareness about international quality, prices and demands. There was more incentive for a farmer to chop down a mango tree and use it for firewood than to harvest the fruit. Aggravating the situation for producers in

Vietnam, there were constant limitations on capital resources and raw material supplies, especially imported ones. Construction periods were typically overrun and numerous projects remained unfinished. Reform or more specifically "renovation" became a necessity.

Major change was introduced towards the end of December 1986, when the Sixth Congress of the National Representatives of the Communist Party of Vietnam approved economic reforms that eliminated much of the basic apparatus of control. This programme was called *Doi-Moi*. Individual entrepreneurs obtained the right to get involved in light industry. Profits were defined as the difference between the value of sales and *allowable* costs; enterprises remained liable for taxes on profits. Restrictions on wages were abolished and firms were given the right to recruit as per their needs.

In contrast to the experiences in Eastern Europe and in the former Soviet Union — where a market economy was decreed to have replaced communism without a long transition period — *Doi-Moi* evolved slowly and gradually, ushering in entrepreneurship initially as a *complement* to state enterprise, rather than as a *replacement*. The *Doi-Moi* Model marked the path to: transition to a market economy; openness to the West; openness to overseas Vietnamese (Viet Kieu); and greater personal freedom. In 1988, the state divided huge co-operative farms into private holdings, releasing private initiative.

In July 1988, the Resolution of New Regulation for the Non-State Economic Sector called for making entrepreneurs important components of the national economy. On September 5, 1988, the Council of Ministries adopted Decree 139, regulating the implementation of the Law on Foreign Investment in Vietnam; this set forth procedures relating to foreign investment and the corresponding tax structure. In the case of a joint venture, the foreign party usually contributes capital and technology.

A further breakthrough in the reintroduction of market-oriented policies followed in 1989, when the predominantly rural population was granted the right to sell output at market prices; furthermore, this right could be inherited. Whereas Vietnam had been near starvation prior to this reform, the nation soon became the world's third largest rice exporter. Without abandoning Marxist ideals, young intellectuals came to the conclusion that a market economy with a private small business sector and entrepreneurship is the quickest means to

Exhibit 17.7   Private Initiative; photo ©2006 Leo Paul DANA

attain the benefits sought out by socialism. The result has been a unique blend of socialist and free enterprise policies whereby the entrepreneur is the agent for social change as described by Barth (1963; 1967), but in a socialist state, i.e., the government affirmed its commitment to socialism. New billboards began to promote *Doi-Moi*, while others continued urging workers to follow socialism.

Most prices in Vietnam were released from centralised control, in 1989. Exceptions were electricity, petrol and transport. This policy enabled entrepreneurs and the small business sector to begin setting prices as a function of market forces, while keeping energy and transportation costs artificially low, thus indirectly subsidising entrepreneurship. That same year, the State Committee for Co-operation and Investment was established, as the body responsible for foreign direct investment and for providing guidance to foreign entrepreneurs. Taiwanese entrepreneurs were among the first to arrive in Vietnam *en masse*, and Singaporeans soon followed.

In 1990, the Ministry for External Economic Relations was absorbed into the Ministry of Commerce. The former had already issued about 100 permits to provincial and local enterprises — and a similar amount to central government firms — permitting them to export directly and allowing them to keep a substantial proportion of the foreign exchange earned. Also in 1990, the Council of Non-State Enterprises was established, specifically to promote the interests of the private sector. Very significant was Decree 28, adopted by the National Assembly on June 30, 1990. The new legislation was named the "Law on Amendments and Additions to a Number of Articles of the Law on Foreign Investment in Vietnam."

Towns and cities sprouted into a plethora of street stalls, restaurants and hotels; by late 1990, Hanoi had a reliable telephone system. Motorcycles, taxis and private cars competed for space. Formerly quiet towns became bustling cities.

Relaxation of regulations made it possible for foreign entrepreneurs to hold 100% of the equity of a business in Vietnam. The Law of Foreign Investment was enacted to protect assets of foreign enterprises from nationalisation. Legislation also made new foreign-owned ventures income-tax exempt for the first four years of operations.

As the law stands, today, foreign direct investment in Vietnam cannot be expropriated or requisitioned by administrative procedure. Investors have complained, nevertheless, as legislation regarding foreigners in Vietnam is open to interpretation, and differences in opinion have caused problems in recent years.

As well, foreign entrepreneurs operating in Vietnam were given the right to remit profits abroad as well as to remit payments abroad for the provision of technology, services and loans. In contrast to China, where only foreign exchange profits could be remitted abroad, Vietnam had no foreign exchange restrictions at the time. Therefore, according to Article 86 of the Foreign Investment Law, profits earned in Vietnam could be converted into hard currency at the Bank of Foreign Trade. These funds could then be repatriated, according to Article 87.

With Decision 25-CP, on January 21, 1991, Vietnam established that all enterprises belonging to the socialist state would develop plans directed by the market. Between June 24 and June 27, 1991, the Seventh Congress of the National Representatives of the Communist Party of Vietnam — also known as the Seventh Party Congress — reaffirmed its commitment to *Doi-Moi*,

Exhibit 17.8   No Longer Quiet; photo ©2006 Leo Paul DANA

showing support for economic reform, while maintaining political stability was held. On the agenda were concerns such as:

> serious inflation; unstable production; increasing unemployment; wages and salaries below subsistence level. . . widespread corruption and other evils. . . an erosion of cultural, spiritual and moral values; and declining confidence in the Party and the State (Communist Party of Vietnam, 1991, p. 150).

Confirming the leading role of the Communist Party of Vietnam, and its adherence to Marxist-Leninism, the Seventh Party Congress renewed the strategy of *Doi-Moi*:

> The overall objectives of this strategy up to the year 2000 are to emerge from crisis, stabilise the socio-economic situation, strive to overcome the condition of poverty and underemployment, improve living conditions for the country to develop more rapidly in the early 21st century. Gross domestic product by the year 2000

will be double of that of 1990 (Communist Party of Vietnam, 1991, p. 157).

In 1991, the Viet Kieu community, numbering 700,000 in the United States alone, contributed approximately $500 million to the Vietnamese economy. In 1992, the Labour Ministry announced a new reform aimed at encouraging new jobs. The minimum wage for employees of foreign firms was *reduced* to $30 monthly. That year, the government began the process of privatising state enterprises. The first to be offered to the private sector was the Legamex garment factory, run by Ms. Nguyen Thi Son in Ho Chi Minh City. This firm exported 1,700,000 jackets to Germany in 1992. The embargo still in effect at the time, entrepreneurs ordered clothing in Hanoi, shipped them to South Korea where South Korean labels were put on them, and re-exported to the United States under their quota.

A tight economic policy succeeded in reducing inflation from over 700% in 1986, to 70% in 1990, 68% in 1991, 18% in 1992 and about 10% in 1993. Per capita GDP in 1992 was $125. In 1994, the United States dropped its trade embargo, and American companies rushed into Vietnam (Dana, 1997a). Per capita income jumped from $190 in 1994, to $275 the following year.

In July 1995, Vietnam became the seventh member of ASEAN. Also in 1995, the National Assembly adopted a new Civil Code, which laid the foundation for a market economy. That same year, import duties of 60% were reduced.

A government resolution, on October 21, 1995, established the Ministry of Planning and Investment. One of 23 ministerial-level offices in Vietnam, it is responsible for decisions, strategy, and plans to develop the national economy.

The Eighth Congress of the Representatives of the Communist Party of Vietnam took place in June 1996. The 1996–2000 Plan called for $21 billion, in foreign investment, to complement an equal amount in local investments.

In 1997, Vietnam's exports grew by 24%, while inflation was 4%. Although the Vietnamese dong depreciated by about 20% compared to the dollar, exports grew by only 3.5% between January and October 1998. Inflation approached 10%. The Asian Crisis had hit Vietnam, and this was of concern because 70% of Vietnam's exports depended on neighbours in the region (Rondinelli and Litvack, 1999).

Exhibit 17.9   Ice for Those with No Refrigerator; photo ©2006 Leo Paul DANA

The state's Central Committee convened in October 1998, to outline a new strategy. In contrast to policy that had, in recent years, designated entrepreneurs as economic engines of growth, the Central Committee decided that state-owned enterprises would lead the Vietnamese economy, giving priority to the local market. The state was neither rushed to privatise state firms, nor to reform the almost obsolete banking sector. Instead, the government decided to focus its efforts, during 1999, on agricultural development, the rural economy and the domestic market. In April 2001, the Ninth Congress initiated further reforms.

Infrastructure

In 1989, Hanoi's electrical system still fluctuated between 80 and 360 volts, and there was not yet a reliable domestic telephone system. Most Vietnamese had yet to see a computer or a photocopier. Because of the embargo, the banking system could handle few transfers; funds were routed via Laos. The state-owned banks favoured state-owned firms.

Exhibit 17.10   Cash City; photo ©2006 Leo Paul DANA

A commercial banking decree, "Decree on Banks, Credit Co-operative and Financial Companies," was promulgated by the Council of Ministers in May 1990. This edict set forth conditions and procedures for establishing commercial banking in Vietnam.

In July 1992, Banque Indosuez of France and Bangkok Bank of Thailand became the first two foreign banks to open branches in Ho Chi Minh City. By 1993, the ANZ Bank had a branch in Hanoi as well as a representative office in Ho Chi Minh City. Other banks, which were quick to enter Vietnam, included Banque Nationale de Paris, Credit Lyonais, Nord-banke, and the Export-Import Bank of Japan. Thus, the banking infrastructure began taking shape and commercial credit slowly began to evolve. Yet, personal cheques for domestic accounts were still unheard of, and most entrepreneurs paid their employees in cash. With the dollar worth over 10,000 dong, and 200-dong notes being common, cash transactions were sometimes bulky.

Meanwhile, foreign banks expressed their concerns: they could only repatriate 30% of their capital, and they were not given the three-year tax holiday granted to foreign entrepreneurs. Furthermore, there was a high tax structure for banks: 50% income tax as well as a turnover tax of 4 to 15%.

By 2002, a plentiful and reliable source of electricity made possible many developments. Computer literacy had long surged with personal computers in urban households and neighbourhood Internet cafés offering affordable rates. International organisations, businesses and foreigners used standard bank transfers. Most international organisations transferred salary payments directly into the private bank accounts of staff.

The Impact of the Doi-Moi *Model*

Vietnam's model of economic transition has been stunning; it is quite a unique model, as it has achieved a harmony between government firms still operating under a system of centralisation, and the small business sector operating independently, yet having access to state alternatives as specified by Resolution No. 16. Whereas transition from centralised planning to market economy in the Soviet bloc was very abrupt and economic reform in Yugoslavia very violent (Dana, 1994d; 2005), the *Doi-Moi* Model of evolutionary change introduced a gradual and smooth transition in Vietnam. Private enterprise is thriving side by side a state-controlled sector.

While many co-operatives have been privatised, most of those still in existence are small to medium-sized businesses. As well, there are countless micro-enterprises in the handicraft and agriculture sectors. The small business sector, including handicrafts as well as small industry, accounts for a significant part of industrial production and exports. Current exports include: bamboo products, bicycle tires and tubes, cotton yarn, glass products, handicrafts, processed forestry products, rubber gloves, and silk yarn.

As a result of *Doi-Moi*, the small business sector in the Socialist Republic of Vietnam now includes co-operatives; family businesses; other private enterprises; and joint ventures between state and private interests. The first three operate free from state control; in the fourth, government influence is limited to contractual agreement.

Although the Socialist Republic of Vietnam has chosen to *retain* socialist ideals, to the ethnographer, Vietnam appears to be thriving more on free enterprise than on Marxist ideology. There is a constant buzz of mercantile energy. Entrepreneurs optimise the use of their minimal resources.

Exhibit 17.11 Micro-enterprise; photo ©2006 Leo Paul DANA

The spirit of entrepreneurship is in the air, even at the subsistence level. One villa advertises — with a spelling mistake — "Telex Coffee Dansing Massage." Not far, a man sits by the roadside with a pump and fills tires, while another rents out the use of a scale. A coconut stand is never very far away, offering fresh coconut water.

In Ho Chi Minh City, one is overwhelmed by entrepreneurial activity; even children sell a variety of merchandise, including pocket video games, T-shirts, cigarettes, fans, money from French Indochina, and stamp collections. The young peddlers follow their prospective clients, for blocks on end, in an attempt to sell their goods.

Nearby, one shed is a pancake restaurant when it is not being used as a bus depot. "Mr. Fix-It" earns his living by selling a wide variety of inventory, ranging from motorcycles and caviar to tiger skins. Not far, a woman sits on the sidewalk, feathering ducks. A man unloads fresh pork from a wooden container onto the street. Nearby, fish are being laid out in tidy rows; some of the fish are still flopping on the merciless, hot pavement.

At the market, items for sale include bananas, coconuts, dragon fruits, grapes, guavas, mint leaves, oranges, papayas, pineapples, and jeruk — green

Exhibit 17.12   Rich with Entrepreneurial Spirit; photo ©2006 Leo Paul DANA

pomelos sweeter and larger than grapefruit. Chicken, duck, fish, and pork are sold alive or dead, or in between. Also for sale is a mixture of green peas, coconut and cane sugar wrapped in palm leaves fashioned into tiny boxes held together by bamboo toothpicks.

Self-employed vendors sell food to passengers on state-run trains. While some children run along the aisles fanning passengers. Others sell sodas; they open the bottles with their teeth.

Wherever the train stops in the morning, locals have washcloths for rent as well as buckets of water for passengers to refresh themselves. Through the windows of the train, merchants sell bread, coconut water, fruit, juice, pastries, and sodas.

Blind musicians come on board the train to sing or play a melody, while an assistant usually holds out a cap for donations. Simultaneously, one may buy a chicken breast with rice cooked in chicken fat, served on a palm leaf, and eaten with one's fingers. Other passengers prefer to crunch a raw, fertilised duck egg, just prior to hatching, feathers, bones and all, lightly salted. Still other passengers enjoy having a local cook board the train and flame a fish at their seat.

Exhibit 17.13   Time to Enjoy; photo ©2006 Leo Paul DANA

A glance out of the open window supplies passengers with constant stimulus. Catholic churches line the railway tracks side by side with Buddhist temples still in use. Farmers in rice fields, with water buffaloes as tractors, work their land in utter peacefulness while but a few kilometres away remnants of a bloody war fill the landscape. Graves with crosses, and graves with dragons adorning them dot the landscape, all with the hatred of war still hanging about them.

Some people live a few feet from the railroad tracks in shacks with no kitchen, toilet or running water. Subtle hands reach into the passenger compartment of the train. Others sling a hammock under the railway cars and alight where they choose, while still others enjoy a warm breeze sitting on top of the wagons as clandestine passengers.

In Hoi-an, an untouched heritage site, the market is the life of the town. For sale at the market are *chuoi tieu*, a variety of bananas with an attractive colour and taste. A few minutes away, peaceful serenity reigns. Lining the

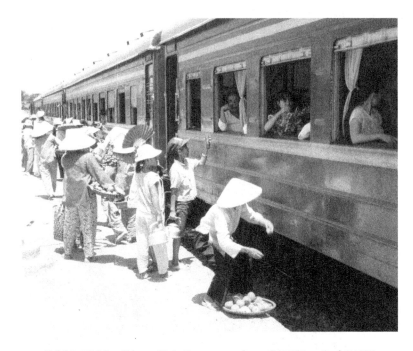

Exhibit 17.14   Sales to Train Passengers; photo ©2006 Leo Paul DANA

waterfront are storefronts untouched for 200 years or more and buildings inscribed with Chinese characters dating back to the era prior to French rule.

Along the road to Hanoi — in addition to modern petrol stations — stalls display one-litre *Coca-Cola* bottles filled with kerosene or petrol for sale. Others sell fuel for cigarette lighters.

Every day, 50,000 peddlers transport their goods between Vietnam and China. Micro-enterprises involve exporters piggybacking freight. Women, less expensive porters than are mules, many carry wicker baskets, each balanced at the end of a pole leaning across the shoulders. In the baskets are cats and dogs destined for Chinese dinner tables.

Pluralism

Ever since the French era, the Hoa — a significant ethnic Chinese minority — were very active in the small business sector of Vietnam; the French — not wanting to deal directly with those they had colonised — encouraged the Hoa to serve as "middleman" entrepreneurs in the region, and these continued to dominate sectors of the economy even after 1954. Auster and Aldrich (1984), Bonacich (1973), Cherry (1990), Dana (1997b), and Loewen (1971) discuss middleman entrepreneurship.

The Chinese in Vietnam — of whom 57% are Cantonese — comprise about 3% of this country's population, but they control a disproportionate percentage of the local economy. Cho Lon — the Chinatown of Ho Chi Minh City — was founded by Chinese immigrants in the 18th century, and the settlement was fused into Saigon in 1932 (Long, 1952). With the exception of scooters, there are relatively few motor vehicles, so *cyclos* can weave their way through traffic. En route, one encounters motorcycles bound for market, carrying bunches of ducks and chickens. Feathers seem to appear everywhere. On many street corners, food is served, including rice soup, fish, duck, chicken, pork, vegetables and coconut paste. Most dishes are served in re-used plastic bowls, not necessarily washed between users.

Most people in Vietnam are Buddhists, Confucians or Taoists. During colonial rule, the French converted 1,600,000 Vietnamese to Catholicism and many of these fled from the north to the south, in 1954 and 1955 (Samuels, 1955).

Toward the Future

In 1952, George W. Long, writing for *National Geographic*, noted a young lieutenant in Vietnam raising his glass and saying: "To our American visitors. I hope they will return someday. And when they do, I hope they will find this country happy, prosperous, and at peace (Long, 1952, p. 328)."

Half a century later, Vietnam is at peace, its people appear happy, and prosperity is spreading. The Vietnam-US Bilateral Trade Agreement established guarantees against expropriation, and mechanisms for dispute resolution. Yet, there is still some concern about property rights.

As discussed by Dollar (1999), it would be misleading to think of Vietnam as having state-sector households distinct from private-enterprise households. Instead, it is common for employees of the state to supplement their incomes with self-employment. Although large state enterprises may be inefficient, people in Vietnam demonstrate a strong work ethic. In contrast to China,

Exhibit 17.15   Strong Work Ethic; photo ©2006 Leo Paul DANA

where individuals dare speak up against their boss, the Vietnamese tend to be very disciplined, and with a mild temperament. As the state enterprises gradually lose their monopolies, a new middle class of *nouveau-riche* entrepreneurs is emerging.

The small business sector will continue to be important to development of the Vietnamese economy in the future. Firms may be established rapidly, and they can produce quick returns on investment. Given the low level of wages, new ventures are likely to utilise labour-intensive technology, creating considerable employment. Small enterprises are flexible as to location, and may be situated in rural areas, thereby reducing development imbalances.

There are nevertheless constraints. Tan and Lim (1993) reported that 80% of business people surveyed in Vietnam found bureaucracy and corruption to be major obstacles to enterprise. More recently, Venard explained:

> Vietnamese corruption arises from four factors: strict relations between the government and some private interests, decentralisation to regional governments which makes them more powerful and less controllable, under-payment of state employees, and vague laws governing commercial transaction (1998, p. 87).

Exhibit 17.16   Flexible as to Location; photo ©2006 Leo Paul DANA

The government is faced with the challenging task of dismantling bureaucratic structures no longer relevant to the economic model of *Doi-Moi*. In addition, Vietnamese entrepreneurs are faced with a complex tariff scale; local taxes; business turnover tax; and a high personal income tax. Entrepreneurs often prefer to bribe an under-paid tax collector than to pay the taxes that they owe. Whereas Vietnamese entrepreneurs are heavily taxed, foreign direct investment is encouraged. Vietnamese entrepreneurs are therefore getting "foreign devil" companies set up in Hong Kong on their behalf. Profits are made in Hong Kong, resulting in less tax and less bureaucratic interference. A reduction in government intervention would allow entrepreneurs to concentrate more on business than on avoiding government regulation. Furthermore, given that Vietnam still has considerable import duties and that large-scale smuggling is known to occur, the entrepreneur who imports legally finds himself at a disadvantage. Appropriate government action should correct this.

Exports of the Socialist Republic of Vietnam were traditionally destined to former East Germany and other socialist countries where demand exceeded supply. Quality, marketing and advertising were not concerns. Vietnamese entrepreneurs have since learned about a service orientation and about marketing, but they do not necessarily understand long-term environmental and sustainability issues. Nor have they come to terms with the fickle

Exhibit 17.17   Underpaid; photo ©2006 Leo Paul DANA

Exhibit 17.18   Smuggling Occurs; photo ©2006 Leo Paul DANA

Exhibit 17.19 Service Orientation; photo ©2006 Leo Paul DANA

Exhibit 17.20 Geared for the Future; photo ©2006 Leo Paul DANA

nature of capitalism, as their coffee rides the market one year but not the next. Government promotion of entrepreneurship should include the training of entrepreneurs, provision of industrial estates and common facility services, including consultant services and labour relations services. Also beneficial would be access to financing for development, industrial research, and assistance in procuring inputs.

Taiwanese entrepreneurs are important investors in Vietnam. They bring technology, they create jobs, and they allow Vietnam to benefit from their marketing skills and networks abroad, contributing to exports. However, these people are concerned about what they perceive to be excessive government intervention in the economy.

In summary, Vietnam has introduced reforms, but has maintained a hands-on approach. Until recently, considerable resources were being expended, in order to spread the socialist model throughout Vietnam. The *Doi-Moi* Model allowed entrepreneurship to gradually play an increasingly important role — without overthrowing the socialist establishment. Institutions and regulatory frameworks are slowly, but continuously, being adapted to the needs of the future.

Chapter 18

Toward the Future

Success depends on good timing, a proper environment and people in harmony.

— Chinese proverb

This book has surveyed the evolution of public policy on entrepreneurship in different contexts. Although governments across Asia recognise the importance of entrepreneurship, their respective promotion efforts differ greatly, reflecting national priorities, demographic factors and cultural values. Likewise, the entrepreneurship sector reflects historical and cultural factors, as well as public policy; in addition, social norms and education have an influence on entrepreneurship.

In Cambodia, the Khmer Rouge extinguished entrepreneurship, a sector which is re-establishing itself, in an environment of uncertainty. In China, entrepreneurship is being promoted as a supplement to the socialist economy. In India, entrepreneurs and their SMEs are helping the country become a superpower. In Indonesia, where the Chinese minority has been at the forefront of entrepreneurship, the state has been trying to promote entrepreneurship among the Indigenous *pribumis*. In Japan, small-scale entrepreneurship complements large corporations, and cultural values propagate inter-firm linkages. Credit policy in Korea resulted in *chaebols* squeezing many entrepreneurs out of business; government measures have since intervened to assist small-scale entrepreneurship. In Laos, cultural values discouraged entrepreneurship among Lao men, resulting in opportunities for women and foreigners.

Exhibit 18.1   Entrepreneurship is a Supplement in Shanghai; photo ©2006 Leo Paul DANA

Exhibit 18.2   Entrepreneurship Complements Multinationals in Japan; photo ©2006 Leo Paul DANA

Exhibit 18.3   Moorish-style Sultan Abdul Samad Building with Clock Tower; photo ©2006 Leo Paul DANA

Exhibit 18.4   Durian Vendor in Singapore's Chinatown; photo ©2006 Leo Paul DANA

Exhibit 18.5   Ho Chi Minh City; photo ©2006 Leo Paul DANA

Exhibit 18.6   Singaporeans Produce Wealth; photo ©2006 Leo Paul DANA

Exhibit 18.7   Singapore Stock Exchange; photo ©2006 Leo Paul DANA

In response to the domination of entrepreneurship in Malaysia, by ethnic-Chinese entrepreneurs, Malaysia adopted a policy of giving preferential treatment to Indigenous *bumiputras*. The Chinese minority also dominates the entrepreneurship sector of the Philippines.

Myanmar is rich in natural resources, but its people are not prosperous. Despite its lack of natural resources, British Singapore's strong legal system, the educational system and security brought prosperity to its immigrants; later, multinationals saturated the domestic markets forcing the internationalisation of formerly local entrepreneurship.

Like in Singapore, Taiwan provided law and order which in turn facilitated entrepreneurship. Taiwan has more entrepreneurs per capita than has any of its neighbours. The Thai government's vision is to make Thailand a knowledge-based society through entrepreneurship and innovation by 2010. In Vietnam, entrepreneurship was introduced as a complement to socialism.

It appears that the ability to produce wealth is more important than simply being endowed with natural resources. The production of wealth, however, requires institutions and the efforts of individuals.

Implications for Public Policy

Different governments have designed a variety of programmes to promote the development of entrepreneurship. Much spending, however, is in vain, as entrepreneurship development programmes alone are insufficient. Programmes may be useful to those who know about them; often, those who could use them the most are unaware of their existence. Furthermore, policies which are not implemented fairly consequently fail to have the desired effect on society. In some economies, bribery, excessive taxation and regulation can inhibit entrepreneurship. Factors that could facilitate entrepreneurship include: education; reductions in barriers to entry; the reduction of excessive regulation, bureaucracy and corruption; flat taxes (as discussed by Forbes, 2006); and the freedom to compete. Also beneficial is a stable legal framework, as discussed by Smith (1892).

A priority for governments should be to determine the appropriate degree of regulation to enact and to enforce, such that the benefits to society exceed the

Exhibit 18.8   Regulation for the Public Good; photo ©2006 Leo Paul DANA

costs of compliance. John Stuart Mill (1869) argued that the only purpose for which power can be rightfully exercised over a member of society, against his will, is to prevent harm onto others. While some regulation is required to ensure order, excessive intervention is counter-productive. Where import duties are considerable, smuggling becomes popular — as is the case in Myanmar and in Vietnam. Even a culture supportive of entrepreneurship benefits from the optimal level of regulation and government intervention.

It appears that the optimal level of regulation and government intervention is culture-specific. Policy-makers should therefore keep in mind that the success of a policy or programme in the West does not guarantee equal success elsewhere. For this reason, it is crucial to avoid trans-locating these from one environment to a different one. To be effective, policies and programmes should be appropriate to the culture of a society. As summarised by Lewis, "If a religion lays stress upon material values, upon thrift and productive investment, upon honesty in commercial relations, upon experimentation and risk-bearing… it will be helpful to growth, whereas in so far as it is hostile to these things, it tends to inhibit growth. Where Theravada Buddhism is the backbone of social and cultural values… it may have a restraining effect on the accumulation of wealth and the rise of an entrepreneurial class (1955, p. 105)." Policy-makers should be aware of the cultural attributes of different ethnic groups, and policy should take these differences into account.

Economic development programmes have been introduced in different contexts. Experts have become sceptical of targeted economic development programmes, because these often subsidise the wrong people, with no lasting benefits. It appears that micro-finance programmes will have greater success. In any case, no funding should be distributed in transitional economies without post-loan or post-grant training. Recipients should be familiarised with finance, tax and payroll issues. Otherwise, of what use is capital unless there is knowledge to invest it?

A problem facing many economies is that social inequities may limit economic development in the future. The challenge facing these countries is

Exhibit 18.9   Poverty Persists in Nepal; photo ©2006 Leo Paul DANA

Exhibit 18.10   Infrastructure in India; photo ©2006 Leo Paul DANA

to identify ways to broaden participation in economic development. Priorities should include:

- Reduction of poverty, by accelerating agricultural development, and in some cases by controlling population growth;
- Improvement of training and vocational education;
- Improvement of property rights;
- Improvement of the legal basis for commerce;
- Improvement of infrastructure;
- Further liberalisation of trade;
- Revision of policies to attract foreign investment;
- Improvement of the management of government expenditures; and
- Reform of tax policies such as to broaden the state's revenue base, in a fair manner.

Implications for Management

If there is one generalisation that can be made about doing business in Asia, it is that across these vast countries, transactions and profits are a function of networks and relationships. Preferential treatment — when reciprocal — reduces overall transaction costs, thus increasing efficiency, competitiveness and profitability. This is generally true, regardless of the specifics of an environment. Nevertheless, one must again be cautious in attempting to generalise across cultures.

In the West, where the firm-type sector prevails, societies tend to take a form specific to them (Geertz, 1963). They resemble each other in their value system, class structure, family organisation, governance, and economic models. Parsons (1951) identified this over half a century ago. It is just as true today, and we have come to refer to this as globalisation. Modern economies in the Occident are democratic and their mainstream society is secular.

Across the nations of Asia, there is more diversity than is the case in other parts of the world. Capitalism in Asia does not necessarily come with democratisation. Political reform is not necessarily part of economic transition. Some governments choose to have greater control than do others.

Likewise, some societies are more religious than others, and there are important differences between religions. Attitudes toward business also vary greatly (Guiso, Sapienza, and Zingales, 2003). Zingales argued that, according to him, "Buddhism and Christianity seem most conducive to capitalism, and Islam least (2006, p. 228)." He wrote, "Jews, Buddhists, Catholics and Protestants (in that order) support competition, while Muslims and Hindus are strongly against it (Zingales, 2006, p. 229)." Nevertheless, capitalism has been very successful in Indonesia and in Malaysia, as demonstrated in the respective chapters in this book. Badawi explained, "Islam is well suited to economic, social and personal development... as long as we interpret it correctly (2006, p. 208)."

Perhaps the most valuable advice one can give to potential investors is that the importance of cultural differences must never be underestimated. There is *neither* one Asian culture, nor one Asian model. Just because people live in the same region, it does not mean that they share the same views about entrepreneurship. Likewise, there is not one standard approach to transition in Asia. This is further complicated in pluralistic societies, where unlike cultures each have their own implicit and explicit assumptions. Risk also varies with different types of pluralism. Melting pot pluralism — the situation prevailing when minorities adapt to a secular mainstream society — is stable. In contrast, when ethnic groups do not share a mainstream society, polarisation can result in violence, as has been the case in Indonesia, Myanmar, and elsewhere. There is no consistency across nations.

Nor is there consistency across time, and managers should keep in mind that in some transitional economies — such as Myanmar — the newly emerging private sector lacks professional, financial and economic structure. Rules change frequently. What is legal today may be banned tomorrow, and vice versa. Also, the ownership of property is not clearly documented, and the liquidity of immoveable assets is often delayed. Where acquisition is not practical, foreign investors may enter markets via networks. Given that communist planners traditionally emphasised vertical integration, managers might find it necessary to explain how, in a market economy, synergy often comes from horizontal integration.

Western management has mastered the art and science of doing business in the firm-type sector. In Asia, many opportunities are to be found in the bazaar and in the state-controlled planned sectors. In the bazaar, the movement of raw materials, processing, distribution and sales are intertwined activities. The focus on relationships supersedes the products and services that are being exchanged. A sliding price system results in prices that are negotiated, reflecting not only the cost or perceived value of a good or service, but also negotiating skills, the relationship between the buyer and the seller, and possibly the time, as well. Also important is an understanding of the parallel sector.

Implications for Educators

Much education has been aimed at teaching managerial content. This is inadequate. Emphasis should also be placed on values, as well as technical content. In the absence of the values related to sustainable long-term entrepreneurship — such as asceticism, frugality, thrift and work ethic (Weber, 1904–5), managerial skills are not being put to optimal use.

Where privatisation and downsizing of state-owned enterprises cause mass unemployment, there is often a mismatch between market demand and skills available in the workforce. The workforce needs retraining in skills that

Exhibit 18.11   Using the Canal for Transport in Shanghai; photo ©2006 Leo Paul DANA

Exhibit 18.12   Cycle-power; photo ©2006 Leo Paul DANA

Exhibit 18.13   New Vehicles; photo ©2006 Leo Paul DANA

Exhibit 18.14   Hong Kong Ferry Service; photo ©2006 Leo Paul DANA

Exhibit 18.15   Cross Harbour Tunnel, Hong Kong; photo ©2006 Leo Paul DANA

are in demand. Consequently, the technical content of courses needs to be adapted to changes in the economy.

Due to the lack of employment opportunities, and in the absence of appropriate retraining, many people have become self-employed, often in informal or covert activities; legitimate entrepreneurship is confused with illegal transactions. It would be beneficial, therefore, for educators to promote acceptance of entrepreneurship.

Exhibit 18.16   Camel Transport in India; photo ©2006 Leo Paul DANA

Exhibit 18.17   Bulls Pulling Mellon-cart in India; photo ©2006 Leo Paul DANA

Exhibit 18.18   Rickshaw in Calcutta; photo ©2006 Leo Paul DANA

Exhibit 18.19   Taxi in Delhi; photo ©2006 Leo Paul DANA

Exhibit 18.20 Using Cattle for Distribution in Myanmar; photo ©2006 Leo Paul DANA

Exhibit 18.21 Using Cattle for Transport in Myanmar; photo ©2006 Leo Paul DANA

Exhibit 18.22   Riding in Nepal; photo ©2006 Leo Paul DANA

Exhibit 18.23   Along the Mekong River; photo ©2006 Leo Paul DANA

Exhibit 18.24   *Cyclo* in Vietnam; photo ©2006 Leo Paul DANA

Where a vibrant entrepreneurial class is absent, this may be due to the public policy environment, or to the lack of inherent entrepreneurial characteristics. Where entrepreneurial spirit exists, new venture programmes may further enhance the environment for entrepreneurship, as is the case in the United States. However, in a transitional society with little experience of legitimate entrepreneurship, education should first focus on encouraging an entrepreneurship-friendly ideology.

As the economy of a nation becomes increasingly complex, marketing functions will mature and become more specialised. Training will be required to help managers solve new problems of planning, distribution and transportation.

Toward Future Research

Entrepreneurship does not guarantee prosperity for a nation. It is important to examine the broader picture. While economic growth has been prescribed as the remedy for poverty, experience shows that growth creates problems of its own. Of what good is rapid transition if its adverse effects are uncontrolled? It is useful to look not only at the creation of wealth, but also at its distribution. Myanmar is an example of rich country with a population that is mostly poor. Class mobility, in such an environment, is often a function of access to bribes rather productive creativity or economic innovation.

It would be a fallacy to attempt to understand entrepreneurship or innovation in isolation. What must change and what need not? The answer depends upon historical context and current situation, as well as the result desired. A variety of models are means to achieve different results. This is where more research is needed.

Classic theories cannot simply be taken and injected into transitional economies, in neglect of the environment in which they are to be placed. Even among members of ASEAN, there are important differences. Historical, socio-cultural and economic contexts appear to be important factors affecting the environment for business; societies cannot all adopt legitimate entrepreneurial systems at an equal pace, nor should they be expected to.

In each economy, the nature of entrepreneurship will evolve in time, but one should *not* expect entrepreneurship to converge across societies. There is no one formula for a "best" policy to promote entrepreneurship. Entrepreneurship is embedded in society, and the latter is affected by historical experience and cultural values. To understand the global nature of entrepreneurship, we must move beyond a universal model or a Western model; entrepreneurship must be understood in the context of national development, and importantly, policy-makers should take note that to be relevant, policies must be culturally sensitive.

The findings of this book suggest that factors which facilitate entrepreneurship include cultural attitude, as well as laws that protect property and facilitate business. Culture is central in explaining the social acceptability and perceived utility of entrepreneurship.

References

Abercrombie, Thomas J. (1964), "Cambodia, Indochina's 'Neutral' Corner," *National Geographic* 126 (4), October, pp. 514–551.

Acs, Zoltan J. and Leo Paul Dana (2001), "Contrasting Two Models of Wealth Redistribution," *Small Business Economics* 16 (2), March, pp. 63–74.

Adas, Michael P. (1974), *The Burma Delta: Economic Development and Local Change on an Asian Rice Frontier 1852–1941*, Madison: University of Wisconsin.

Ahlstrom, David and Gary D. Bruton (2002), "An Institutional Perspective on the Role of Culture in Shaping Strategic Actions by Technology-focused Entrepreneurial Firms in China," *Entrepreneurship Theory and Practice* 26 (4), pp. 53–69.

Alderman, Liz (2006), "'Weak links' raise anxiety on growth," *International Herald Tribune*, Thursday, January 26, p. 12.

Aldrich, Howard E., Trevor P. Jones and David McEvoy (1984), "Ethnic Advantage and Minority Business Development," in Robin Ward and Richard Jenkins, eds., *Ethnic Communities in Business: Strategies for Economic Survival*, Cambridge: Cambridge University Press, pp. 189–210.

Aldrich, Howard E., Ben Rosen and William Woodward (1987), "The Impact of Social Networks on Business Foundings and Profit in a Longitudinal Study," *Frontiers of Entrepreneurship Research*, Wellesley, Massachusetts: Babson College, pp. 154–168.

Aldrich, Howard E. and Roger David Waldinger (1990), "Ethnicity and Entrepreneurship," in W. Richard Scott and Judith Blake, eds., *Annual Review of Sociology* 16, pp. 111–135.

Aldrich, Howard E. and Catherine Zimmer (1986), "Entrepreneurship Through Social Networks," in Donald L. Sexton and Raymond W. Smilor, eds., *The Art and Science of Entrepreneurship*, Cambridge, Massachusetts: Ballinger, pp. 3–24.

Ali, Abbas J., Mona Lee and Robert C. Camp (2002), "Export Attitudes of Taiwanese Executives," *Journal of Global Marketing* 16 (1–2), pp. 27–46.

Anderson, Alistair R., Jin-Hai Li, Richard T. Harrison and Paul J. A. Robson (2003), "The Increasing Role of Small Business in the Chinese Economy," *Journal of Small Business Management* 41 (3), July, pp. 310–316.

Anderson, Poul H. (1995), *Collaborative Internationalisation of Small and Medium-Sized Enterprises*, Copenhagen: DJOF.

Arnold, General H. H. (1944), "The Aerial Invasion of Burma," *National Geographic* 86 (2), August, pp. 129–148.

331

Auster, Ellen and Howard E. Aldrich (1984), "Small Business Vulnerability, Ethnic Enclaves and Ethnic Enterprise," in Robin Ward and Richard Jenkins, eds., *Ethnic Communities in Business: Strategies for Economic Survival*, Cambridge: Cambridge University Press, pp. 39–54.

Aw, Bee Yan (2002), "Productivity Dynamics of Small and Medium Enterprises in Taiwan," *Small Business Economics* 18 (1–3), February, pp. 69–84.

Badawi, Abdullah Ahmad (2006), "Islam and Development," *Global Agenda: The Magazine of World Economic Forum Annual Meeting* 4, February, pp. 208–209.

Bainbridge, Oliver (1907), "The Chinese Jews," *National Geographic* 18 (10), October, pp. 621–632.

Balakrishna, Ramachandra (1961), *Review of Economic Growth in India*, Bangalore: Bangalore Press.

Bandura, Albert (1982), "Self-Efficacy Mechanism in Human Agency," *American Psychologist* 36, pp. 122–147.

Bandura, Albert and Nancy E. Adams (1977), "Analysis of Self-Efficacy Theory of Behavioral Change," *Cognitive Theory and Review* 1, pp. 287–310.

Barth, Frederik, ed., (1963), *The Role of the Entrepreneur in Social Change in Northern Norway*, Bergen: Norwegian Universities' Press.

Barth, Frederik (1966), *Models of Social Organization*, London: Royal Anthropological Institute.

Barth, Frederik (1967a), "Economic Spheres in Darfur," in Raymond Firth, ed., *Themes in Economic Anthropology*, London: Tavistock, pp. 149–174.

Barth, Frederik (1967b), "On the Study of Social Change," *American Anthropologist* 69 (6), December, pp. 661–669.

Barth, Frederik (1981), *Process and Form in Social Life*, London: Routledge and Kegan Paul.

Beach, William W., and Gerald P. O'Driscoll (2001), "Factors of the Index of Economic Freedom," in Gerald P. O'Driscoll, Kim R. Holmes and Melanie Kirkpatrick, *2001 Index of Economic Freedom*, New York: The Wall Street Journal.

Becker, Jasper (2004), "China's Growing Pains: More Money, More Stuff, More Problems," *National Geographic* 205 (3), March, pp. 68–95.

Begley, Thomas M. and David P. Boyd (1987), "Psychological Characteristics Associated With Performance in Entrepreneurial Firms and Smaller Businesses," *Journal of Business Venturing* 2 (1), pp. 79–93.

Bhagwati, Jagdish (2006), "The Big Debate: Setting the Business Agenda," Statement at the World Economic Forum, Davos, January 25.

Bishop, Isabella L. (1899), *The Yangtze Valley and Beyond*, London: John Murray.

Boissevain, Jeremy and Hanneke Grotenbreg (1987), "Ethnic Enterprise in the Netherlands: The Surinamese of Amsterdam," in Robert Goffee and Richard Scase, eds., *Entrepreneurship in Europe*, London: Croom Helm, pp. 105–130.

Bonacich, Edna (1973), "A Theory of Middleman Minorities," *American Sociological Review* 38 (5), October, pp. 583–594.

Boulnois, Luce (1963), *La Route de la Soie*, Paris: Arthaud.

Brenner, Gabrielle A. and Jean-Marie Toulouse (1990), "Business Creation among the Chinese Immigrants in Montreal," *Journal of Small Business and Entrepreneurship* 7 (4), July, pp. 38–44.

Brockhaus, Robert H., Sr. (1982), "The Psychology of the Entrepreneur," in Calvin A. Kent, Donald L. Sexton and Karl H. Vesper, eds., *Encyclopedia of Entrepreneurship*, Englewood Cliffs, New Jersey: Prentice Hall, pp. 39–57.

Brown, Josephine A. (1944), "6,000 Miles over the Roads of Free China," *National Geographic* 85 (3), March, pp. 355–384.

Brown, MacAlister and Joseph Jermiah Zasloff (1999), *Cambodia Confounds the Peacemakers, 1979–1998*, Ithaca: Cornell University Press.

Brown, MacAlister, Joseph Jermiah Zasloff and Richard F. Staar (1986), *Apprentice Revolutionaries: The Communist Movement in Laos 1930–1985*, Hoover Institution Press.

Cantillon, Richard (1755), *Essai sur la Nature du Commerce en Général*, London and Paris: R. Gyles; translated into English in 1931, by Henry Higgs, London: MacMillan and Co.

Carsrud, Alan L., Connie Marie Gaglio and Kenneth W. Olm (1986), "Entrepreneurs – Mentors, Networks and Successful New Venture Development: An Exploratory Study," *Frontiers of Entrepreneurship Research*, Wellesley, Massachusetts: Babson College, pp. 229–243.

Castle, William R., Jr. (1932), "Tokyo To-day," *National Geographic* 61 (2), February, pp. 131–162.

Chadwick, Douglas H. (1987), "At the Crossroads of Kathmandu," *National Geographic* 172 (1), July, pp. 32–65.

Chadwick, Douglas H. (2005), "Thailand's Urban Giants," *National Geographic* 208 (4), October, pp. 98–117.

Chamard, John and Michael Christie (1996), "Entrepreneurship Education Programs: A Change in Paradigm is Needed," *Entrepreneurship, Innovation, and Change* 5 (3), September, pp. 217–226.

Chandler, David P. (1999), *A History of Cambodia*, Boulder, Colorado: Westview Press.

Chandler, David P., Ben Kiernan and Chanthou Boua (1988), *Pol Pot Plans the Future*, New Haven: Yale.

Chandra, Nayan and Rodney Tasker (1992), "The Gem Stampede," *Far Eastern Economic Review*, July 30, p. 20.

Chantrabot, Ros (1993), *La Republique Khmère (1970–1975)*, Paris: Les Editions L'Harmattan.

Chapman, H. Owen (1928), *The Chinese Revolution 1926–27: A Record of the Period Under Communist Control as Seen from the Nationalist Capital, Hankow*, London: Constable & Co.

Chetwode, Penelope (1935), "Nepal, the Sequestered Kingdom," *National Geographic* 67 (3), March, pp. 319–352.

Chen, Kuang-Jung (1997), "The Sari-Sari Store," *Journal of Small Business Management* 35 (4), October, pp. 88–91.

Cherry, Robert (1990), "Middleman Minority Theories: Their Implications for Black-Jewish Relations," *The Journal of Ethnic Studies* 17 (4), Winter, pp. 117–138.

Chinh, Truong (1977), "Firmly Grasp the Proletarian Dictatorship," *Vietnam* 225, September, p. 1.

Chitty, J. R. (1922), *Things Seen in China*, London: Seeley, Service & Co.

Chow, K.W. Clement and W. K. Eric Tsang (1995), "Entrepreneurs in China: Development, Functions and Problems," *International Small Business Journal* 1, pp. 63–77.

Christian, John LeRoy (1942), *Modern Burma*, Berkeley, California: University of California Press.

Christian, John LeRoy (1943), "Burma: Where India and China Meet," *National Geographic* 84 (4), October, pp. 489–512.

Clark, Milton J. (1954), "How the Kazakhs Fled to Freedom," *National Geographic* 106 (5), November, pp. 621–644.

Communist Party of Vietnam (1991), *Seventh National Congress Documents*, Hanoi: Vietnam Foreign Languages Publishing House.

Coville, Lilian Grosvenor (1933), "Here in Manchuria: Many Thousand Lives Were Lost and More Than Half the Crops Destroyed by the Floods of 1932," *National Geographic* 63 (2), February, pp. 233–256.

Cummings, Scott, ed., (1980), *Self-Help in Urban America: Patterns of Minority Business Enterprise*, Port Washington, New York: Kennikat, pp. 33–57.

Curzon-of-Kedleston, Marquess (1924), "In the Diamond Mountains," *National Geographic* 66 (4), October, pp. 353–374.

Dalgic, Tevfik (1998), "Dissemination of Market Orientation in Europe," *International Marketing Review* 15 (1), pp. 45–60.

Dana, Leo Paul (1992), "Entrepreneurship, Innovation and Change in Developing Countries," *Entrepreneurship, Innovation, and Change* 1 (2), June, pp. 231–242.

Dana, Leo Paul (1993), "A Goods and Services Tax (GST) and the Small Business Sector: Some Canadian Reflections," *Australian Journal of Public Administration* 52 (4), December, pp. 457–464.

Dana, Leo Paul (1994a), "A Marxist Mini-Dragon? Entrepreneurship in Today's Vietnam," *Journal of Small Business Management* 32 (2), April, pp. 95–102.

Dana, Leo Paul (1994b), "Economic Reform in the New Vietnam," *Current Affairs* 70 (11), University of Sydney, May, pp. 19–25.

Dana, Leo Paul (1994c), "The *Doi-Moi* Model: An Ethnographic Account of Entrepreneurship, Innovation and Change in Former French Indo-China," *Entrepreneurship, Innovation, and Change* 3 (1), March, pp. 61–84.

Dana, Leo Paul (1994d), "The Impact of Culture on Entrepreneurship, Innovation, and Change in the Balkans: The Yugopluralist Model," *Entrepreneurship, Innovation, and Change* 3 (2), June, pp. 177–190.

Dana, Leo Paul (1995a), "Entrepreneurship in a Remote Sub-Arctic Community: Nome, Alaska," *Entrepreneurship: Theory and Practice* 20 (1), Fall, pp. 57–72.

Dana, Leo Paul (1995b), "Small Business in a Non-Entrepreneurial Society: The Case of the Lao People's Democratic Republic (Laos)," *Journal of Small Business Management* 33 (3), July, pp. 95–102.

Dana, Leo Paul (1997a), "Pepsi, Vietnam," *Management Case Quarterly* 2 (3), Autumn, pp. 11–13.

Dana, Leo Paul (1997b), "The Origins of Self-Employment," *Canadian Journal of Administrative Sciences/Revue Canadienne des Sciences de l'Administration* 14 (1), April, pp. 99–104.

Dana, Leo Paul (1997c), "Vongpackdy, Laos," *Management Case Quarterly* 2 (3), Autumn, pp. 29–32.

Dana, Leo Paul (1998a) "Small Business in Xinjiang," *Asian Journal of Business and Information Systems* 3 (1), Summer, pp. 123–136.

Dana, Leo Paul (1998b), "Small But Not Independent: SMEs in Japan," *Journal of Small Business Management* 36 (4), October, pp.73–76.

Dana, Leo Paul (1999a), "Entrepreneurship as a Supplement in the People's Republic of China," *Journal of Small Business Management* 37 (3), July, pp. 76–80.

Dana, Leo Paul (1999b), *Entrepreneurship in Pacific Asia: Past, Present & Future*, Singapore, London and Hong Kong: World Scientific.

Dana, Leo Paul, ed. (1999c), *International Entrepreneurship: An Anthology*, Singapore: ENDEC.

Dana, Leo Paul (1999d), "Kentucky Fried Chicken in Shanghai," *British Food Journal* 101 (5–6), May, pp. 293–495.

Dana, Leo Paul (1999e), "The Development of Entrepreneurship in Macao and Hong Kong: A Comparative Study," *Public Administration and Policy*, March, pp. 61–72.

Dana, Leo Paul (2000a), "Creating Entrepreneurs in India," *Journal of Small Business Management* 38 (1), January, pp. 86–91.

Dana, Leo Paul (2000b), *Economies of the Eastern Mediterranean Region: Economic Miracles in the Making*, Singapore, London and Hong Kong: World Scientific.

Dana, Leo Paul (2000c), "International Management: Culture is of the Essence in Asia," Invited Essay in *Financial Times*, Mastering Management Special Section, November 27, pp. 12–13.

Dana, Leo Paul (2001), "Networks, Internationalization and Policy," *Small Business Economics* 16 (2), March, pp. 57–62.

Dana, Leo Paul (2002), *When Economies Change Paths: Models of Transition in China, the Central Asian Republics, Myanmar, and the Nations of Former Indochine Française*, Singapore, London and Hong Kong: World Scientific.

Dana, Leo Paul (2005), *When Economies Change Hands: A Survey of Entrepreneurship in the Emerging Markets of Europe from the Balkans to the Baltic States*, Binghamton: International Business Press.

Dana, Leo Paul (2006), *Entrepreneurship & SMEs in the Eurozone: Toward a Theory of Symbiotic Enterprises*, London: Imperial College Press.

Dana, Leo Paul, Hamid Etemad and Richard W. Wright (2000), "The Global Reach of Symbiotic Networks," in Leo Paul Dana, ed., *Global Marketing Co-operation and Networks*, Binghamton: International Business Press, pp. 1–16.

Deering, Mabel Craft (1933), "Chosen – Land of Morning Calm," *National Geographic* 64 (4), October, pp. 421–448.

Desjardins, Thierry (1997), "Le Cambodge, royaume de la corruption," *Figaro*, January 1, p. 4B.

Dilke, Charles Wentworth (1894), *Greater Britain: A Record of Travel in English-speaking Countries*, London: Macmillan and Co.

Dinh, Tran Van (1989), "Hue," *National Geographic* 176 (5), November, pp. 595–603.

Djamour, Judith (1959), *Malay Kinship and Marriage in Singapore*, London: Athlone.

Dollar, David (1999), "The Transformation of Vietnam's Economy: Sustaining Growth in the 21st Century," in Jennie I. Litvack and Dennis A. Rondinelli, eds., *Market Reform in Vietnam: Building Institutions for Development*, Westport, Connecticut: Quorum, pp. 31–46.

Drabble, John H. (1973), *Rubber in Malaya, 1876–1922: The Genesis of the Industry*, Kuala Lumpur: Oxford University Press.

Dubini, Paola and Howard E. Aldrich (1991), "Personal and Extended Networks are Central to the Entrepreneurship Process," *Journal of Business Venturing* 6 (5), September, pp. 305–313.

Dunung, Sanjyot P. (1995), *Doing Business in Asia*, New York: Lexington Books.

Dyer, Linda M. and Christopher A. Ross, (2000), "Ethnic Enterprises and Their Clientele," *Journal of Small Business Management* 38 (2), April, pp. 48–66.

Ear, Sophal (1995), "Cambodia's Economic Development in Historical Perspective: 1953–1970," *Berkeley McNair Journal* 3, Summer, pp. 25–37.

Edwards, Mike (2004), "Han Dynasty," *National Geographic* 205 (2), February, pp. 2–29.

Eigner, Julius (1938), "The Rise and Fall of Nanking," *National Geographic* 73 (2), February, pp. 189–224.

El-Namaki, M. S. S. (1988), "Encouraging Entrepreneurs in Developing Countries," *Long Range Planning* 21 (4), pp. 98–106.

Evans, Joel R. and Richard L. Laskin (1994), "The Relationship Marketing Process: A Conceptualization and Application," *Industrial Marketing Management* 23 (5), pp. 432–452.

Far Eastern Economic Review (1994), "Indochina," May 5, p. 60.

Feige, Edgar L. and Katarina Ott (1999), eds., *Underground Economies in Transition: Unrecorded Activity, Tax, Corruption and Organized Crime*, Aldershot: Ashgate.

Forbes, Steve (2006), "Flat Taxes, Higher Revenues," *Global Agenda: The Magazine of World Economic Forum Annual Meeting* 4, February, pp. 118–119.

Freedman, Maurice (1961), "Immigrants and Associations: Chinese in Nineteenth-century Singapore," *Comparative Studies in Society and History* 3, pp. 25–48.

Furnivall, John Sydenham (1956), *Colonial Policy and Practice: A Comparative Study of Burma and Netherlands India*, New York: New York University Press.

Furnivall, John Sydenham (1957), *A Study of the Social and Economic History of Burma*, Rangoon.

Gadgil, Dhananjaya Ramchandra (1959), *Origins of the Modern Indian Business Class*, New York: Institute of Pacific Relations.

Garrett, W. E. (1971), "Pagan, on the Road to Mandalay," *National Geographic* 139 (3), March, pp. 343–365.

Garrett, W. E. (1974), "The Hmong of Laos," *National Geographic* 145 (1), January, pp. 78–111.

Gasse, Yvon (1982), "Elaborations on the Psychology of the Entrepreneur," in Calvin A. Kent, Donald L. Sexton and Karl H. Vesper, eds., *Encyclopedia of Entrepreneurship*, Englewood Cliffs, New Jersey: Prentice Hall, pp. 57–66.

Geertz, Clifford (1963), *Peddlers and Princes: Social Development and Economic Change in Two Indonesian Towns*, Chicago, Illinois: University of Chicago Press.

Ghosh, Ratna, Meenakshi Gupta and S. Nina Dhar (1998), "Women and Entrepreneurship in India," in Rabindra N. Kanungo, ed., *Entrepreneurship & Innovation: Models for Development*, New Delhi: Sage, pp. 156–175.

Glinkina, Svetlana (1999), "Russia's Underground Economy During the Transition," in Edgar L. Feige and Katarina Ott, eds., *Underground Economies in Transition: Unrecorded Activity, Tax, Corruption and Organised Crime*, Aldershot: Ashgate, pp. 101–116.

Gomes-Casseres, Benjamin (1997), "Alliance Strategies of Small Firms," *Small Business Economics* 9 (1), February, pp. 33–44.

Goodnow, Frank Johnson (1927), "The Geography of China: The Influence of Physical Environment on the History and Character of the Chinese People," *National Geographic* 51 (6), June, pp. 651–664.

Gray, Denis D. (2001), "Working Elephants Make Last Stand in Myanmar," *The Jerusalem Post*, March 13, p. 7.

Griffis, William Elliot (1923), "The Empire of the Risen Sun," *National Geographic* 44 (4), October, pp. 415–443.

Griffis, William Elliot (1933), "Japan, Child of the World's Old Age: An Empire of Mountainous Islands, Whose Alert People Constantly Conquer Harsh Forces of Land, Sea, and Sky," *National Geographic* 63 (3), March, pp. 257–301.

Gronroos, Christian (1989), "Defining Marketing: A Market-Oriented Approach," *European Journal of Marketing* 23 (1), pp. 52–59.

Grossman, Gregory (1977), "The Second Economy of the USSR," *Problems of Communism* 26 (5), pp. 25–40.

Guiso, Luigi, Paola Sapienza and Luigi Zingales (2003), "People's opium? Religion and Economic Attitudes," *Journal of Monetary Economics* 50 (1), pp. 225–282.

Hagen, Everett E. (1962), *On the Theory of Social Change: How Economic Growth Begins*, Homewood, Illinois: Dorsey.

Hagen, Toni (1960), "Afoot in Roadless Nepal," *National Geographic* 117 (3), March, pp. 361–405.

Hakansson, Hakan, ed. (1982), *International Marketing and Purchasing of Industrial Goods: An Interaction Approach*, Chicester: John Wiley and Sons.

Haley, George T. and Usha C. V. Haley (1998), "Boxing With Shadows," *Journal of Organisational Change Management* 11 (4), pp. 301–320.

Haley, George T., Chin Tiong Tan and Usha C. V. Haley (1998), *New Asian Entrepreneurs*, Oxford: Butterworth-Heinemann.

Halloran, James W. (1991), *Why Entrepreneurs Fail*, New York: Liberty Hall.

Hamel, Bernard (1993), *Sihanouket le Drame Cambodgien*, Paris: L'Harmattan Broché.

Harvey, Charles and Boon-Chye Lee (2002), "The Study of Small and Medium Sized Enterprises in East Asia," in Charles Harvey and Boon-Chye Lee, eds., *Globalisation and SMEs in East Asia*, Cheltenham, United Kingdom: Edward Elgar, pp. 1–9.

Haskell, Martin R. and Lewis Yablonsky (1974), *Crime and Delinquency*, Chicago: Rand McNally.

Hazlehurst, Leighton W. (1966), *Entrepreneurship and the Merchant Castes in a Punjabi City*, Durham, North Carolina: Duke University Commonwealth Studies Center.

Henker, Julia Kreisinger (1999), "Hot Breads," in Richard G. Linowes, ed., *Portraits of Business Practices in Emerging Markets: Cases for Management Education*, Washington, DC: Institute of International Education and US Agency for International Development, Volume 2, pp. 174–180.

Henry, Stuart (1978), *The Hidden Economy: The Context and Control of Borderline Crime*, London: Martin Robertson.

Herald Tribune (1988), "U Ne Win is Removed From Office in Burma," July 26, p. 2.

Hipwell, William T. (2005), "Re-Constructing Nature and Reterritorialising Alishan: Taiwan's Cou Nation and the Making of Danayigu," presented at the Association of American Geographers' 2005 Annual Meeting, Denver, Colorado, April 5–9.

Hirsh, Michael and Ron Moreau (1995), "Risky Business," *Newsweek*, June 19, p. 10.

Hla, Lludu U. (1975), *Rice*, Mandalay: Kyipwaye Press.

Hodgson, Bryan (1984), "Time and Again in Burma," *National Geographic* 166 (1), July, pp. 90–121.

Hoge, James F. (2006), "The Emergence of India," Statement at the World Economic Forum, Davos, January 25.

Hong, Ma (1990), *Modern China's Economy and Management*, Beijing: Foreign Languages Press.

Hornaday, John A. (1982), "Research About Living Entrepreneurs," in Calvin A. Kent, Donald L. Sexton, and Karl H. Vesper, eds., *Encyclopedia of Entrepreneurship*, Englewood Cliffs, New Jersey: Prentice Hall, pp. 20–38.

Hull, David, John J. Bosley and Gerald G. Udell (1980), "Renewing the Hunt for the Heffalump: Identifying Potential Entrepreneurs by Personality Characteristics," *Journal of Small Business Management* 18 (1), January, pp. 11–18.

Huntington, Samuel P. (1996), *The Clash of Civilization and the Remaking of World Order*, New York: Simon and Schuster.

Hwang, Eui-Gak (1993), *The Korean Economies: A Comparison of North & South*, Oxford: Clarendon.

Iyer, Gopalkrishnan and Jon M. Shapiro (1999), "Ethnic Entrepreneurship and Marketing Systems: Implications for the Global Economy," *Journal of International Marketing* 7 (4), pp. 83–110.

Jackson, Karl D., ed., (1989), *Cambodia 1975–1978*, Princeton, New Jersey: Princeton University Press.

Jain, Anita (2006), "A Dramatic Change in Shopping," *Financial Times*, Wednesday, June 28, p. 4.

Japan Times (1999), "Bear Market," March 7, p. 11.

Jenkins, Richard (1984), "Ethnicity and the Rise of Capitalism in Ulster," in Robin Ward and Richard Jenkins, eds., *Ethnic Communities in Business: Strategies for Economic Survival*, Cambridge: Cambridge University Press, pp. 57–72.

Johanson, Jan and Associates (1994), *Internationalization, Relationships and Networks*, Stockholm: Almquist and Wiksell International.

Johnson, Jo (2006), "Surging with Self-confidence and Ambition," *Special Report on the World's Fastest Growing Democracy*, London: Financial Times, January 26.

Kahin, George M. (1952), *Nationalism and Revolution in Indonesia*, Ithaca: Cornell University Press.

Kakar, Sudhir (1978), *The Inner World: A Psycho-Analytic Study of Hindu Childhood and Society*, Oxford University Press, London.

Kanitkar, Ajit and Nalinee Contractor (1992), *In Search of Identity: The Women Entrepreneurs of India*, Ahmedabad: Entrepreneurship Development Institute of India.

Khatiwada, Yuba Raj (2002), "Banking Sector Reforms for Nepal: Implications for Corporate Governance," in John Adams, Bishwa K. Maskay, and Sugandha D. Tulandhar, eds., *Corporate Governance in Nepal*, Kathmandu: Centre for Development and Governance.

Khup, San (1996), "Macroeconomic Policies with Special Emphasis on Infrastructural Development," in Tan Teck Meng, Low Aik Meng, John J. Williams, and Ivan P. Polunin, eds., *Business Opportunities in Myanmar*, Singapore: Prentice Hall, pp. 69–79.

Kinyanjui, Mary Njeri (1993), "Finance Availability of Capital and New Firm Formation in Central Kenya," *Journal of East African Research and Development* 23, pp. 63–87.

Kipling, Rudyard (1890), *Letters from the East,* New York: Frank F. Lovell.

Kirjassoff, Alice Ballantine (1920), "Formosa the Beautiful," *National Geographic* 37 (3), March, pp. 247–292.

Kirzner, Israel M. (1973), *Competition and Entrepreneurship,* Chicago: University of Chicago Press.

Kirzner, Israel M. (1979), *Perception, Opportunity, and Profit*, Chicago: University of Chicago Press.

Kirzner, Israel M. (1982), *Method, Process and Austrian Economics*, Lexington, Massachusetts: Lexington Books.

Kirzner, Israel M. (1985), *Discovery and the Capitalist Process*, Chicago: University of Chicago Press.

Kunstadter, Peter (1972), "Spirits of Change Capture the Karens," *National Geographic* 141 (2), February, pp. 267–285.

Kyi, Khin Maung (1970), "Western Enterprises and Economic Development in Burma," *Journal of Burma Research Society* 53 (1), June, pp. 25–49.

Lamb, David (2004), "Hanoi: Shedding the Ghosts of War," *National Geographic* 205 (5), May, pp. 80–97.

Lasserre, Philippe and Hellmut Schütte (1995), *Strategies for Asia Pacific*, London: Macmillan.

Lee, Byoung-Hoon (2003), "Globalization and Industrial Relations in Korea," *Korean Journal* 43 (1), pp. 261–288.

Lee, Byoung-Hoon and Seong Kyeun Kwun (2003), "Public Policy Toward the Innovation-driven Economy in Korea," *International Journal of Entrepreneurship and Innovation Management* 3 (3), pp. 267–281.

Lee, Choong Y. (1998), "Quality Management by Small Manufacturers in Korea: An Exploratory Study," *Journal of Small Business Management* 36 (4), October, pp. 73–76.

Lee, Joseph S. and Jiann-Chyuan Wang (2003), "Public Policies for the Promotion of an Innovation-driven Economy in Taiwan," *International Journal of Entrepreneurship and Innovation Management* 3 (3), pp. 227–248.

Leong, Choon Chiang (2004), "Government Development Assistance Programmes (GDAPs) for Small- and Medium-sized Enterprises (SMEs) in a Knowledge-based Economy," *International Journal of Entrepreneurship and Innovation Management* 4 (2–3), pp. 124–137.

Lewis, W. Arthur (1955), *The Theory of Economic Growth*, Homewood, Illinois: Richard D. Irwin.

Light, Ivan (1972), *Ethnic Enterprise in America: Business and Welfare among Chinese, Japanese and Blacks*, Berkeley, California: University of California Press.

Light, Ivan (1984), "Immigrant and Ethnic Enterprise in North America," *Ethnic and Racial Studies* 7 (2), pp. 195–216.

Light, Ivan and Edna Bonacich (1988), *Immigrant Entrepreneurs: Koreans in Los Angeles 1965–1985*, Berkeley, California: University of California Press.

Lin, Carol Yeh-Yun (1998), "Success Factors of Small and Medium-Sized Enterprises in Taiwan," *Journal of Small Business Management* 36 (4), October, pp. 43–56.

Loewen, James W. (1971), *The Mississippi Chinese: Between Black and White*, Cambridge: Harvard University Press.

Long, George W. (1952), "Indochina Faces the Dragon," *National Geographic* 102 (3), September, pp. 287–328.

Long, George W. (1954), "Hong Kong Hangs On," *National Geographic* 105 (2), September, pp. 239–272.

Lowdermilk, Walter C. (1945), "China Fights Erosion with U.S. Aid," *National Geographic* 87 (6), June, pp. 641–680.

Luo, Jar-Der (1997), "The Significance of Networks in the Initiation of Small Businesses in Taiwan," *Sociological Forum* 12, pp. 297–317.

Macaulay, R. H. (1934), *History of the Bombay Burmah Trading Corporation, Ltd., 1864–1910*, Colchester, London and Eton: Spottiswoode, Ballantyne and Co.

MacDonald, Don (2005), "China's Challenges to Growth," *The Gazette*, Saturday, October 1, pp. B.1–2.

Marx, Karl and Friedrich Engels (1848), *Manifest der Kommunisitischen Partei*, London: J. E. Burghard.

Maung, Mya (1991), *The Burma Road to Poverty*, New York: Praeger.

May, Daw Khin San (1996), "Mandalay: The Handicraft Centre of Myanmar," in Tan Teck Meng, Low Aik Meng, John J. Williams and Ivan P. Polunin, eds., *Business Opportunities in Myanmar*, Singapore: Prentice Hall, pp. 47–52.

McClelland, David Clarence (1961), *The Achieving Society*, Princeton, New Jersey: D. Van Nostrand.

McClelland, David Clarence (1975), *Power*, New York: Free Press.

Medhora, Phiroze B. (1965), "Entrepreneurship in India," *Political Science Quarterly* 80 (4), Summer, pp. 558–559.

Mill, John Stuart (1869), *On Liberty*, London: Longman, Roberts & Green.

Min, Pyong Gap (1984), "From White-Collar Occupation to Small Business: Korean Immigrants' Occupational Adjustment," *Sociological Quarterly* 25 (3), Summer, pp. 333–352.

Min, Pyong Gap (1986–7), "Filipino and Korean Immigrants in Small Business: A Comparative Analysis," *Amerasia* 13 (1), Winter, pp. 53–71.

Min, Pyong Gap (1987), "Factors Contributing to Ethnic Business: A Comprehensive Synthesis," *International Journal of Comparative Sociology* 28 (3–4), September-December, pp. 173–193.

Min, Pyong Gap and Charles Jaret (1985), "Ethnic Business Success: the Case of Korean Small Business in Atlanta," *Sociology and Social Research* 69 (3), April, pp. 412–435.

Minniti, Maria, William D. Bygrave and Erkko Autio (2006), *Global Entrepreneurship Monitor: 2005 Executive Report*, London: London Business School.

Mishra, Atul (2005), "Entrepreneurial Motivations in Start-up and Survival of Micro- and Small Enterprises in the Rural Non-Farm Economy," *Journal of Small Business and Entrepreneurship* 18 (3), pp. 289–326.

Moore, W. Robert (1930), "Among the Hill Tribes of Sumatra," *National Geographic* 57 (2), February, pp. 187–227.

Moore, W. Robert (1933), "The Glory that Was Imperial Peking," *National Geographic* 63 (6), June, pp. 745–780.

Moore, W. Robert (1950), "Strife-torn Indochina," *National Geographic* 98 (4), October, pp. 499–510.

Moore, W. Robert (1954), "War and Quiet on the Laos Frontier," *National Geographic* 105 (5), May, pp. 665–680.

Moore, W. Robert (1963), "Burma: Gentle Neighbor of India and Red China," *National Geographic* 123 (2), February, pp. 153–199.

Moore, W. Robert and Maynard Owen Williams (1951), "Portrait of Indochina," *National Geographic* 99 (4), April, pp. 461–490.

Moser, Don (1977), "The Philippines: Better Days Still Elude an Old Friend," *National Geographic* 151 (3), March, pp. 360–391.

Mydans, Seth (2005), "In Aceh, Empty Spaces Won't Be Filled Soon," *International Herald Tribune*, Saturday-Sunday, June 25–26, p. 2.

Nafziger, E. Wayne (1971), "Indian Entrepreneurship: A Survey," in Peter Kilby, *Entrepreneurship and Economic Development*, New York: The Free Press, pp. 287–316.

Ngudup, Penjor, Jason C. H. Chen and Binshan Lin (2005), "E-commerce in Nepal: A Case Study of an Underdeveloped Country," *International Journal of Management and Enterprise Development* 2 (3–4), pp. 306–324.

North, Douglass (1990), *Institutions, Institutional Change and Economic Performance*, Cambridge: Harvard University Press.

O'Driscoll, Gerald P., Kim R. Holmes and Melanie Kirkpatrick (2001), *2001 Index of Economic Freedom*, New York: The Wall Street Journal.

Orwell, George (1930), *Burmese Days*, New York: Harcourt-Brace Co.

Outram, Frank and G. E. Fane (1940), "Burma Road, Back Door to China," *National Geographic* 78 (5), November, pp. 629–658.

Parnwell, Mike and Sarah Turner (1998), "Sustaining the Unsustainable? City and Society in Indonesia," *Third World Planning Review* 20 (2), pp. 147–163.

Parsons, Talcott (1951), *The Social System*, Glencoe, Illinois: Free Press.

Parsons, Talcott and Neil Smelzer (1956), *Economy and Society*, Glencoe, Illinois: Free Press.

Passantino, Joseph E. (1946), "Kunming, Southwestern Gateway to China," *National Geographic* 90 (2), August, pp. 137–168.

Patel, V. G. (1987), *Entrepreneurship Development Programme in India and Its Relevance to Developing Countries*, Ahmedabad: Entrepreneurship Development Institute of India.

Patric, John (1936), "Friendly Journeys in Japan: A Young American Finds a Ready Welcome in the Homes of the Japanese During Leisurely Travels Through the Islands," *National Geographic* 69 (4), April, pp. 441–480.

Peng, Michael W. and Peggy Sue Heath (1996), "The Growth of the Firm in Planned Economies in Transition: Institutions, Organizations, and Strategic Choice," *Academy of Management Review* 21 (2), pp. 492–528.

Perazic, Elizabeth (1960), "Little Laos Next Door to Red China," *National Geographic* 117 (1), January, pp. 46–69.

Perlez, Jane (2006), "Women Caught in a More Radical Indonesia," *International Herald Tribune*, Wednesday, June 28, p. 2.

Pio, Edwina (2005a), "A Change Process Imbued with an Eastern Ethos Revitalizes an Indian Business," *Journal of Organizational Excellence* 24 (3), Summer, pp. 3–10.

Pio, Edwina (2005b), "A Time to Sew: Work, Culture and Organic Cotton at Knitex India," *Management Case Study Journal* 5 (2), pp. 69–82.

Ponchaud, François (1977), *Cambodia*, New York: Holt, Rinehart and Winston.

Porter, Elaine G. and K. V. Nagarajan (2005), "Successful Women Entrepreneurs as Pioneers: Results from a Study Conducted in Karaikudi, Tamil Nadu, India," *Journal of Small Business and Entrepreneurship* 18 (1), Winter, pp. 39–52.

Portes, Alejandro and Robert C. Bach (1985), *Latin Journey*, Berkeley, California: University of California Press.

Portes, Alejandro and Leif Jensen (1987), "What's an Ethnic Enclave? The Case for Conceptual Clarity," *American Sociological Review* 52 (6), December, pp. 768–771.

Portes, Alejandro and Leif Jensen (1989), "The Enclave and the Entrants: Patterns of Ethnic Enterprise in Miami Before and After Mariel," *American Sociological Review* 54 (6), December, pp. 929–949.

Portes, Alejandro and Leif Jensen (1992), "Disproving the Enclave Hypothesis," *American Sociological Review* 57 (3), June, pp. 418–420.

Prasso, Sheridan T. (2001), "The Riel Value of Money: How the World's Only Attempt to Abolish Money Has Hindered Cambodia's Economic Development," *Asia Pacific Issues* 49, January, pp. 1–8.

Prud'Homme, Remy (1969), *L'économie du Cambodge*, Paris: Presses Universitaires de France.

Raghavendra, N. V. and M. H. Bala Subrahmanya (2005), "Collective Efficiency and Technological Capacity on Small Firms: Evidence from Two Foundry Clusters in South India," *International Journal of Management and Enterprise Development* 2 (3–4), pp. 325–348.

Redding, Gordon (1990), *The Spirit of Chinese Capitalism*, Berlin: de Gruyter.

Rigg, Jonathan (1997), *Southeast Asia: The Human Landscape of Modernization and Development* London: Routledge.

Roberts, William H. (1931), "The Five Thousand Temples of Pagan," *National Geographic* 60 (4), October, pp. 445–454.

Robinson, H. W. (1923), "The Hairnet Industry in North China," *National Geographic* 44 (3), September, pp. 327–336.

Rock, Joseph F. (1924), "Banishing the Devil of Disease among the Nashi," *National Geographic* 66 (5), November, pp. 473–499.

Rock, Joseph F. (1930), "Seeking the Mountains of Mystery: An Expedition on the China-Tibet Frontier to the Unexplored Amnyi Machen Range, One of Whose Peaks Rivals Everest," *National Geographic* 57 (2), February, pp. 131–185.

Rock, Joseph F. (1935), "Sungmas, the Living Oracles of the Tibetan Church," *National Geographic* 68 (4), October, pp. 475–478.

Rondinelli, Dennis A. and Jennie I. Litvack (1999), "Economic Reform, Social Progress, and Institutional Development: A Framework for Assessing Vietnam's Transition," in Jennie I. Litvack and Dennis A. Rondinelli, eds., *Market Reform in Vietnam: Building Institutions for Development*, Westport, Connecticut: Quorum, pp. 1–30.

Rosenbloom, Alfred and Bijay K.C. (2005), "Management Education in Nepal: A View from the High Country," in John R. McIntyre and Ilan Alon, eds., *Business and Management Education in Transitioning and Developing Countries: A Handbook*, Armonk, New York: M. E. Sharpe, pp. 69–82.

Roth, Siobhan (2006), "Marrying Young," *National Geographic* 209 (5), May, p. 26.

Rothenberger, Catherine (1999), "Growing Pains: Management Challenges in an Emerging Financial Market," in Richard G. Linowes, ed., *Portraits of Business Practices in Emerging Markets: Cases for Management Education*, Washington, DC: Institute of International Education and US Agency for International Development, Volume 2, pp. 164–173.

Roy, Denny (2003), *Taiwan: A Political History*, Ithaca: Cornell University Press.

Samuels, Gertrude (1955), "Passage to Freedom in Viet Nam," *National Geographic* 107 (6), June, pp. 858–874.

Sanders, Jimmy M. and Victor Nee (1987), "Limits of Ethnic Solidarity in the Enclave Economy," *American Sociological Review* 52 (6), December, pp. 745–767.

Sanghavi, Nitkin (2002), "Franchising as a Growth Strategy in the Japanese Retail Market," in Dianne N. B. Welsh and Ilan Alon, eds., *International Franchising in Industrialized Markets: North America, the Pacific Rim, and Other Countries*, Chicago: CCH, pp. 269–286.

Say, Jean Baptiste (1816), *Catechism of Political Economy: Or, Familiar Conversations of the Manner in Which Wealth is Produced, Distributed, and Consumed by Society*, London: Sherwood.

Schaper, Michael and Thierry Volery (2004), *Entrepreneurship and Small Business: A Pacific Rim Perspective*, Milton, Queensland: John Wiley & Sons.

Schive, Chi and Ming-Wen Hu (2001), "The Evolution and Competitiveness of Taiwan's SMEs," in Chao-Cheng Mai and Chien-Sheng Shih, eds., *Taiwan's Economic Success Since 1980*, Cheltenham, UK: Edward Elgar, pp. 248–274.

Schumpeter, Joseph Alois (1912), *Theorie der wirtschaftlichen Entwicklung*, Munich and Leipzig: Dunker und Humblat.

Schumpeter, Joseph Alois (1928), "The Instability of Capitalism," *Economic Journal* 38, November, pp. 361–386.

Schumpeter, Joseph Alois (1934), *The Theory of Economic Development: An Inquiry into Profits, Capital, Credit, Interest, and the Business Cycle*, Cambridge, Massachusetts: Harvard University Press.

Schumpeter, Joseph Alois (1939), *Business Cycles: A Theoretical, Historical and Statistical Analysis of the Capitalist Process*, New York: McGraw Hill.

Schumpeter, Joseph Alois (1942), *Capitalism, Socialism and Democracy*, New York: Harper and Row.

Schumpeter, Joseph Alois (1947), "The Creative Response in Economic History," *Journal of Economic History* 7, November, pp. 149–159.

Schumpeter, Joseph Alois (1949), "Economic Theory and Entrepreneurial History," in *Change and the Entrepreneur: Postulates and Patterns for Entrepreneurial History*, Cambridge, Massachusetts: Harvard University Press, pp. 63–84.

Scidmore, Eliza R. (1910), "Mukden, the Manchu Home, and Its Great Art Museum," *National Geographic* 21 (4), April, pp. 289–320.

Scidmore, Eliza R. (1914), "Young Japan," *National Geographic* 26 (1), July, pp. 54–64.

Sebastian, Jose and Sanjay Thakur (1994), *Not Born – The Created Entrepreneurs*, Ahmedabad: Entrepreneurship Development Institute of India.

Seglin, Jeffrey L. (1990), *The McGraw Hill 36-Hour Marketing Course*, New York: McGraw Hill.

Sein, Thaung (1950), *Problems of the Burmese Film*, Rangoon: Bamakhit Press.

Sharma, S.V.S. (1979), *Small Entrepreneurial Development in Some Asian Countries: A Comparative Study*, New Delhi: Light and Life.

Shor, Franc (1960), "The City They Call Red China's Showcase," *National Geographic* 118 (2), August, pp. 192–223.

Silcock, Thomas H. (1967), *Thailand: Social and Economic Studies in Development*, Durham, North Carolina: Duke.

Simon, Scott (2005), "Scarred Landscapes and Tattooed Faces: Poverty, Identity and Land Conflict in a Taiwanese Indigenous Community," in Robyn Eversole, John-Andrew McNeish, and Alberto D. Cimadamore, eds., *Indigenous Peoples and Poverty: An International Perspective*, London: Zed, pp. 53–68.

Simpich, Frederick (1926), "Singapore, Crossroads of the East: The World's Greatest Mart for Rubber and Tin Was in Recent Times a Pirate-haunted, Tiger-infested Jungle Isle," *National Geographic* 49 (3), March, pp. 235–269.

Simpich, Frederick (1929), "Manchuria, Promised Land of Asia: Invaded by Railways and Millions of Settlers, This Vast Region Now Recalls Early Boom Days in the American West," *National Geographic* 56 (4), October, pp. 379–428.

Singh, Manmohan (2006), "India's Economic Challenge," in George Skaria, ed., *India 2006: Taking India to the World*, London: World Link, pp. 12–14.

Sinha, Jai B. P. (1978), "Superior Subordinate Relationship and Alienation," *National Labour Institute Bulletin* 4, pp. 209–223.

Sinha, Jai B. P. (1984), "A Model of Effective Leadership Style in India," *International Studies of Management and Organization* 14, pp. 86–98.

Skaria, George, ed. (2006), *India 2006: Taking India to the World*, London: World Link.

Smith, A. W. (1930), "Working Teak in the Burma Forests: The Sagacious Elephant Is Man's Ablest Ally in the Logging Industry of the Far East," *National Geographic* 68 (2), August, pp. 239–256.

Smith, Adam (1892), *Inquiry into the Nature and Causes of the Wealth of Nations*, Vols. I & II (reprinted from the sixth edition with an introduction by Ernest Belfort Bax), Covent Garden, London: George Bell & Sons, York Street.

Smith-Hunter, Andrea E. (2006), *Women Entrepreneurs Across Racial Lines: Issues of Human Capital, Financial Capital and Network Structures*, Cheltenham, United Kingdom: Edward Elgar.

So-young, Kim and Shin Hae-in (2005), "176 Public Agencies to be Relocated Out of Seoul by 2012," *The Korea Herald* 16,060, Saturday, June 25, p. 1.

Sochurek, Howard (1964), "Slow Train Through Viet Nam's War," *National Geographic* 126 (3), September, pp. 412–444.

Soh-jung, Yoo (2005), "Jobless Rate Higher than Official Figure," *The Korea Herald* 16,060, Saturday, June 25, p. 5.

Somavia, Juan (2006), "SMEs," Statement at the World Economic Forum, Davos, January 26.

Speece, Mark and Phyu Phyu Sann (1998), "Problems and Conflicts in Manufacturing Joint Ventures in Myanmar," *Journal of Euro-Asian Management* 4 (3), December, pp. 19–43.

Steinberg, David I. (1982), *Burma: A Socialist Nation of Southeast Asia*, Boulder, Colorado: Westview Press.

Steinberg, David J. (1959), *Cambodia*, New Haven: Human Relations Area Files Press.

Stewart, B. Anthony (1944), "Salt for China's Daily Rice," *National Geographic* 86 (3), September, pp. 329–336.

Štulhofer, Aleksandar (1999), "Between Opportunism and Distrust: Socio-Cultural Aspects of the Underground Economy in Croatia," in Edgar L. Feige and Katarina Ott, eds.,*Underground Economies in Transition: Unrecorded Activity, Tax, Corruption and Organized Crime*, Aldershot: Ashgate, pp. 43–63.

Swe, Myint (1972), *History of Burmese Printed Books*, Rangoon: Kayathuka Press.

Swerdlow, Joel L. (1995), "Burma: The Richest of Poor Countries," *National Geographic* 188 (1), July, pp. 70–97.

Swierczek, Frederic William and Somkid Jatusripatak (1994), "Exploring Entrepreneurship Cultures in Southeast Asia," *Journal of Enterprising Culture* 2 (2), July, pp. 687–708.

Tambunan, Tulus T. H. (1992), "The Role of Small Firms in Indonesia," *Small Business Economics* 4 (1), March, pp. 59–77.

Tambunan, Tulus T. H. (2005), "Promoting Small and Medium Enterprises with a Clustering Approach: A Policy Experience from Indonesia," *Journal of Small Business Management* 43 (2), April, pp. 138–154.

Tan, Cheng Leong and Terence S. Lim (1993), *Vietnam: Business and Investment Opportunities*, Singapore: Cassia.

Thein, Myat (1996), "Socio-economic and Cultural Background of Myanmar," in Tan Teck Meng, Low Aik Meng, John J. Williams and Ivan P. Polunin, eds., *Business Opportunities in Myanmar*, Singapore: Prentice Hall, pp. 17–24.

Turnbull, Constance M. (1977), *A History of Singapore 1819–1975*, Oxford, United Kingdom: Oxford University Press.

Turner, Sarah (2003a), *Small Entrepreneurs in Indonesia: Trading on the Margins*, London: Routledge Curzon.

Turner, Sarah (2003b), "Speaking Out: Chinese Indonesians After Suharto," *Asian Ethnicity* 4 (3), pp. 337–352.

Venard, Bernard (1998), "Vietnam in Mutation: Will it Be the Next Tiger or a Future Jaguar?" *Asia Pacific Journal of Management* 15, pp. 77–99.

Wai, U Tun (1955), *Burma's Currency and Credit*, Calcutta: Orient Longmans.

Waldinger, Roger David (1984), "Immigrant Enterprise in the New York Garment Industry," *Social Problems* 32 (1), October, pp. 60–71.

Waldinger, Roger David (1986a), "Immigrant Enterprise: A Critique and Reformulation," *Theory and Society* 15 (1–2), pp. 249–285.

Waldinger, Roger David (1986b), *Through the Eye of the Needle: Immigrants and Enterprise in New York's Garment Trades*, New York: New York University Press.

Waldinger, Roger David and Howard E. Aldrich (1990), "Trends in Ethnic Business in the United States," in Roger David Waldinger, Howard E. Aldrich, Robin Ward, and Associates, *Ethnic Entrepreneurs: Immigrant Business in Industrial Societies*, Newbury Park, California: Sage, pp. 49–78.

Waldinger, Roger David, Howard E. Aldrich and Robin Ward (1990), "Opportunities, Group Characteristics and Strategies," in Roger David Waldinger, Howard E. Aldrich, Robin Ward, and Associates, *Ethnic Entrepreneurs: Immigrant Business in Industrial Societies*, Newbury Park, California: Sage, pp. 13–48.

Waldinger, Roger David, David McEvoy and Howard E. Aldrich (1990), "Spatial Dimensions of Opportunity Structures," in Roger David Waldinger, Howard E. Aldrich, Robin Ward, and Associates, *Ethnic Entrepreneurs: Immigrant Business in Industrial Societies*, Newbury Park, California: Sage, pp. 106–130.

Walsh, James and Philip Anderson (1995), "Owner-Manager Adoption/Innovation Preference and Employment Performance," *Journal of Small Business Management* 33 (3), July, pp. 1–8.

Wang, Yueping and Yang Yao (2002), "Market Reforms, Technological Capabilities, and the Performance of Small Enterprises in China," *Small Business Economics* 18 (1–3), February, pp. 197–211.

Wani, V. P., T. K. Garg and S. K. Sharma (2003), "The Role of Technical Institutions in Developing a Techno-entrepreneurial Workforce for Sustainable Development of SMEs in India," *International Journal of Management and Enterprise Development* 1 (1), pp. 71–88.

Wani, V. P., T. K. Garg and S. K. Sharma (2005), "Engineer as Entrepreneur: A Necessity for Successful Product Innovation in the Small-scale Industry Sector in India," in John

R. McIntyre and Ilan Alon, eds., *Business and Management Education in Transitioning and Developing Countries: A Handbook,* Armonk, New York: M. E. Sharpe, pp. 39–57.

Ward, Robin (1987), "Ethnic Entrepreneurs in Britain and in Europe," in Robert Goffee and Richard Scase, eds., *Entrepreneurship in Europe: The Social Processes,* London: Croom Helm, pp. 83–104.

Ward, Robin and Richard Jenkins, eds. (1984), *Ethnic Communities in Business: Strategies for Economic Survival,* Cambridge: Cambridge University Press, pp. 105–124.

Weber, Max (1904–5), "Die protestantische Ethik und der Geist des Kapitalismus," *Archiv für Sozialwissenschaft und Sozialpolitik* (20–21); translated (1930) by Talcott Parsons, *The Protestant Ethic and the Spirit of Capitalism,* New York: George Allen & Unwin.

Weber, Max (1924), *The Theory of Social and Economic Organization,* New York: The Free Press.

Weber, Max (1958), *The Religion of India — The Sociology of Hinduism & Buddhism,* New York: The Free Press.

Webster, Donovan (2003), "Blood, Sweat, and Toil along the Burma Road," *National Geographic* 204 (5), May, pp. 84–103.

Webster, Frederick E. (1992), "The Changing Role of Marketing in the Corporation," *Journal of Marketing* 53, October, pp. 1–17.

Wei, Liu (2001), "Incentive Systems for Technical Change: The Chinese System in Transition," *International Journal of Entrepreneurship and Innovation Management* 1 (2), pp. 157–177.

White, Peter T. (1961a), "Report on Laos," *National Geographic* 120 (2), August, pp. 241–275.

White, Peter T. (1961b), "South Viet Nam Fights the Red Tide," *National Geographic* 120 (4), October, pp. 445–489.

White, Peter T. (1967), "Behind the Headlines in Viet Nam," *National Geographic* 131 (2), February, pp. 149–193.

White, Peter T. (1968), "The Mekong River of Terror and Hope," *National Geographic* 134 (6), December, pp. 737–787.

White, Peter T. (1982), "Kampuchea Wakens From a Nightmare," *National Geographic* 161 (5), May, pp. 590–623.

White, Peter T. (1987), "Laos Today," *National Geographic* 171 (6), June, pp. 772–795.

Williams, Maynard Owens (1919), "The Descendants of Confucius," *National Geographic* 36 (3), September, pp. 253–265.

Williams, Maynard Owens (1935), "By Motor Trail across French Indo-China," *National Geographic* 68 (4), October, pp. 487–534.

Williams, Maynard Owens (1942), "New Delhi Goes Full Time," *National Geographic* 82 (4), October, pp. 465–494.

Williamson, Oliver E. (1985), *The Economic Institutions of Capitalism,* New York: Free Press.

Williamson, Oliver E. (1996), *The Mechanisms of Governance,* New York: Oxford University Press.

Wong, Bernard (1987), "The Role of Ethnicity in Enclave Enterprises: A Study of the Chinese Garment Factories in New York City," *Human Organization* 66 (2), Summer, pp. 120–130.

Wong, How-Man (1984), "Peoples of China's Far Provinces," *National Geographic* 165 (3), March, pp. 283–333.

Wong, Poh Kam, Finna Wong, Lena Lee and Yuen Ping Ho (2005), *Global Entrepreneurship Monitor,* Singapore: National University of Singapore.

Wu, Yuan Li (1983), "The Role of Alien Entrepreneurs in Economic Development: An Entrepreneurial Problem," *American Economic Review* 73 (2), May, pp. 112–117.

Wulsin, Frederick R. (1926), "The Road to Wang Ye Fu: An Account of the Work of the National Geographic Society's Central-China Expedition in the Mongol Kingdom of Ala Shan," *National Geographic* 69 (2), February, pp. 195–234.

Yang, Sung-jin (2005), "Beyond Dichotomy between Growth and Distribution," *The Korea Herald* 16,060, Saturday, June 25, p. 12.

Yeung, Henry Wai-Chung (1999), "The Internationalization of Ethnic Chinese Business Firms from Southeast Asia: Strategies, Processes and Competitive Advantage," *International Journal of Urban and Regional Research* 23 (1), pp. 103–127.

Yu, Junbo and Roger R. Stough (2006), "The Determinants of Entrepreneurship Development in China," *International Journal of Management and Enterprise Development* 3 (1–2), pp. 30–52.

Zainol, Vivi (2005), "Govt Okays Youths' Ideas for Change," *The Straits Times,* Wednesday, June 8, p. 1.

Zasloff, Joseph Jermiah, ed., (1988), *Postwar Indochina: Old Enemies and New Allies,* Washington, DC: US Government Printing Office.

Zasloff, Joseph Jermiah and Leonard Unger (1990), *Laos: Beyond the Revolution,* New York: St. Martin's Press.

Zineldin, Mosad Amin (1998), "Towards an Ecological Collaborative Relationship Management," *European Journal of Marketing* 32 (11–12), pp. 1138–1164.

Zingales, Luigi (2006), "Gods and Mammon," *Global Agenda: The Magazine of World Economic Forum Annual Meeting* 4, February, pp. 228–229.

Index

Printed in the United States
By Bookmasters